Blind Spot

Blind Spot

When Journalists Don't Get Religion

EDITED BY

PAUL MARSHALL

LELA GILBERT

ROBERTA GREEN AHMANSON

OXFORD
UNIVERSITY PRESS

2009

OXFORD
UNIVERSITY PRESS

Oxford University Press, Inc., publishes works that further
Oxford University's objective of excellence
in research, scholarship, and education.

Oxford   New York
Auckland   Cape Town   Dar es Salaam   Hong Kong   Karachi
Kuala Lumpur   Madrid   Melbourne   Mexico City   Nairobi
New Delhi   Shanghai   Taipei   Toronto

With offices in
Argentina   Austria   Brazil   Chile   Czech Republic   France   Greece
Guatemala   Hungary   Italy   Japan   Poland   Portugal   Singapore
South Korea   Switzerland   Thailand   Turkey   Ukraine   Vietnam

Published by Oxford University Press, Inc.
198 Madison Avenue, New York, New York 10016

www.oup.com

Oxford is a registered trademark of Oxford University Press.

Library of Congress Cataloging-in-Publication Data
Blind spot : when journalists don't get religion / edited by Paul Marshall,
Lela Gilbert, Roberta Green Ahmanson.
    p. cm.
ISBN 978-0-19-537436-0; 978-0-19-537437-7 (pbk.)
1. Religion and the press.   I. Marshall, Paul A., 1948–   II. Gilbert,
Lela.   III. Green, Roberta.
PN4756.B62, 2008
070.4'492—dc22   2008012185

9 8 7 6 5 4 3 2 1

Printed in the United States of America
on acid-free paper

To Abe Rosenthal,
Leonard Rossman,
Ray Griffith,
and Ellen Bevier

Acknowledgments

The editors have benefited from assistance, conversations, and advice with and from a wide range of people, including James Kurth, Peter Berger, Samuel Huntington, Dan Philpott, Philip Jenkins, David Aikman, Francis Beckwith, Tom Farr, Abe Rosenthal, John Green, Kenneth Woodward, Louis Bolce, Gerald De Maio, Rodney Stark, Tom Farr, Walter Russell Mead, Dallas Willard, and Luis Lugo, and we would like to thank them for their time and help.

The staff of Fieldstead and Co., including Ann Hirou, Thelma Dunaitis, Lisa May, Steve Ferguson, Doug Swardstrom, Clara Payne, Terrie Campos, and Kirk Stone, have been of immense aid. Guidance was provided by the staff and board of the media project of the Oxford Center for Religion and Public Life—Caroline Comport, Arne Fjeldtad, Jody Hassett Sanchez, Vinay Samuel, Hillel Fradkin, and Doug LeBlanc. Nina Shea and Grace Terzian of the Hudson Institute provided important advice, and Beth Kerley performed her usual assiduous editorial work.

We would especially like to thank Cynthia Read of Oxford University Press for her advice, encouragement, and enthusiasm.

Contents

Contributors

Roberta Green Ahmanson is a writer and philanthropist. Born in 1949 in Perry, Iowa, Ahmanson is also an award-winning journalist, and coauthor of *Islam at the Crossroads*, an attempt to outline the issues facing contemporary Muslims. Mrs. Ahmanson is a graduate of Calvin College. She holds a master's degree in English from the University of Michigan and has completed a year of graduate study in journalism at the University of Missouri. She was also the recipient of a fellowship in the Program for Religious Studies for Journalists at the University of North Carolina–Chapel Hill. After working as a freelance writer in Toronto, Canada, Mrs. Ahmanson moved to California, where she was Religion Editor of the *Sun* newspaper in San Bernardino and Religion Reporter for the Orange County *Register*. She has received journalism awards from Gannett News Service, the Religious Public Relations Council of New York, the Orange County Press Club, and the Roman Catholic Diocese of Orange County, California. In 1982 the Religion Newswriters Association listed her among the nation's ten best religion reporters. Roberta Green Ahmanson is also a trustee of Fieldstead and Company, Inc., a private philanthropy founded by her husband, Howard Ahmanson, in 1979.

John J. DiIulio Jr. is the Frederic Fox Leadership Professor of Politics, Religion, and Civil Society and Professor of Political Science at the University of Pennsylvania. During his leave from Penn in academic year 2000–2001, he served as Assistant to the President of the

United States, and first Director of the White House Office of Faith-Based and Community Initiatives. He is a Non-Resident Senior Fellow at the Brookings Institution, where he directed the Center for Public Management. For thirteen years, he was Professor of Politics and Public Affairs at Princeton University. He is author, coauthor, or editor of a dozen books. His most recent major publications are *Godly Republic: A Centrist Blueprint for America's Faith-Based Future* (University of California Press, 2007), and *American Government: Institutions and Policies* (with James Q. Wilson; Houghton Mifflin and Company, 2007, 11th edition). Dr. DiIulio received his Ph.D. from Harvard University, where he also served as a Head Resident Tutor. He won the David N. Kershaw Award of the Association of Public Policy Analysis and Management, and the Leonard D. White Award of the American Political Science Association (APSA). He has served as chairman of APSA's standing committee on professional ethics.

Michael J. Gerson is the Roger Hertog Senior Fellow at the Council on Foreign Relations, a columnist syndicated with the *Washington Post* Writers Group, a contributor to *Newsweek,* and the author of *Heroic Conservatism.* He has been Assistant to the President for Policy and Strategic Planning (2005–2006); Assistant to the President for Speechwriting and Policy Adviser (2002–2005); Deputy Assistant to the President and Director of Presidential Speechwriting (2001–2002); Chief Speechwriter and Senior Policy Adviser, Bush Presidential Campaign (1999–2000); and Senior Editor, Politics, *U.S. News and World Report.*

Lela Gilbert is a freelance writer and editor who has authored or coauthored more than sixty published books. She writes primarily in the field of ecumenical Christian nonfiction, and her work includes the award-winning 1997 survey of anti-Christian persecution, *Their Blood Cries Out,* coauthored with Paul Marshall, and a primer on the Muslim faith, *Islam at the Crossroads.* She was also senior editor of the award-winning bestseller *A Table in the Presence: The Dramatic Account of How a U.S. Marine Battalion Experienced God's Presence amidst the Chaos of the War in Iraq,* by Lt. Carey H. Cash. She has authored her own published fiction, children's books, and poetry.

James L. Guth is William R. Kenan Jr. Professor of Political Science at Furman University. He received his B.S. from the University of Wisconsin and his Ph.D. from Harvard University. He is the coauthor of *The Bully Pulpit: The Politics and Protestant Clergy* (University Press of Kansas, 1998), *Religion and the Culture Wars: Dispatches from the Field* (Rowman and Littlefield, 1996), and *The Bible and the Ballot Box* (Westview, 1991). His articles have appeared in the *American Journal of Political Science, Journal of Politics, Political Science*

Researcher, American Politics Research, Social Science Quarterly, Journal for the Scientific Study of Religion, Sociology of Religion, Journal of Common Market Studies, European Union Politics, and many other journals. He is currently co-editing the forthcoming *Oxford Handbook of Religion and American Politics.*

Allen Hertzke is Presidential Professor of Political Science at the University of Oklahoma. He is author of *Representing God in Washington,* an award-winning analysis of religious lobbies, which has been issued in a Chinese-language translation; and *Echoes of Discontent,* an account of church-rooted populist movements; he coauthored *Religion and Politics in America,* a comprehensive text now in its third edition. His latest book is titled *Freeing God's Children: The Unlikely Alliance for Global Human Rights.* A frequent news commentator, Hertzke has been featured in such outlets as the *New York Times, Washington Post, Wall Street Journal, London Times, Time Magazine, New Republic, USA Today, Christian Science Monitor, Los Angeles Times, San Francisco Chronicle,* and *Weekly Standard,* and on the BBC World Service, PBS, National Public Radio, and Swedish Radio. A winner of numerous teaching awards, Dr. Hertzke has lectured at the National Press Club, the U.S. Holocaust Memorial Museum, the Council on Foreign Relations, and the Carnegie Council on Ethics and International Affairs, and before numerous audiences in China.

Jeremy Lott is a contributing editor to *Books & Culture* and author of *In Defense of Hypocrisy* and *The Warm Bucket Brigade,* a history of the vice-presidency. He served for a time as the foreign press critic for GetReligion.org, a Web site that analyzes how the press covers religion. His writing has appeared in nearly a hundred publications in the United States, Canada, the United Kingdom, and the Netherlands, and been praised by critics as disparate as Charles Colson, founder of Prison Fellowship Ministries and broadcaster of the Breakpoint radio commentaries, and Chris Mooney, author of *The Republican War on Science.* He lives in Fairfax, Virginia, and Lynden, Washington.

Paul Marshall is Senior Fellow at the Hudson Institute's Center for Religious Freedom. For eight years before joining Hudson, he worked at Freedom House, as Senior Fellow at the Center for Religious Freedom. He is the author and editor of more than twenty books on religion and politics, especially religious freedom, including more recently, *Radical Islam's Rules: The Worldwide Spread of Extreme Sharia Law* (2005), *The Rise of Hindu Extremism* (2003), *Islam at the Crossroads* (2002), *God and the Constitution* (2002), *The Talibanization of Nigeria* (2002), *Massacre at the Millennium* (2001), *Religious Freedom in the World* (2000), *Egypt's Endangered Christians* (1999), *Just Politics* (1998), *Heaven Is Not*

My Home (1998), *A Kind of Life Imposed on Man* (1996), and the best-selling, award-winning survey of religious persecution worldwide *Their Blood Cries Out* (1997). He is the author of several hundred articles, and his writings have been translated into Russian, German, French, Dutch, Spanish, Portuguese, Norwegian, Danish, Albanian, Japanese, Malay, Korean, Arabic, Farsi, and Chinese. He is a frequent demand for lectures and media appearances including interviews on ABC Evening News; CNN; PBS; Fox News; the British, Australian, Canadian, South African, and Japanese Broadcasting Corporations; and Al Jazeera. His work has been published in or the subject of articles in the *New York Times, Wall St. Journal, Washington Post, Los Angeles Times, Washington Times, Boston Globe, Dallas Morning News, Christian Science Monitor, First Things, New Republic, Weekly Standard, Reader's Digest,* and many other newspapers and magazines.

Terry Mattingly writes the nationally syndicated "On Religion" column for the Scripps Howard News Service in Washington, D.C., and is director of the Washington Journalism Center at the Council for Christian Colleges and Universities. He has worked as a reporter and religion columnist at the *Rocky Mountain News* in Denver, the *Charlotte Observer,* and the *Charlotte News.* His writing also appears in *Again Magazine,* the Poynter Institute's "Journalism with a Difference" column, Beliefnet, and numerous other publications. He is the author of the book *Pop Goes Religion: Faith in Popular Culture.*

Michael Rubin is editor of the *Middle East Quarterly,* a resident scholar at the American Enterprise Institute, and author of *Eternal Iran: Chaos and Continuity* (2005). Between 2002 and 2004, he served as an Iran and Iraq staff advisor in the Office of the Secretary of Defense. He has written for the *Washington Post, Wall St. Journal, New Republic, National Review,* and many other publications, and lectured at the Land Warfare Study Center, Marshall Center for European Strategic Studies, Woodrow Wilson School, Council on Foreign Relations, and elsewhere. Rubin is featured on Fox News and/or CNN a couple of times per month and speaks frequently on NPR radio programs. His most recent op-eds have been in the *Washington Post, National Review,* and *New York Sun.* Rubin also lectures frequently to audiences both military (Land Warfare Study Center, Marshall Center for European Strategic Studies) and nonmilitary (Woodrow Wilson School, American Council on Foreign Relations in Wichita, Indianapolis, Des Moines, etc.). He thanks his research assistant Suzanne Gershowitz for her valuable assistance with this chapter.

Timothy Samuel Shah is Senior Research Scholar at the Institute on Culture, Religion and World Affairs at Boston University and Adjunct Senior Fellow for

Religion and Foreign Policy at the Council on Foreign Relations, and formerly Senior Fellow in Religion and World Affairs at the Pew Forum on Religion & Public Life. He is editor of a series of volumes on evangelical Protestantism and democracy in Africa, Asia, and Latin America to be published by Oxford University Press in 2008. He also serves as a principal researcher for the Religion in Global Politics research project at Harvard University. Shah's work on religion and politics has appeared in the *Journal of Democracy*, *SAIS Review of International Affairs*, *Political Quarterly*, and *Foreign Policy*. His Harvard government department Ph.D. dissertation was awarded the Aaron Wildavsky Award for Best Dissertation in Religion and Politics by the American Political Science Association in 2003.

Monica Duffy Toft is Associate Professor of Public Policy at the Kennedy School of Government, Harvard University. She holds a Ph.D. and M.A. from the University of Chicago and a B.A. in Political Science and Slavic Languages from the University of California, Santa Barbara. Professor Toft was the Assistant Director of the John M. Olin Institute for Strategic Studies at Harvard University from 1999 to 2006 and served as a research intern at the RAND Corporation and a consultant for an international firm for four years. She served in the U.S. Army in Germany as a Russian linguist. Her interests include international relations, nationalism and ethnic conflict, civil and interstate wars, demography and security, military and strategic planning, and religion and global politics. Professor Toft is the author of *The Geography of Ethnic Violence* (Princeton, 2003) and an edited volume, *The Fog of Peace* (Routledge, 2006). She is completing a book on the termination of civil wars and state building, *Peace through Victory: The Durable Settlement of Civil Wars*. She is the author of several articles on religion in international affairs and civil wars, is working on a book manuscript on the global resurgence of religion, and directs the Initiative on Religion in International Affairs at Harvard University.

C. Danielle Vinson is Associate Professor of Political Science at Furman University. She authored *Local Media Coverage of Congress and Its Members*, has authored or coauthored articles on media and the courts and campaign finance, and is researching communication in political campaigns and communication in Congress.

Amy Welborn has been writing for the Catholic press for fifteen years, has been published in *Commonweal*, *Liguorian*, *First Things*, and *Writer's Digest*, is the author of several books, and is a regular columnist for the *Florida Catholic*, *Our Sunday Visitor*, and *Catholic News Service*. Currently, the bulk of her energy is directed at blogging (amywelborn.typepad.com) and writing books.

Foreword

Michael J. Gerson

In the heat of the 2000 election, then-Governor George W. Bush of Texas made an off-the-cuff statement that we ought take the log out of our own eye before calling attention to the speck in the eye of our neighbor. The *New York Times* reported the remark as a minor gaffe—what it termed "an interesting variation on the saying about the pot and the kettle." The reporter—actually a fine and balanced journalist—did not recognize the biblical reference. Neither did his editors. And this, of course, was not an obscure biblical reference. Not only is it found in the red letters of the New Testament, it is taken from the Sermon on the Mount.

This is a small matter raising a large issue. The problem in many cases such as these is not just biblical literacy—though that is a problem. The lack of biblical literacy is often accompanied by an assumption among many journalists, and, more broadly, the "knowledge class." In these circles, it is often believed that public expressions of religion are themselves offensive—a violation of the truce of tolerance. Religious belief, in this view, is protected by the Constitution, but for the sake of pluralism must be confined to the private sphere. And it certainly cannot be the basis for laws and public policy because this would be to impose a narrow set of beliefs on dissenters.

This kind of secularism can lead to indifference—and, when religion becomes an unavoidable topic, to suspicion. As a citizen,

I believe this makes for bad political philosophy. As a former reporter, I know it makes for bad journalism.

A journalism that ignores or dismisses the role of religion in our common life misses the greatest stories of our time.

First, a journalist with secular blinders will miss the main source of reform and hope in the American story. Religious communities have always provided men and women with a source of support in times of oppression and a vision of social justice that stands above the status quo. This was true of Quakerism, which motivated so much early abolitionism; nineteenth-century evangelicalism, which continued and completed that fight; and African American Christianity, which, with tremendous spiritual resources, opposed segregation. And the central role of religion in social reform is clear today, from the pro-life movement, to antiwar activism, to growing concerns with global poverty, disease, sexual trafficking, and genocide.

American journalists have a history of missing this fascinating story. One of Rev. Martin Luther King Jr.'s lieutenants, Andrew Young, recalls of the civil rights era: "Even then, see, people didn't want to think of Martin Luther King as a minister. Most of our white supporters kind of tolerated our religion, but they really didn't take it seriously, and most of the press, too." But King took religion seriously. After the Montgomery bus boycott began in 1955, King was receiving dozens of death threats a day. One evening around midnight, a call came promising to blow up his home, and King began to despair. He prayed aloud: "Lord, I'm down here trying to do what's right. . . . But, Lord, I must confess that I'm weak now; I'm faltering; I'm losing my courage." He went on to say, "It seemed at that moment that I could hear an inner voice saying to me, 'Martin Luther, stand up for righteousness, stand up for justice, stand up for truth. And lo I will be with you, even until the end of the world.' And I'll tell you, I've seen the lightning flash. I've heard the thunder roll. I felt sin-breakers dashing, trying to conquer my soul. But I heard the voice of Jesus saying still to fight on. He promised never to leave me, never to leave me alone. No, never alone. No, never alone. He promised never to leave me, never to leave me alone."

This is quite a story—the voice of God, urging persistence in a movement of social reform that transformed America. And it is not uncommon in our history, because dissent often requires courage, and courage is often rooted in faith. Any journalist who cares about dissent and reform must take religion seriously.

Second, a journalist with secular blinders will not be able to see some of the most important historical trends of our time. Many of those trends, of course, concern Islam—its nature and future. The events of 9/11, and the wars in Iraq and Afghanistan, have exposed Americans to a bewildering array of theological and historical debates within Islam. The participants in those debates consider them deadly serious. But the coverage of those religious arguments in Western journalism—with some notable exceptions—has been less than serious. High-quality journalism on Islam is not an option but a requirement in the modern world.

But there are other important trends being missed as well. We are witnessing a historic shift of the center of gravity of world Christianity to the global south. There are now more evangelical Christians in Nigeria and Brazil combined than there are in the United States. African church officials are engaged in active missions to North America. This trend is already causing disagreement within many global denominations; it is forging stronger ties between American Christians and their developing-world brothers and sisters; it is igniting new movements to fight poverty and disease; and it is exposing a fault line of conflict between Christianity and Islam across the center of Africa. A journalist who ignores this trend is missing a fascinating story.

Third, a journalist with secular blinders ignores some of the deepest philosophic views and moral convictions of Americans. The great influence of religion has not been its eschatology or soteriology—those teachings have little public importance—but its anthropology, its view of human beings. From the beginning, a Judeo-Christian view of human rights and dignity has informed the American experiment, along with the philosophic views of the Enlightenment. Religion provides a transcendent basis for human dignity and equality, which skepticism and moral relativism do not supply.

A Canadian newspaper once cited as evidence of resurgent American extremism that President Bush claimed that "God wants people to be free." That, of course, is the extremism of the Declaration of Independence. It is the extremism of Abraham Lincoln, who argued that "nothing stamped with the divine image and likeness was sent into the world to be trodden on, and degraded, and imbruted by its fellows." It is the extremism of Franklin D. Roosevelt, who proclaimed that "man, born to freedom in the image of God, will not forever suffer the oppressors' sword." A journalist who ignores or dismisses this kind of public argument is ignoring a central tenet in the philosophy of freedom.

This timely, lively volume explores a variety of issues where religion and journalism intersect—from Islam, to human rights, to Mel Gibson. Taken together, these essays make an important case: The more sophisticated our knowledge of religion, the more sophisticated our knowledge of the world.

G. K. Chesterton once called secularism "a taboo of tact or convention, whereby we are free to say that a man does this or that because of his nationality, or his profession, or his place of residence, or his hobby, but not because of his creed about the very cosmos in which he lives."

Good journalism should be concerned with all of life, including our nationality, our professions, the places we live, and the interests that engage us. But journalism is radically incomplete without also covering the creeds we hold about the cosmos in which we live.

PART I

Background

Introduction

Paul Marshall

This book is about media coverage of major news stories in which religion is a major component and how journalists often miss, or misunderstand, these stories because they do not take religion seriously, or misunderstand religion when they do take it seriously. Jeff Sharlot, editor of the *Revealer,* New York University's online review of religion and the press, suggests, "Religion in the true, broad sense underlies, controls, permeates at least half the stories in the news, probably a lot more."[1] Obviously, we can argue about the proportion of reports affected, but, as Tim Shah's and Monica Toft's opening chapter "Why God Is Winning" shows, religion is a major and growing factor in human affairs throughout the world and, hence, in major news stories. Therefore, if reporters do not understand it, they will be poorer reporters. To the extent that journalists do not grasp events' religious dimensions, both global and local, they are hindered from, and sometimes incapable of, describing what is happening.

Several years ago Edward Luttwak noted that analysts and commentators, including journalists, who are ever ready to "interpret economic causality, who are apt to dissect social differentiations more finely, and who will minutely categorize political affiliations, are still in the habit of disregarding the role of religion, religious institutions, and religious motivations in explaining politics and conflict, and even in reporting their concrete modalities."[2] As CNN political analyst William Schneider opined, "On the national level, the press is one of the most secular institutions in American society. It just doesn't get religion or any idea that flows from religious conviction. The press is not necessarily contemptuous of serious religion. It's just uncomprehending."[3]

This attitude has persisted despite the fact that on September 11, 2001, the United States was attacked by an explicitly religiously based enemy. As Paul Marshall notes in his chapter, much commentary has sought to make bin Laden and his cadres theoretically domesticated by reducing their concerns to issues of poverty or globalization or U.S. foreign policy, or even sexual frustration, or just about anything except the terrorists' repeatedly stated desire to restore a worldwide caliphate ruled by Islamic law.

Some journalists, like Schneider, realize there is a problem. E. J. Dionne records how, in covering a papal tour and reading through John Paul II's speeches, his Associated Press colleague Victor Simpson appealed to his fellow reporters in mock alarm, "What are we going to write about? There's nothing but religion here."[4] Jim Hoagland notes what he calls a "professional dichotomy": "By instinct and training, we journalists are skeptics about religious activists. . . . Editors reinforce reporters' instincts to treat religion politely but suspiciously. Ours is a secular trade honoring information more than faith."[5] In the aftermath of the 2004 elections, *Nation* columnist Alexander Cockburn, pointing to the influence of "moral values" in voting, mocked his fellow writers: "Moral values brings us to the well-known fact (greeted with amazement on Wednesday morning by the pundits) that the United States is a Christian nation. Tocqueville noticed this some time ago and anyone driving today down any county road or state highway will see a lot of churches." He added that, even when journalists do notice that they are writing about one of the most religious countries on the face of the earth, their response is often distant and alienated: "Even though the highest reading on any chart of Intolerance is that nourished towards Christians by secular liberals (after all, Christians believe in forgiveness and the possibility of redemption) I suppose we'll have to put up with much earnest journalism from sensitive liberal writers driving into the Christian heartland to inspect and commune with the natives. I read one patronizing prospectus from a Californian free-lancer that sounded like an application by an anthropologist in 1925 for funding to inspect an African tribe."[6]

As Terry Mattingly describes in his chapter, Roy Peter Clark, a senior scholar at the Poynter Institute, a premier center for media studies, admitted his own alienation and ignorance and noted that it makes for poor journalism:

> I stood on line for two hours Tuesday to vote, predicting that a big
> turnout of young people and new voters would push John Kerry over
> the top. This morning I'm looking in the mirror, wondering, as a

journalist and a citizen, if there is something fundamentally myopic about how I see the world. . . .

I am now taking seriously the theory that we mainstream journalists are different from mainstream America. "Different" is too pale a word. We are alienated. . . . The churched people who embrace Bush, in spite of a bumbling war and a stumbling economy, are more than alien to me. They are invisible. . . .

I don't know the difference between evangelical and charismatic, but I can argue about who has sluttier videos, Britney or Christina.

I know little about the "born again" experience but can celebrate the narrative structure of Queer Eye for the Straight Guy.

I've never listened to a religious radio program or attended a church supper, but I can tell you whatever you want to know about Howard Stern and Bubba the Love Sponge.

I attend Catholic Mass most Sundays, but in my life as a citizen I am a thorough secularist. . . . My blind spots blot out half of America. And that makes me less of a citizen, and less of a journalist.[7]

As one corrective to this ignorance, *New York Times* columnist Nicholas Kristof suggested "more diverse newsrooms." He wrote, "When America was struck by race riots in the late 1960s, major news organizations realized too late that their failure to hire black reporters had impaired their ability to cover America. In the same way, our failure to hire more red state evangelicals limits our understanding of and ability to cover America today."[8] In June 2005 *New York Times* executive editor Bill Keller said the paper would indeed make "an extra effort to focus on diversity of religious upbringing and military experience, of region and class." He also endorsed the paper's Credibility Committee's recommendation that "we cover religion more extensively. . . . Not because we want to appease believers . . . but because good journalism entails understanding more than just the neighborhood you grew up in."[9]

These are good observations, but it's not entirely clear why having more reporters with a "religious upbringing" or religious beliefs really addresses the problem. After all, Clark says he goes to mass "most Sundays" but confesses he doesn't understand the religious dimensions of American culture. Whether Kristof's "red state evangelicals" could help would depend on how they integrated their understanding of religion with the nature of news. Nor is the problem adequately addressed by stories that focus specifically on religion, necessary as they are: though there are still problems, as Terry Mattingly's chapter points out, many current religion reporters are good at their trade. Another important question is how well other reporters, regardless of their own religious beliefs, grasp the importance of religion in covering what are often misnamed "secular" news stories.

The chapters by Marshall, Rubin, Hertzke, Vinson and Guth, Welborn, and Lott explore this issue by describing an important event, issue, trend, problem, or situation, seeking to show the centrality of religion to the story, then outlining how journalists actually covered it, and finally explaining how they often got it wrong because they missed or misunderstood the relevant religious dynamics. The chapters also suggest how the media can improve coverage in this area. Some of the authors are academics, some journalists, and some have experience in both fields. This leads to differing approaches to their material, but both groups reach similar conclusions.

As our major, though not exclusive, focus is on "secular" news, most of the chapters focus on issues, such as Iraq or presidential elections, which are not usually thought of as specifically religious. However, we have included two chapters that deal with more specifically religious topics: these are Amy Welborn's chapter on the popes, and Jeremy Lott's on the movie *The Passion of the Christ*. One reason for this is that interest in and coverage of these issues went far beyond the religion pages and became front-page news. The death of John Paul II received the type of extended wall-to-wall coverage more often reserved for elections or Hollywood scandals, while the *The Passion of the Christ* was the most talked about movie of 2004, and perhaps of the decade, so that we believe their media coverage deserves attention. Finally, the two concluding chapters focus on ways of correcting the problems that the earlier chapters describe. Mattingly describes barriers to taking religion seriously and well in the newsroom: his focus is on problems affecting what is called religion coverage, but the practices that he suggests also apply to religious dimensions of the "secular." Ahmanson also describes such barriers but with a focus on the conceptual issues that often hinder journalists in taking religious issues, particularly religious knowledge, seriously.

Tim Shah's and Monica Toft's chapter, "Why God Is Winning," a longer version of a cover story in *Foreign Affairs* (Summer 2006), does not try to review media coverage. Its purpose is to set the stage, so to speak, by giving an overview of the influence of religion on world politics in recent decades. They show that global politics is increasingly marked by what could be called "prophetic politics," in which voices claiming transcendent authority are filling public spaces and winning key political contests. Of course, some political prophets, like al Qaeda, act through violence; others, like American evangelicals, act through elections; still others, like Hamas and some Indian Hindu revivalists, combine the two. But the overall trend is clear. Whether the field of battle is democratic elections or the more inchoate struggle for global public opinion, religious groups are increasingly competitive, putting secular movements on the defensive. Shah and Toft suggest that "God is on a winning streak" and that the spread of democracy, far from checking the power of religious activists, has often only expanded their reach. In fact, many political prophets have emerged from democratic processes more organized, more popular, and more legitimate—but sometimes no less violent. Democracy is giving the world's peoples their voice, and many want to talk about God.

Paul Marshall's chapter "Religion and Terrorism: Misreading al Qaeda" describes Osama bin Laden's and other Islamist terrorists' developed ideology and view of history and how, to them, this explains and justifies their brutalities. He then contrasts their stated motives and rationales with press coverage of their and their confreres' attacks in Yemen, Bali, Iraq, Pakistan, and Saudi Arabia, seeking to show that both the terrorists' goals and the identity of their victims are repeatedly misstated. Whereas al Qaeda consistently describes its intended targets in religiously loaded terms—as Christians, Jews, Crusaders, followers of the cross, Hindus, Buddhists, apostates, idolaters, infidels, and polytheists—and will frequently spare people, even Americans, if they are Muslims, many journalists consistently describe al Qaeda strikes as attacks on "Westerners," "non-Arabs," or "Americans" and their allies. Marshall shows how, as a result, the connection between Australian and United Nations actions in East Timor and the bombings in Bali and of the UN compound in Baghdad were missed almost entirely. The result is that the nature and goals of Islamist terrorism are frequently described erroneously, to the detriment not only of the press but of all people threatened by terrorism.

In "Three Decades of Misreporting Iran and Iraq," Michael Rubin examines coverage of Iran and Iraq and shows how it has veered from underestimating the political force in Iran of the Ayatollah Khomeini's heterodox innovations to overestimating the political ambitions of Iraq's Shiite leaders. He shows how ignorance about Shiite and Sunni beliefs and practices, including the role of Shiite shrines and Sufi brotherhoods, has lead to misreporting major political divisions in Iraq, and even its day-to-day politics. In the process, he gives a marvelous overview of current religious dynamics in both countries. It has become a commonplace that the U.S. administration was insufficiently aware of the religious complexities of Iran and Iraq when it led the invasion of Iraq in 2003: it is less commonly noted that press coverage has suffered from the same problem.

Allen Hertzke, in "The Faith-Based Human Rights Quest: Missing the Story," describes what he maintains is the most important human rights story since the end of the cold war, the growth in the United States of a broad movement for international human rights that draws in evangelicals, Catholics, Jews,

Buddhists, Baha'is, African Americans, and feminists. This movement has pushed successfully for legislation and active policy on international religious freedom, Sudan, sexual trafficking, debt forgiveness, AIDS, and North Korea. Despite its repeated successes, it has often been ignored by journalists, or else its programs and personnel have been misstated, so that the broadest coalition in foreign policy is sometimes reduced to the purported politics of the "Christian Right." The result is that this major evolution in U.S. human rights concerns and in U.S. foreign policy has been missed or misunderstood.

Danielle Vinson and James Guth analyze coverage of religious dimensions of the 2004 presidential election and conclude that journalists were consistently "misunderestimating" religion. They illustrate how the labels often used by journalists to categorize religious adherents missed many of the most important political cleavages and what makes religious voters tick. One result was that Bush's religious beliefs and appeal were mischaracterized, while Kerry's religious beliefs were usually ignored. The same pattern held for coverage of evangelical and African American churches. After the election, general ignorance about America's religious dynamics led to widespread media surprise that the increased youth and general-voter turnout had helped Bush rather than Kerry.

In "The Popes," Amy Welborn describes the coverage of Pope John Paul II's funeral and the accompanying retrospectives on his life and influence, and the appraisals of the incoming Benedict XVI, formerly Cardinal Ratzinger. She argues that coverage of the occasions themselves was usually very good, especially because experts were drawn in to comment, particularly on television. However, the assessments of the two men, especially in the print media, were frequently askew because journalists knew very little about the history and the authority structure of the Catholic Church, and equally little about current trends within Catholicism. While there was considerable attention to the pope's role in undercutting Communism, something that journalists felt more at home covering, much of the portrayal remained fixed within a template of "authoritarian popes versus U.S. liberal Catholics." The extensive criticism that John Paul II received from conservative Catholics was neglected, as was the fact that during his papacy there were in fact very few acts of Church discipline, especially as compared to, say, recent years in the U.S. Episcopal Church, and that the most important disciplinary actions were directed at conservatives. The features of the pope's career most often noted by Catholics, his theology of the body, the new catechism, and the rapid rise of new ecclesiastical orders, were bypassed entirely.

Jeremy Lott's "Jesus Christ, Superstar: The Passion of the Press" takes a tour of the reporting on and critical coverage of Mel Gibson's *The Passion of the Christ* and finds almost no attempt to understand or portray the movie on its own terms—in other words, no acknowledgment that it was not an effort at a literal portrayal of the gospels but was structured around a very specifically Catholic piety centered on the Stations of the Cross and the Eucharistic sensibility of Christ's body and blood. Because they did not grasp these liturgical dimensions, the media instead focused on the controversies about the movie's purported anti-Semitism, its bloodiness, and its supposed literalism. This led to many wrong predictions, including that this movie in Aramaic would bomb at the box office, that "Mad Mel" would lose his fortune, and that the film would ignite a wave of anti-Semitism, and missed a major story—that millions of American evangelicals flocked to and warmly embraced a picture of very Roman Catholic sensibility.

Terry Mattingly explores the barriers in the newsroom to covering religion well, and much of the chapter draws on a series of interviews he conducted with journalists and editors generally believed to be doing a good job of connecting religion and journalism. He highlights the need for journalists to examine the religious language and labels that they use, the need for diversity of religious knowledge and awareness in newsrooms, the role of editors in offering better training and resources both to those identified as religion reporters and to others whose work veers into religious territory, and the need to strive to get inside the daily lives and mindset of the people covered.

Roberta Green Ahmanson also explores newsroom barriers to covering news with religious content well, but with a different focus. She outlines some of the conceptual barriers that journalists face in covering religion, particularly a common modern assumption, shared by many journalists, that religions cannot be understood as forms of knowledge. She recommends that journalists first strive to understand what religion is, try to take seriously an individual's faith or lack thereof, take history seriously, question their own assumptions and the assumptions of our time, consciously try to avoid "pack journalism," and realize that even in religious affairs, details matter a great deal. This is a tall order and will never be fully met, but it can be attempted.

The purpose of this book is not to make journalists or others into believers, or to convince them or anyone else that religion is good: in fact, most of the authors think that religion can be good or bad. Our concern is to emphasize that religion is important even in secular news, so that it is vital for journalists to take religion seriously and to know about it in order to properly report the news. We also want to emphasize that religious beliefs and practices are usually varied and complex, which means that learning about them will take some work, but such work is indispensable to good journalism.

I

God Is Winning: Religion in Global Politics

Timothy Samuel Shah and Monica Duffy Toft

Prophet-Driven Politics

God won again. After Hamas achieved a decisive victory in the January 2006 Palestinian elections, one of its first acts was to replace the PLO flag flying over parliament with its emerald-green banner heralding, "There is no God but God, and Muhammad is His Prophet." Days after the Prophet's banner was unfurled in Ramallah, thousands of Muslims mounted a vigorous and sometimes violent defense of the Prophet's honor in cities as diverse as Jakarta, New Delhi, Beirut, and London. Protesting cartoons of Muhammad originally published in Denmark, numerous Islamic groups, governments, and individuals staged demonstrations, boycotts, and embassy attacks. If their aim was to discourage the publication of such images, they achieved some success. Most American media declined to publish the cartoons, and President Bush appeared sympathetic to the protestors' cause when he said that freedom of the press comes with "the responsibility to be thoughtful about others."[1]

Although these events burst suddenly onto the world stage early in 2006, they dramatized a deep undercurrent that has been gathering force for decades and holds much more than the Muslim world in its grip. Global politics as a whole is increasingly becoming what could be called "prophetic politics," in which voices claiming transcendent authority are filling public spaces and winning key political contests. Whether the field of battle is democratic elections or the more inchoate struggle for global public opinion, religious groups are increasingly competitive—and victorious. And the trend continues. In July 2007, in an election that was deliberately cast and widely perceived as a contest between the militant secularism of the Turkish military and the mild Islamism of the Justice and Development (AK) Party, the Islamists and their liberal supporters won a resounding victory.[2] The result is that if there is any consistent loser in the proverbial "battle for the world's hearts and minds," it is secularism, including secular leaders, ideologies, and regimes. If there is any consistent winner, it may be none other than God himself.[3]

Though America has been affected by prophetic politics for almost the entire postwar period (the civil rights movement offers but one instance)—and particularly since the avowedly born again Jimmy Carter burst onto the U.S. political scene more than thirty years ago—no one has been more astonished by fundamentalist religion's global political comeback than America and its foreign policy elite. U.S. foreign policy has been blasted—and blindsided—by one divine thunderbolt after another, from the 1979 Iranian Revolution, to the 9/11 terror attacks, to the Shia Revival and religious strife in postwar Iraq, right up to the Hamas victory in 2006. And not all the thunderbolts have been hurled by Allah. Hindu nationalists in India rocked the international community when they held true to their ideologically inspired strategic agenda and tested nuclear weapons in May 1998, and American evangelicals continue to surprise the U.S. foreign policy establishment with their increasing activism and influence on international issues like religious freedom and Africa policy. Offering an apt if unintended summary of the whole history of America's tumultuous dealings with conservative religious activists over the last few decades, Secretary of State Condoleezza Rice confessed after the Hamas win, "I don't know anyone who wasn't caught off guard."[4]

It's time the United States stopped being shocked, surprised, and caught off guard. Prophetic politics did not arrive on the political scene yesterday. In fact, by our reckoning, religious conservatives have enjoyed a political winning streak stretching back nearly forty years. What is more, prophetic politics' more recent winning streak suggests that the spread of democracy, far from checking the power of conservative religious activists, will probably only enhance the global reach of prophetic political movements, some of which will emerge from democratic processes more organized, more popular, and more legitimate—but quite possibly no less violent.

God's Greatly Exaggerated Demise

"Is God Dead?" a *Time* magazine cover story asked on April 8, 1966. The mid-1960s marked the apex of secularism's dominance over modern world affairs.

As *Time*'s cover dramatized, the conventional wisdom shared by many intellectual and political elites the world over was that modernization would inevitably extinguish religion's vitality. With ever-expanding material security and education, fewer people would turn to religion either for comfort or knowledge, and its power—above all, its *public* power—would inevitably diminish to the vanishing point.

This secularist consensus had been developing for some time. In 1952 eminent Indian historian and diplomat K. N. Panikkar predicted that Christianity throughout Asia and Africa would collapse once the coercive pressures of Western colonialism were removed.[5] In 1958 Daniel Lerner's hugely influential work on modernization in the Middle East, *The Passing of Traditional Society*, cited a consensus of scholars in support of its conclusion that Islam was "absolutely defenseless" in the face of the rationalist and positivist spirit of modernity and that secularization would inevitably follow the rapid urbanization of Egypt and other Arab countries.[6] By 1968 eminent British historian Arnold Toynbee wrote with breathtaking sweep and confidence that "*all* current religions . . . have been losing their hold on the hearts and consciences and minds of their former adherents" and underscored that he had more than just the West in mind by adding that "*all* the non-Western religions . . . are now experiencing the same crisis of faith and allegiance that the Western Christian churches had begun to experience before the close of the 17th century."[7]

In part, this conventional wisdom reflected the contours of world politics, in which the all-consuming struggles between Western capitalist democracy and Soviet Communism and between colonialism and third world nationalism were defined largely in terms of competing secular ideologies.

But if 1966 was the zenith of secularism's global self-confidence, 1967 marked the beginning of the end of its global hegemony. In that year the leader of secular Arab nationalism, Gamal Abdel Nasser, suffered a humiliating defeat at the hands of the Israeli army during the Six-Day War. From that point onward, the legitimacy and popularity of Nasserite Arab nationalism suffered a precipitous decline. By the end of the 1970s, hardly more than ten years after *Time*'s "death of God" cover, Iran's Ayatollah Khomeini, born again U.S. president Jimmy Carter, television evangelist Jerry Falwell, and Pope John Paul II had dramatically demonstrated the increasing political clout of religious movements and their leaders.

Ten years later, devout Catholic Solidarity workers in Poland and Kalashnikov-wielding mujahideen in Afghanistan helped defeat atheistic Soviet Communism, leading French political scientist Gilles Kepel to observe that it was more accurate to talk about the "revenge of God" than about the death of God.[8] After yet another decade, nineteen hijackers transformed world politics and the strategic priorities of the world's most powerful state by crashing passenger jets into the World Trade Center and the Pentagon, crying "God is great" as they did so.[9]

In sum, reports of God's demise have been greatly exaggerated. We now live in an era when religion is a robust global force. Whether in the form of Islamic radicalism, evangelical Protestantism, Hindu nationalism, Eastern Orthodoxy, Buddhist revivalism, or Jewish Zionism, religion is increasingly vibrant, assertive, and politicized the world over.

The Roots of Resurgence

Why have religious motives and movements become so politically vital and influential in recent years? Some have suggested that religion's intense political activity in the modern world is best interpreted as a sign of embattlement, weakness, and decline.[10] If religion's societal position and influence were really secure, as they were in pre-modern traditional society, it would not need to resort to extraordinary political means to advance its influence, or so the argument goes.[11] "[Religious radicals] and their devout followers fight back in their own ways against the spreading vulgarization and secularization of societies that seem tempted to dispense with religion altogether," wrote *Washington Post* columnist Jim Hoagland in early 2006. "These are by and large counterrevolutionary movements, out of step with a secularizing march by history that many of them would destroy rather than accept."[12]

In fact, with the exception of Europe and a few other places (discussed below), global religion shows little sign of declining in the face of modernization or any "secularizing march by history." On the contrary, the modern world has proven remarkably hospitable to religious vitality. Any number of objective measures reveals that religiosity is robust across the globe.[13] In fact, these measures demonstrate that the period in which economic and political modernization has been most intense and globally expansive—that is, the last thirty to forty years—has witnessed an increase in religious vitality the world over. This increase in religious vitality, along with global declines in secular ideologies and movements and the global expansion of democracy, has been a major driver of the resurgence in prophetic politics.

First, in terms of the sheer number of adherents, the world's largest religions have expanded at a rate that exceeds that of global population growth. Consider the two largest Christian confessions, Catholicism and Protestantism, and the two largest non-Christian religions, Islam and Hinduism. According to the *World Christian Encyclopedia*, the most comprehensive and up-to-date publication on global religious demographics available, a greater *proportion* of the world's population adhered to *each* of these religious systems in 2000 than in 1900. At the beginning of the twentieth century, a bare majority of the world's people, 50 percent, were Catholic, Protestant, Muslim, or Hindu. At the beginning of the twenty-first century, however, nearly 64 percent of the world's people belonged to one of these four religious groupings.[14]

Both the timing and the character of this spiritual transformation are noteworthy. The overwhelming preponderance of this growth occurred during the astonishingly short span of thirty years, between 1970 and 2000. Furthermore, almost the entire shift occurred because Islam and Protestantism experienced particularly rapid growth, accounting for 12 percent out of the 14 percent increase in the world population share of these four faiths.[15]

Also noteworthy is the geography of this spiritual transformation. Islam continues a massive expansion in the vast arc of Muslim-majority countries stretching across the earth's middle, from Morocco to Indonesia, while Christianity's growth has occurred throughout the so-called global South—Africa, Asia, and Latin America. Indeed, as Philip Jenkins has dramatized in *The Next Christendom*, Christianity's share of the global South population has skyrocketed in the course of the twentieth century.[16] The result of Christian growth in the global South is that Protestants and Catholics now together constitute a slightly higher share of global South population than Muslims do (24% vs. 23%), whereas these Christian confessions were dwarfed by Islam in that region at the beginning of the twentieth century (7% vs. 17%).[17]

Just as the sheer *quantity* of religious adherents demonstrates religion's continuing vitality, measures of religious *quality* reveal much the same thing. In a 2002 survey by the Pew Global Attitudes Project, 80 percent or more of respondents in each of the ten African countries surveyed and majorities in seven Latin American countries all said that religion is "very important" to them, as did more than 85 percent of respondents in each of four Asian countries: Indonesia, India, the Philippines, and Bangladesh.[18] Furthermore, the World Values Survey and the European Values Survey suggest that levels of religiosity are not only high but increasing in most of the world. These surveys, which provide data from countries containing more than 85 percent of the world's population, have been conducted in five successive waves between 1981 and 2005. They demonstrate that the most populous and fastest-growing countries in the world—including the United States—are witnessing measurable increases in religiosity, based on responses to questions concerning belief in God, importance of God in one's life, importance of religion in one's life, whether people were raised religiously at home, how much comfort people find in religion, and frequency of attendance at church or religious services. People surveyed in country after country, including China, Brazil, Nigeria, Russia, South Africa, and the United States, showed *increased* levels of religious belief and behavior in the course of the 1990s.[19]

Of course, signs of religious renewal and politicization have been less robust in some parts of the world—particularly in Europe. European respondents who said that religion was "very important" to them in the 2002 Pew survey ranged from only 11 percent in the Czech Republic and France to 36 percent in Poland.[20] But Europe, along with Japan and relatively sparsely populated European settler societies such as Canada, Australia, and New Zealand, are clearly the secular exception to the global rule of religious vitality. Furthermore, Europe's secular exceptionalism will become more and more exceptional in the next several decades as Europe experiences an absolute population decline. According to the United Nations Population Division, Europe's fertility rate between 2000 and 2005 was 1.4 children per woman, compared to 2.9 for the world's "less developed regions," well below the population-replacement level of 2.1 children per woman. The report estimates that between 2005 and 2050, Europe's population will decrease from 728 to 653 million.[21]

One reason for Europe's population decline appears to be a negative link between secularity and fertility, which obtains not just in Europe but in the world as a whole. The countries examined in the World Values Survey can be divided into three categories—"most secular," "moderate," and "most religious"— based on the average response to the question, "How important is God in your life?" Pippa Norris and Ronald Inglehart found that from 1975 to 1997, the annual population growth rate of the "most religious" societies was 2.2 percent, whereas it was only 0.7 percent for the "most secular" societies. From 1997 to 2015, it is estimated that population growth in religious societies will have declined to 1.5 percent, but this will still constitute substantial growth. In the most secular societies, the average growth rate has already plunged to 0.2 percent, and the rate in some of these countries has become negative. Based on this data and other findings from the four iterations of the World Values Survey, Inglehart and Norris conclude that "the world as a whole now has more people with traditional religious beliefs than ever before—and they constitute a growing proportion of the world's population."[22] Declining fertility, Inglehart declared in 2006, makes secularization "its own gravedigger."[23]

Even apart from the population issue, evidence suggests that faith has a great deal more staying power in the secular strongholds of Europe, Canada, and Japan than many people generally assume. For one thing, although Ronald Inglehart is generally a strong proponent of secularization theory, he believes that, even in Europe, faith and spirituality are showing some signs of a comeback, with evidence of at least slight upticks in some indicators of religiosity in the latest iteration of the World Values Survey and a significant increase in the percentage of people who say that they often spend time thinking about the meaning and purpose of life. "This is a growing phenomenon," according to Inglehart, and the result is that "spiritual concerns take on a new lease in life" even in the otherwise secular, postindustrial societies of Europe.[24] In Canada, too, recent research by one of the country's premier sociologists, Reginald Bibby, suggests that church attendance is increasing, particularly among conservative Protestants.[25]

In the United States, religion appears as robust as ever. On the questions of whether religion is very important and whether one has to believe in God to be moral, Americans are closer to Africans and Latin Americans than to Europeans. In the 2002 Pew survey, 59 percent of Americans surveyed said that religion is "very important" to them, and 58 percent of Americans stated that it is necessary to believe in God to be moral.[26] Furthermore, in 2000, Andrew Kohut, John Green, Scott Keeter, and Robert Toth published evidence of *increases* in key measures of religiosity among Americans in the course of the 1990s. According to Kohut and his colleagues, between 1987 and 1997, increases of 10 percent or more occurred in the proportions of Americans surveyed who "strongly agreed" that there was no doubt God existed, that inevitably they would have to answer for their sins before God on Judgment Day, that God performed miracles in today's world, that prayer was an important part of their daily life, and that clear guidelines distinguishing good from evil apply to everyone everywhere.[27] These increases occurred among every major religious category: evangelical, mainline, and black Protestants; Catholics; and even seculars![28]

The evidence suggests that modernization theorists were half right. By several objective measures, the world has indeed become more modern. It enjoys more political freedom, more democracy, and more education than perhaps at any time in history. According to Freedom House, the number of "Free" and "Partly Free" countries jumped from 91 to 148 between 1976 and 2006.[29] UNESCO estimates that adult literacy rates doubled in Sub-Saharan Africa, the Arab States, and South and West Asia between 1970 and 2000.[30] Furthermore, the average proportion of people in developing regions living on less than a dollar a day fell from nearly one third to one fifth between 1990 and 2002, according to World Bank estimates.[31]

But like an earlier set of thinkers, modernization theorists also predicted that in becoming more modern, the world would also become more secular.[32] "The philosophers of the eighteenth century," wrote Alexis de Tocqueville in 1835, "explained the gradual weakening of beliefs in an altogether simple fashion. Religious zeal, they said, will be extinguished as freedom and enlightenment increase." As Tocqueville commented even then, "It is unfortunate that the facts do not accord with this theory."[33] As the world has become more free, more enlightened, and more prosperous, it has also become more religious.

Public and Private

Not only have the world's major religious communities expanded and religious commitment intensified, but religion has become much more politicized in nearly every part of the globe. Beginning in the middle of the 1970s, evidence mounted that religion not only remained a vital part of people's private lives but also was beginning to play an increasingly influential role in public life. While secular leaders such as Nasser, ideologies such as Communism, and forms of nationalism such as those of Nkrumah in Africa and Nehru in India began to falter, religious beliefs, leaders, and institutions inspired public confidence and fostered dramatic political change.

In the developing world in particular, secular leaders and ideologies that seemed in the 1950s and early 1960s to be the harbingers of modern progress—particularly because many had been instrumental in third world decolonization—began to falter shortly thereafter. Nehru's death in 1964 brought a spurt of challenges to the hegemony of the secularist Congress Party, including from Hindu-nationalist elements. (A proposal to create a new militant Hindu organization was floated only three months after Nehru's death, and by 1966 it had taken shape as the Vishva Hindu Parishad or "World Hindu Council."[34]) Nasser, who dominated the Middle East with his secular brand of pan-Arabism for nearly twenty years, suffered a humiliating defeat in the 1967 Arab-Israeli War and died three years later. The legitimacy of the secular and Western-oriented shah of Iran declined in the 1970s, and the Iranian Revolution of 1979 brought the Ayatollah Khomeini and an Islamic theocracy to power. In Pakistan, Bangladesh, and Sri Lanka, secular concepts of national identity gave way to more religious forms of nationalism in the 1970s, a trend that has continued to this day.

Greatly accelerating God's "winning streak" was the decline of Soviet Communism in the 1970s and early 1980s, which system was perhaps the most politically powerful and globally successful antireligious movement in history. Partly due to religious groups such as the Catholic Church in Poland and the mujahideen in Afghanistan (not to mention the publication of Aleksandr Solzhenitsyn's *Gulag Archipelago* in 1973), Communism was increasingly on the moral and military defensive from the mid-1970s onward. The eventual collapse of the Soviet socialist model created a political vacuum in numerous developing countries, which some religious groups, such as Islamists in the

Middle East, were able to fill. The collapse of Soviet Communism also embold-
ened some religious groups—above all Osama bin Laden's al Qaeda—to seek
a wider field of operations, and to target a longer list of enemies, including the
United States.

The end result of religion's deepening and spreading politicization is that
it has become an important factor in almost every major area of world politics. Today religion is the most common source of civil wars currently raging.
Monica Toft has shown that from the 1940s to the 1960s, religious conflicts
represented no more than a quarter of civil wars, but in the 1970s, they jumped
to 36 percent, then to 41 percent in the 1980s, and up to 43 percent in the
1990s. Since 2000, fully 47 percent of civil wars have been religious.[35] Furthermore, religious ideology is a leading motivation for most transnational terrorist
attacks, particularly but not exclusively those committed by al Qaeda.[36] At the
same time, religion has mobilized millions of people to oppose authoritarian
regimes, inaugurate democratic transitions, support respect for human rights,
and relieve human suffering. It is also a growing source of ethnic and national
identity.[37] Religion contains an immense capacity to define and mobilize people within and across state boundaries, both for good and for ill.

Manipulative Elites?

Some dismiss religion's increasing worldwide politicization as a product of
manipulative elites who merely use sacred symbols to mobilize ignorant
masses for their own political purposes. In a major speech in October 2005,
for instance, President Bush proclaimed that "[Islamic radicals] exploit resent-
ful and disillusioned young men and women, recruiting them through radical mosques as the pawns of terror."[38] He added that radical Islamic ideology
"exploits Islam for political ends and defiles a noble faith." This widespread
view presupposes a top-down or instrumentalist theory of religion: elites use
religion for their own ends.[39] The corollary is that religion serves as the pal-
liative of the masses or the weak, as compensation for material insecurity or
psychological inadequacy.[40]

On this theory, religion is afforded little or no independent role in moving
people to act. Rather, it is seen as both passive and pathological—a secondary
symptom of societal dysfunction. In a normal, modern society, religion would
be little cause for concern, or if it were, it would only be because a few nefarious
elites manipulated it for their own ends.

Clearly the role of manipulative religious and political leaders, whether a
Jim Jones or an Osama bin Laden, should not be denied altogether. But it is

simply inadequate as a comprehensive explanation of the massive and global entry of religion into public life in so many different contexts from the 1970s onward. For even if one grants that elite manipulation of religion explains much of its worldwide salience in public life, a crucial though neglected question is why religion is the chosen instrument of such elites.

The answer, of course, is that it is chosen because it is effective. And it is effective because it has enjoyed a durable hold on popular imaginations in country after country, while secular nationalisms and ideologies like pan-Arabism and Communism suffered increasing blows to their legitimacy in the late 1960s, 1970s, and 1980s. In other words, the marriage of religion with politics is not necessarily imposed on people, but welcomed, if not demanded, by them.[41]

The independent force of religion is clearly demonstrated by polling data, which reveal that large percentages of people demand that religion play a greater role in their politics. According to the Pew Global Attitudes Project, in surveys of Muslims in Pakistan, Turkey, Uzbekistan, Nigeria, and Indonesia in 1999 and 2002, respondents were asked whether they believed that "religious leaders should play a larger role in politics." In all of the countries except Indonesia, the percentage of those surveyed who said they completely or mostly agreed increased between 1999 and 2002, with a notable jump among Nigerian Muslims from 72 percent in 1999 to 91 percent in 2002.[42] In a six-nation survey conducted by Shibley Telhami in May 2004, pluralities of people in Jordan, Saudi Arabia, and the United Arab Emirates said that they wanted the clergy to play a bigger role in their political system.[43] In the same survey, majorities or pluralities of people in Jordan, Morocco, Saudi Arabia, and the United Arab Emirates cited their Islamic identity as their preeminent identity, trumping their national identity, among others. Recent events underscore this tendency. The collapse of the quasi-secular Ba'athist dictatorship in Iraq was immediately followed by the reemergence of religious and ethnic allegiances combined with an insistence that Shia Islam play a dominant role in the country's political life, including in its constitution.[44]

Even in highly developed countries with traditionally secular politics, the public salience of religion cannot be ignored. Consider Europe. A number of Europe's most contentious public controversies, such as Turkish accession to the European Union, immigration, and terrorism, involve Islam and the role of religion in European identity. Survey after survey demonstrates that large numbers of Europeans—including many Turks—believe that Turkey is too Islamic ever to join the European Union. This is despite the strenuous efforts of the vast majority of Europe's political elite to persuade them otherwise. Even in secular France, one of the most important reasons given by those surveyed by *Le Figaro* in 2004 for opposing Turkish accession to the European Union was that there are "too many religious and cultural differences" between Europe and Turkey.[45] Remarkably, this is true in a France in which only 11 percent say that religion is "very important" to them.[46]

Religious issues and individuals are increasingly shaping the public agenda in "secular" Japan and Canada as well. In Japan the ruling Liberal Democratic Party announced in 2005 that it would try to change the constitution to relax the traditional separation of religion and state—mostly to deflect domestic criticism of the prime minister's regular visits to Yasukuni, the controversial Shinto shrine for Japanese war dead.[47] And in Canada the country's prime minister since January 2006, Stephen Harper, is an evangelical and arguably the country's most openly religious politician in decades.

Why do so many modern people warmly welcome religious ideas, leaders, and movements into public life? No doubt part of the reason lies in the comprehensiveness and stability of religious frameworks. For many people, religion permeates all aspects of life, serving as a map for what the universe is really like and a navigation system for how to conduct one's life.[48] Some have argued that such maps are implausible or otherwise unsustainable in the modern world. In fact, however, the rapid technological and social changes associated with modernization and globalization give people new and increasingly plausible reasons to turn to these maps for guidance. Indeed, as Walter Mead has suggested, the perceived utility of these maps arguably *increases* as people's social, political, and economic lives change in more and more basic ways and at a faster and faster rate.

At a more basic level, when so many people are religious "in private," we should not be surprised when they seek to be religious "in public." Although separation of the personal and public is considered by some to be essential to civil and democratic politics,[49] in practice it is psychologically difficult, especially because many religions purport to provide a comprehensive moral compass whose scope is intrinsically difficult to restrict.[50] People's attachment to their religious and moral compasses becomes even more intense with increased anxiety concerning perceived threats to their way of life. Global attitudes seem to underscore this. In the vast majority of countries surveyed by the Pew Global Attitudes Project in 2002, large majorities of the population fear that their "traditional way of life is getting lost."[51] For example, not just conservative Christians but Americans across the religious spectrum have concluded that religion is an answer—if not necessarily *the* answer—to America's moral problems. According to a 2000 Public Agenda survey, "Americans strongly equate religion with personal ethics and behavior, considering it an antidote to the moral decline they perceive in our nation today."[52] For reasons both logical and psychological, many people regard the public reaffirmation of their religious identity as an effective and perhaps indispensable means of strengthening traditional forms of morality, community, and identity.

Divinity and Democracy

Many Americans have been educated to believe that democracy and secularism go hand in hand, with democracy requiring that religion be separate from their public lives and policy making. It is widely believed that the U.S. Constitution requires the state to keep its distance from religion. The integrity of American liberal democracy requires that religion be kept private—on the assumption that religion would otherwise threaten liberal democracy.[53] This is a normative view borne of centuries in which the marriage of power and faith in Europe resulted in horrendous bloodshed. The insistence on a secular state—which has usually amounted to the subordination of faith to state power, rather than their separation—is a direct product of this unique historical experience.[54] In this view, isn't the global, political upsurge of religion in the modern world a terrible thing?

In fact, the states of Europe sought and often achieved a coercive subordination of religious institutions to government power in the seventeenth century under very special political circumstances—that is, in the aftermath of approximately eighty years of brutal intra-Christian warfare. The Treaties of Westphalia of 1648 aimed to prevent future wars by resolving three fundamental issues: the sovereignty of states, the identity of their citizens, and the role of religion. A system of states with inviolable borders emerged. Within those borders, the religious identities of citizens became a function of the religious loyalties and political interests of state leaders. Religious identity and allegiance were defined by sovereign states, in varying degrees of coordination with religious authorities, and then imposed coercively on the people as a necessary condition of full membership in the political community.[55]

However, subsequent history demonstrates that religion and democracy can enjoy a symbiotic relationship that fosters political inclusion, equality, and contestation—the hallmarks of democracy. In seventeenth-century Europe and eighteenth-century America, Protestantism helped give birth to democracy and religious freedom,[56] whereas in the nineteenth century, religious political parties (mostly Christian Democratic) were among the most welcoming and expansive in terms of membership, helping push for universal suffrage and mobilizing religious citizens to enter the political process and protect their rights.[57] As a historical matter, a close interaction between religion and state has not necessarily undermined democracy. In fact, a 2007 empirical survey found that very few of the world's democracies—including Western liberal democracies—practice a complete separation of religion and state, and concluded that, no matter how the concept is defined, it "is not necessary for a functioning democracy or liberal democracy."[58]

In other words, modernity assumed a trajectory quite different from the one envisioned by either the architects of Westphalia or the prophets of the Enlightenment. Reality first began to diverge dramatically from their expectations when, from the late eighteenth century onward, "the people" in both Europe and America became increasingly sovereign over both their governments and their religious identities. Despite the statist and anti-populist prejudices of many statesmen and intellectuals, such as Grotius, Hobbes, Burke, Bentham, and Kant, modernity was increasingly characterized by a transition from elite sovereignty to popular sovereignty.[59] This transition to greater popular sovereignty was in fact hastened and deepened by populist religious forces, particularly dissenting and evangelical forms of Protestantism. In addition, it strongly promoted both the norm of democracy in politics and the norm of individual freedom of conscience in the realm of religion.[60] While this epochal empowerment of the *demos* is often portrayed as an inevitable defeat for religion's traditional authority, it often intensifies religion's influence in at least three respects.

First, the political norm of popular sovereignty presupposes that the people and their interests can be coherently defined and represented—that "the people" are sovereign presupposes that "the people" have a coherent identity. In many historical cases, the basis for defining the national identity of the people has been religion,[61] and today religion is increasingly playing a nation-defining role in several major democracies, such as India, Israel, Turkey, and even the United States.[62] Recent electoral battles in these and other democracies—such as the 2000 and 2004 elections in the United States, the 1999 and 2004 elections in India, the 2002 and 2007 elections in Turkey, the 2001 elections in Bangladesh, and the 2004 elections in Sri Lanka—have often at least partly become battles over whether religion should play a greater role in defining national identity and public life.

Second, the rise of popular sovereignty and the global expansion of freedom have contributed not only to the "desecularization" of national identities but also to a much wider "sacralization" of public life. In other words, not only has religion contributed to democracy and democratization, but democracy and democratization have empowered religion.

Thanks to the "third wave" of democratization and to smaller waves of freedom that have occurred since, people in dozens of countries have been empowered to shape their public lives in ways that were inconceivable in the

1950s and 1960s. A pattern emerged as they exercised their new political free-doms. In country after country, politically empowered groups began to chal-lenge the secular constraints imposed by the first generation of modernizing, post-independence leaders. Often, as in communist countries, secular strait-jackets had been imposed by sheer coercion; in other cases, as in Ataturk's Tur-key, Nehru's India, and Nasser's Egypt, secularism retained legitimacy partly because the political systems afforded little effective competition and partly because elites considered it essential to national integration, economic develop-ment, and social modernization—and, at least in the case of these three leaders, partly because of their sheer charisma. In Latin America, both left-wing secu-lar movements such as the Mexican Revolution and right-wing dictatorships, sometimes in league with the Catholic Church, severely restricted the activi-ties and influence of grassroots religious actors on public life, with the former focusing their restrictions on Catholic groups and the latter focusing them on evangelicals and Pentecostals.

As politics gradually liberalized and democratized in countries such as Mexico, Nigeria, Turkey, Indonesia, and India (after Indira Gandhi's suspen-sion of democracy between 1975 and 1977), religion's influence on political life increased dramatically.[63] Even in the United States, evangelicals exercised a growing, grassroots influence on the Republican Party in the 1980s and 1990s partly because the presidential nomination process depended more on popu-lar primaries and less on the decisions of party bosses meeting behind closed doors.[64] In short, to the extent that political systems reflect the voice and values of the people, they reflect the religiosity of the people.

Third, the pluralistic condition of modernity is no longer one in which reli-gion is inherited or taken for granted but rather one in which socially empow-ered individuals can choose to reject it, embrace it, or ignore it.[65] When religion is self-consciously chosen by people under these conditions, the form in which it is chosen can often be intense, public, and conservative. "Pluralistic moder-nity can promote the vitality of culturally well-equipped traditional religions," observes sociologist Christian Smith. "Far from necessarily undermining the strength of orthodox faith, modernity creates the conditions in which tradi-tional religion may thrive."[66] Many people who are free to choose religion under modern and democratic circumstances often choose to adopt forms of religious identity that are morally demanding and publicly assertive.

Far from stamping out religion, modernization has spawned a new genera-tion of savvy, activist, organizationally sophisticated, and technologically adept religious movements, including evangelical Protestantism in America and much of the "global South," "Hindutva" in India, Salafist and Wahhabi forms of Islam in the Middle East, "engaged" Buddhism in South and Southeast Asia,

Pentecostalism in Africa and Latin America, and revivalist forms of Catholicism exemplified by groups such as Opus Dei and Communion and Liberation. "Religious actors appear to have an incredible capacity to draw on traditional beliefs and practices of faith and adjust them to a variety of social situations, including modern structures, imperatives, and sensibilities."[67] In other words, the most dynamic religiosity is not so much "old-time religion" or stubbornly separatist "fundamentalism" as activist forms of religion that creatively combine tradition and modernity in order to appeal to modern people—often urban, middle-class people—in modern circumstances. Today's religious upsurge is less a return of rigid religious orthodoxies than an explosion of "neo-orthodoxies."

A common denominator of these neo-orthodoxies is the deployment of sophisticated and politically capable organizations. These modern organizations effectively marshal specialized institutions in addition to the latest technologies to recruit new members, strengthen connections with old adherents, deliver social services, and press their agenda in the public sphere. The Vishva Hindu Parishad, formally established in 1966, "saffronized" large swaths of India through its religious and social activism and (working closely with its parent body, the Rashtriya Swayamsevak Sangh or "National Volunteer Organization," founded in 1925) laid the groundwork for the Bharatiya Janata Party's electoral successes in the late 1980s and 1990s. Similar groups in the Islamic world include the Muslim Brotherhood in Egypt and Jordan, a succession of Islamist parties in Turkey (such as the Welfare Party, the Virtue Party, and today's Justice and Development Party), Hamas in the Palestinian territories, Hezbollah in Lebanon, and Muhammadiyah and the Nahdlatul Ulama in Indonesia. In Brazil, Pentecostals have organized their own legislative caucus, representing about 10 percent of the national congress. Religious communities are also developing remarkable transnational capabilities, appealing to foreign governments and international bodies deemed sympathetic to their cause.

As some of these religious movements gained greater influence with the decline of secularism's legitimacy and effective political authority, they helped usher in the "third wave" of democracy in Latin America, Eastern Europe, Sub-Saharan Africa, and Asia from the mid-1970s to the early 1990s, in addition to a few smaller waves of democracy since.[68] The post–Vatican II Catholic Church played a particularly important role in opposing authoritarian regimes and mobilizing and organizing frustrated populations in all these regions. In the Philippines, for example, Cardinal Sin and Catholic organizations openly condemned the policies and electoral fraud of President Ferdinand Marcos and often ran several steps ahead of the Vatican.[69]

A key question is the ongoing relationship between activist, neo-orthodox religion and democratization. Are they compatible? The answer may depend partly on the strength and autonomy of the religious institutions in which religious leaders operate.[70] For example, if politics is a balancing of interests, the post–Vatican II Catholic Church was—and is—well positioned to play an active role in regime transitions. Catholicism's highly centralized and organized character made it an effective "peer competitor" with the authoritarian states it sought to democratize.[71] Catholicism also enjoyed an institutional capacity to adapt to democracy in the sense that it had a centralized and authoritative mechanism whereby it could embrace liberal democratic principles on the basis of its deepest theological resources, and then disseminate this doctrinal development to the faithful.

Whereas the earlier "third wave" of democracy was largely a Catholic wave, the $64,000 question is whether there can be a "fourth-wave" of democratization in the Muslim world. In 2006 only three of the world's forty-seven Muslim-majority countries—Mali, Senegal, and Indonesia—lived under regimes Freedom House classifies as "free." Unlike Catholicism, Islam is not centralized under a single leadership and doctrine capable of playing a balancing, mediating, and consensus-building role on political and social issues. Instead, local or national leaders define the religion's response to local and national conditions. Unfortunately, such leaders have several disadvantages when it comes to democratization. They often promote different and mutually competitive interpretations of texts—some democratic and liberal, others undemocratic and illiberal. Furthermore, lacking recognized authority and broad constituencies, they are either easily subverted or co-opted by authoritarian states or tend toward violent radicalism to compensate for their weakness vis-à-vis the state. The story of the major country where Muslim actors have been successful in promoting democracy—Indonesia—supports this analysis: these actors were successful not only because they adopted democratic political theologies but also because they were organized around two powerful civil society institutions—Muhammadiyah and Nahdlatul Ulama—that enjoyed substantial autonomy from state control.[72]

Conversely, the lack of a centralized authority structure in Islam may be one reason most religious civil wars are within Muslim societies, with Muslim fighting Muslim.[73] These religious civil wars are fought over the proper role of religion in relation to the state and interpretations of holy texts. The trajectory of the cleric Moqtada al-Sadr in postwar Iraq is thus not unusual. Religious and political elites are competing—violently if necessary—for the mantle of providing the one true and orthodox interpretation. The 1990s witnessed the widespread phenomenon of ethnic elites using hostile and extreme nationalist rhetoric to ethnically outbid opponents.[74] The vulnerable and defensive position in which some ethnic groups perceived themselves to be often favored elites who adopted the most extremist positions. Just as ethnic outbidding plagued democratization efforts then, often resulting in violence, a similar dynamic of "religious outbidding" dogs democratization efforts today.

Conclusions

What may be most surprising and disturbing about the increasing power of religion in global politics is not the trend itself but the fact that so many foreign-policy makers, analysts, and journalists around the world persist in finding it so surprising and disturbing. Earth-shattering as they may appear, the thunder-bolts of prophetic politics can no longer be seen as bolts out of the blue. They have now become too frequent to be deemed unexpected and unpredictable. And the worldwide politicization of religion began too long ago, has built up too much momentum, and is rooted in factors too enduring and pervasive to be a blip on the geopolitical radar screen.

The belief that religion's global upsurge is a parenthetical and abnormal exception to the iron laws of modernization and secularization was perhaps plausible in 1966 when *Time* asked, "Is God Dead?" But when radical reli-gious mobilization is characterized as "out of step with a secularizing march by history" in 2006, it becomes harder to make excuses.[75] For some people, secularism may be desirable as a social ideal. But as a framework for describ-ing, explaining, and predicting the course of global politics in the real world, it has become a serious liability. Believers in iron laws of history are usually disappointed in the end. Believers in a "march by history" toward some secular end-state are headed for more disappointment than most.

Due partly to social science theories like modernization and partly to for-eign policy paradigms like "realism," American policy analysts and decision makers have long been imprisoned within conceptual straitjackets that consis-tently underrate religious vitality and its political impact in the modern world. The secularist expectations generated by these models not only yielded what proved to be costly decisions, but also ensured that U.S. policymakers would continually be surprised and blindsided by a vast array of global religious move-ments. When in the mid-1970s the CIA dismissed an internal proposal to study religious leaders in pre-revolutionary Iran as useless "sociology," it was guilty of more than a poor judgment call.[76] When, in early 2003, U.S. prewar plan-ners expected that Iraq would democratize easily because it was assumed to be an essentially secular and middle-class society, the problem was not merely that they happened to be wrong.[77] These were not retail mistakes resulting from inadequate information, but wholesale strategic failures resulting from a deep-seated and pervasive mindset. In the words of David Brooks, it is high time that the world's policy makers and opinion shapers kick what has proven to be an extraordinarily stubborn "secularist habit."[78]

Contrary to the influential scholarly theories of the 1950s and 1960s, religion is not dying with modernization. Contrary to conventional wisdom, religion plays an independent and powerful role in how people view themselves and how states conduct their affairs. And, contrary to the assumptions of recent U.S. foreign policy, democracy promotion may only increase the political role of religion—including radical religion—throughout the world, most immediately in Iraq and other parts of the Middle East. God is winning in global politics. And modernization, democratization, and globalization have only made him stronger.

PART II

Case Studies

2

Religion and Terrorism: Misreading al Qaeda

Paul Marshall

"This war is fundamentally religious. . . . Those who try to cover this crystal clear fact, which the entire world has admitted, are deceiving the Islamic nation. This war is fundamentally religious. . . . This fact is proven in the book of God Almighty and in the teachings of our messenger, may God's peace and blessings be upon him. This war is fundamentally religious. Under no circumstances should we forget this enmity between us and the infidels. For, the enmity is based on creed."
                                        —Osama bin Laden, November 3, 2001

"It is a religious-economic war. . . . Therefore, religious terms should be used when describing the ruler who does not follow God's revelations and path and champions the infidels by extending military facilities to them or implementing the UN resolutions against Islam and Muslims. Those should be called infidels and renegades. . . . The confrontation and conflict between us and them started centuries ago. The confrontation and conflict will continue because the conflict between right and falsehood will continue until Judgment Day."
                                        —Osama bin Laden, March 2004

The United States, and much of the rest of the world, is suffering attacks by a variety of extremist Islamic groups, most notably an apparently apocalyptic religious network or franchise usually referred to by its nickname "al Qaeda," which has also styled itself more formally as the "World Islamic Front for Holy War against Jews and Crusaders." The attacks perpetrated by this network have usually been accompanied by a plethora of videotapes, audiotapes, declarations, books, letters, fatwas, magazines, e-mails, and Web sites that present and explain its theology, its view of history and the political order, and its understanding of contemporary events, in order to explain and justify its actions in terms of its version of Islamic teaching, law, history, and practice. These extensive materials, now collected in several volumes, expound a religiously shaped program that announces as its general goal a plan to unite Muslims worldwide into one people, the *ummah,* with one divinely sanctioned leader, a caliph, governed by a reactionary version of *shari'a* (Islamic law), and organized to wage *jihad* (in this context, divinely sanctioned war) on the rest of the world.[1] Its primary target was initially local Muslim regimes and their supporters, which al Qaeda usually refers to as "apostates" from Islam, but now also includes those it maintains have supported such regimes and who are now allegedly waging war around the world on the true Muslims. These latter opponents are referred to variously as "Crusaders," "followers of the cross," "Jews," or "infidels."

Consequently, the network's attacks have not been confined to America or "the West"; in fact, most of its victims are non-Westerners and Muslims. Its members have sought to kill, injure, or silence those opposed to its version of Islam and the caliphate, whether Muslim or non-Muslim, on the Left or on the Right, American, British, Israeli, Australian, French, Indian, Algerian, Sudanese, Indonesian, Thai, or Filipino, and whether or not supported by the United Nations. Its justification for this breadth of attacks is found in its stated global goals and its global reading of history.

One illustration is the grievances listed in its manual. The manual begins not by recalling the birth of Israel or the Soviet invasion of Afghanistan but an event often little noted in America: "the fall of [the] orthodox Caliphates on March 3, 1924." That this same event and historical period is a source of continuing grievance is shown in Osama bin Laden's November 3, 2001, videotape, which similarly proclaims, "Following World War I, which ended more than 83 years ago, the whole Islamic world fell under the Crusader banner." For bin Laden, his followers, and his imitators, one of the key turning points of history was the ending of the Ottoman Empire and the fragmentation of the Muslim ummah by Turkish leader Mustafa Kemal Atatürk through his creation of modern secular Turkey and abolition of the caliphate. Their most fundamental grievance, continually expressed, is the modern collapse of the Islamic world in the face of "Christendom," a collapse that they argue can be explained only by Muslims' weakness due to their apostasy from true, pure Islam and can be reversed only by returning to the radicals' version of Islam.

These themes are repeated in the network's statements, yet much of our media ignore or downplay this explicitly religious narrative, rationale, and motive, instead referring only to al Qaeda ("the base"), and often interpreting its actions by means of a grid of Western concerns and preconceptions such as third world liberation, economics, and recent events in the Middle East. However, bin Laden's and Ayman al-Zawahiri's complaints are set within a context of Islamic history and teaching quite distinct from the nostrums of Western Enlightenment and post-Enlightenment thought.

There are now many radical Islamist terrorist groups and tendencies, even within the al Qaeda network itself, and they often have disagreements with each other—perhaps the best known being elucidated in Zawahiri's January 2004 letter to Abu Musab al-Zarqawi, then the leader of al Qaeda in Iraq, criticizing him for his attacks on Shiites. There are also a variety of theorists and writers, such as Abu Musab al-Suri and Abu Muhammad al-Maqdisi, who are less well known to people in the West but are very influential with their extremist audience. But here I will concentrate on the ideology of the network now known colloquially as al Qaeda, and in particular the statements of its two senior figures, Osama bin Laden and Ayman al-Zawahiri, because their writings and speeches have, for excellent reasons, drawn most media attention, and they seem to have the same general ideology.

The World Islamic Front's Ideology

On August 23, 1996, bin Laden issued a "Declaration of War against the Americans Occupying the Land of the Two Holy Places." Its focus was, as its title implies, the Arabian Peninsula, where it indicted the Saudis for the religious offense of "Suspension of the Islamic Shari'ah law and exchanging it with man made civil law." However, the declaration mentioned much of the world and also described Muslims whose "blood has been spilled in Palestine and Iraq." It continued, "The horrifying pictures of the massacre of Qana, in Lebanon, are still fresh in our memory. Massacres in Tajikistan, Burma, Kashmir, Assam, Philippine, Patani, Ogadin, Somalia, Erithria, Chechnya and in Bosnia-Herzegovina took place, massacres that send shivers through the body and shake the conscience." It also expounded on what it claims is worldwide war against Islam waged by Indian Hindus; Burmese Buddhists; Russian, Ethiopian, and Eritrean Orthodox; and, above all, Zionist Jews, with crusader Americans leading the cabal. The declaration's grievances culminated with what it described as "the latest and greatest of these aggressions, the greatest incurred by the Muslims since the death of the Prophet," the presence of the "American Crusaders and their allies" in Islam's holiest places.[2] In response to these alleged crimes, remembering that Muslims had fought against "the' Russians in Afghanistan, the Serbs in Bosnia-Herzegovina," and today are fighting in Chechnya . . . [and] in Tajikistan," bin Laden called for "fighting [jihad] against the disbelievers in every part of the world."[3]

Bin Laden did mention the Palestinians, but because he believes that nationalism is anti-Islamic and is even a form of apostasy from Islam, his concern was not with a people fighting for a homeland but rather with the fact that infidels were in control of the Al-Aqsa Mosque, often thought by Muslims to be the site of the Furthest Mosque, the destination of the Prophet's night journey, and as such Islam's third-holiest place.[4] He also described Israel and the Palestinian areas as part of the Arabian Peninsula, and hence accused the Israelis of "annexing" the "northerly part" of the land of the two holy places, so that all three of Islam's holiest places lay under the feet of infidels.

While regaining control of the three holiest places remained central to bin Laden's agenda, he also insisted that all lands that have ever been ruled by Muslims must now be returned to their control. In the year following his "Declaration of War," he reiterated that "Jihad will remain an individual obligation until all other lands that were Muslim are returned to us so that Islam will reign again: before us lie Palestine, Bokhara, Lebanon, Chad, Eritrea, Somalia, the Philippines, Burma, Southern Yemen, Tashkent, and Andalusia (Spain)."[5]

On February 23, 1998, he and Zawahiri, along with "Abu-Yasir Rifa'i Ahmad Taha, Egyptian Islamic Group, Shaykh Mir Hamzah, secretary of the Jamiat-ul-Ulema-e-Pakistan, and Fazlul Rahman, amir of the Jihad Movement in Bangladesh," released the manifesto of their "World Islamic Front for Holy War against Jews and Crusaders." It echoed previous statements and called for attacks on Americans, based on charges that "for over seven years America has occupied the holiest parts of the Islamic lands, the Arabian peninsula, plundering its wealth, dictating to its leaders, humiliating its people, terrorizing its neighbors and turning its bases there into a spearhead with which to fight the neighboring Muslim peoples."[6] Later that year, in December, the "World Front for Jihad against Jews and Crusaders" announced, "There are two parties to the conflict: World Christianity, which is allied with Jews and Zionism, led by the United States, Britain and Israel. The second part is the Islamic world."[7] It also repeated the demand for the return of "Andalusia" to Islam.[8]

Following September 11, 2001, bin Laden reemphasized the religious nature of his side of the war: "This war is fundamentally religious. . . . Those who try to cover this crystal clear fact, which the entire world has admitted, are deceiving the Islamic nation. This war is fundamentally religious. . . . This fact is proven in the book of God Almighty and in the teachings of our messenger, may God's peace and blessings be upon him. This war is fundamentally religious. Under no circumstances should we forget this enmity between us and the infidels. For, the enmity is based on creed. . . . The unequivocal truth is that Bush has carried the cross and raised its banner high."

He went on: "Following World War I, which ended more than 83 years ago, the whole Islamic world fell under the crusader banner—under the British, French, and Italian governments. They divided the whole world, and Palestine was occupied by the British." In response, he called for "revenge for those innocent children in Palestine, Iraq, southern Sudan, Somalia, Kashmir and the Philippines. . . . Take for example the Chechens." He said, "They are a Muslim people who have been attacked by the Russian bear which embraces the Christian Orthodox faith."

He then castigated the United Nations for its purported attempt "to divide the largest country in the Islamic world. . . . This criminal, Kofi Annan, was . . . putting pressure on the Indonesian government, telling it, you have twenty-four hours to divide and separate East Timor from Indonesia by force. The crusader Australian forces were on Indonesian shores, and, in fact, they landed to separate East Timor, which is part of the Islamic world."[9]

The consistent themes of these lengthy statements, declarations, and manifestos revolve around the occupation of the three Muslim holy places and the purported worldwide war waged by infidels against Muslims, both of which are part of a religious struggle that will continue until Judgment Day. The language use is explicitly religious and embedded in a version of Islam and of religious history without which it would make no sense. He castigates regimes throughout the world and describes Russia, like the United States, as a Christian power attacking Islam, with Vladimir Putin purportedly demanding "that the cross and the Jews should stand by him."

This language and pattern of argument have continued in the utterances of bin Laden and Zawahiri and their confreres. However, there are some exceptions, in which, in addresses aimed at English speakers, though not in those targeting Arabic speakers, he has tried to submerge his basic and explicitly religious agenda and instead harp on some peculiarly Western grievances such as environmentalism or campaign finance reform. These pronouncements usually show a marked change in tone, as if he had taken public relations advice that his previous statements had played well in Peshawar but not in Peoria or Paris. His October 6, 2002, "Letter to America" mentioned the Kyoto accord on global warming, environmental problems, election campaign finances, and the use of nuclear weapons on Japan—matters he had consistently ignored in the previous decade. He also added mention of President Clinton's "immoral acts" in the Oval Office, homosexuality, intoxicants, gambling, charging interest, and using women in advertising. Even in this somewhat crude attempt to play to American prejudices, he returned to his basic religious message and, above all, condemned the U.S. constitution for not enshrining Islamic shari'a and instead allowing the American people to make their own laws. He concluded with a fervent appeal to Americans to repent and become Muslim: "The first thing we are calling you to is Islam."[10] Meanwhile, his addresses to his primary, Muslim, audience focused on his longstanding concerns. His January 2004 message "to the Muslim nation" emphasized that, because the West "invaded our countries more than 2,500 years ago," "It is a religious-economic war. . . . Therefore, religious terms should be used when describing the ruler who does not follow God's revelations and path and champions the infidels by extending military facilities to them or implementing the UN resolutions against Islam and Muslims. Those should be called infidels and renegades. . . . [T]he confrontation and conflict between us and them started centuries ago. The confrontation and conflict will continue because the conflict between right and falsehood will continue until Judgment Day."[11]

At the end of 2004, he lamented the "control exerted by the Zionists and the Cross worshippers" and described the world conflict once again as "a struggle between two camps," contending, "One camp is headed by America, and it represents the global Kufr [infidelity], accompanied by all apostates. The other camp represents the Islamic Ummah [nation] headed by its Mujahideen Brigades."[12] Similarly, his December 27, 2004, "Letter to the Iraqi People" referred to the war as a conflict "between the army of Mohammed, the army of belief, and the people of the cross." He stressed the primacy of Islamic law and warned Iraqis not to participate in the January 30, 2005, elections because the Iraqi constitution is "a Jahiliyya [pre-Islamic] constitution that is made by man," and Muslims may elect only a leader for whom "Islam is the only source of the rulings and laws." Voting in Afghanistan was likewise forbidden on the grounds that the Karzai government is "apostate." Finally, on similar grounds, he forbade voting in Palestinian Authority elections because "the constitution of the land is a Jahili made by man," and added the novel, but certainly religiously loaded, claim that Fatah candidate Mahmoud Abbas "is a Baha'i."[13] Since Baha'is are regarded as apostates who should be killed, this was a grave and dangerous charge.[14]

These religious themes have continued. On April 23, 2006, while castigating the United Nations, bin Laden denounced "pagan Buddhists," presumably the Chinese. He claimed that the "world's crusaders, alongside pagan Buddhists, hold the five permanent seats" in the UN Security Council. (The following year, Indian police spokesman Prem Lal said Lashkar-e-Toiba, an al Qaeda affiliate in South Asia, had threatened to kill the Dalai Lama "on the directions of a foreign organisation," which he declined to name.[15]) Bin Laden also stressed India's role and referred to a "Crusader-Zionist-Hindu war against the Muslims," even seeking to blame Hindus for their role in the alleged conspiracy to separate East Timor from Indonesia. In addition, he complains at length about the 2001 Sudan Peace Act passed by Congress, which facilitated an end to the North–South civil war in that country and may allow the southern part, largely Christian and animist, to separate from the rest and to be exempt from shari'a. Bin Laden tied the fate of Sudan to the earlier destruction of the Ottoman state and the ending of the caliphate, and the subsequent division of the area by the British in 1956. He claimed that the infidels are again using Darfur to divide the Muslim world, and calls on the mujahideen to gather landmines, anti-armor grenades, and rocket-propelled grenades and go to Darfur to fight the infidels. He also condemned the Danish cartoonists at the center of the 2005–2006 Muhammad cartoon controversy as well as "free thinkers" and heretics among Muslims, especially Muslim reformers in Kuwait and Saudi Arabia, asserting that all of these supposed offenders should be killed.[16]

Meanwhile, Zawahiri was echoing the same themes. On June 9, 2006, he claimed that the United Nations was preparing to occupy and divide Darfur.[17] On June 23 he interrupted his praise of Zarqawi to denounce U.S. ambassador to Iraq Zalmay Khalilzad as "the Afghan apostate" and to denounce Turkey for being secular.[18] In September 2006 he emphasized threats to Darfur once again and responded to what he regarded as Pope Benedict XVI's criticism of Islam. His response went on at length, condemning and refuting Christianity, and criticizing Christian views of the nature of Christ, the sanctity of the Church, the crucifixion, the resurrection, and the Holy Spirit. He concluded that Benedict's comments, in addition to Salman Rushdie's books and the cartoons of Muhammad published in the Danish newspaper *JyllandsPosten*, are part of the "War on Islam."[19]

Infidels and Massacres

This religious focus on infidels, rather than Americans or "Westerners," emerged chillingly in the May 29, 2004, Khobar killings in Saudi Arabia. An interview with Fawwaz bin Muhammad Al-Nashami, who commanded the Al-Quds Brigade that took responsibility for the massacre, published on the al Qaeda–linked Web site Sawt Al-Jihad, describes that murderous rampage.[20]

We tied the infidel [a Briton] by one leg [behind the car]. . . . Everyone watched the infidel being dragged. . . . The infidel's clothing was torn to shreds, and he was naked in the street. The street was full of people, as this was during work hours, and everyone watched the infidel being dragged, praise and gratitude be to Allah. . . .

We entered one of the companies' [offices], and found there an American infidel who looked like a director of one of the companies. I went into his office and called him. When he turned to me, I shot him in the head, and his head exploded. We entered another office and found one infidel from South Africa, and our brother Hussein slit his throat. We asked Allah to accept [these acts of devotion] from us, and from him. . . . [W]e found a Swedish infidel. Brother Nimr cut off his head, and put it at the gate so that it would be seen by all those entering and exiting. . . .

We found Filipino Christians. We cut their throats and dedicated them to our brothers the Mujahideen in the Philippines. [Likewise], we found Hindu engineers and we cut their throats, too, Allah be praised. That same day, we purged Muhammad's land of many Christians and polytheists. . . . Then we went up to the next floor, found several Hindu dogs, and cut their throats. . . .

The Indian Muslims told us that their manager was a vile Hindu who did not permit them to pray, and that he would arrive shortly. When [the manager] arrived, we verified his religion by means of his identifying documents, and we kept him with us for a short time [before killing him].

. . . brother Hussein was on the stairs and noticed an Italian infidel. He aimed his gun at him and told him to come closer. The infidel came closer. We saw his identifying documents . . . afterwards we would cut his throat and dedicate him to the Italians who were fighting our brothers in Iraq and to the idiotic Italian president who wants to confront the lions of Islam.

Consistently, the attackers described their enemies, whatever their country or race or politics, as "infidels" or "polytheists." They were especially joyful at the killing of an Italian, a Briton, and Filipinos, whose countries were participants in the coalition in Iraq. But they also killed a Swede and a South African, whose countries took no part in the invasion of Iraq, and their greatest frisson seemed to come from killing Hindus, who, as purported polytheists, are even further down al Qaeda's religious scale than "people of the book," such as Christians and Jews.

While America is consistently seen by al Qaeda as the greatest power among the infidels, nevertheless, after debating the matter, the terrorists spared an American because he was himself a Muslim. They even apologized to him for getting blood on his carpet. Meanwhile, they happily killed Filipino, Swedish, British, Italian, and South African Christians and Indian Hindus—just as their allies in Thailand kill Buddhists such as the sixty-three-year-old rubber-tapper Sieng Patkaoe, who was beheaded the same month.

Missing Religious References

The al Qaeda network has consistently explained and justified its actions with a narrative centered on the fall and anticipated rise of the caliphate, the restoration of shari'a, and the inevitable conflict between true Muslim believers and apostates and infidels destined to last until the day of judgment. Many journalists have, however, tended to ignore this fundamental religious dimension and instead concentrated on those terrorist statements that might fit into secular Western preconceptions about oppression, economics, freedom, and progress. One small but telling example is the *New York Times* reference to one Iraqi insurgent; the paper reported, "the man's long speech is addressed to President Bush, who is called a dog at one point." In fact, the man called Bush a "Christian dog," a much more illuminating phrase.[21] The religious dimension was obscured, even obliterated.

Similarly, when Al Jazeera broadcast bin Laden applauding an attack on a tanker off the coast of Yemen, the Associated Press accurately quoted his praise for the heroism "of the faithful holy warriors in Yemen against a crusader oil tanker . . . [that] hit the umbilical cord and lifeline of the crusader community," but then offered its own erroneous guidance by suggesting that Islamist terrorists "often referred to the United States as 'crusaders.'" This attempt to equate the religious designation of crusaders not with Christians but with the United States was especially confusing since the tanker in question was French.[22]

When the Afghan government made public its draft constitution enshrining an undefined Islam as the source of law, a document the U.S. Commission on International Religious Freedom described as "Taliban-lite," the *Washington Post* headlined its story "Proposed Afghan Constitution Fits U.S. Model." But, while under the document's provisions Afghanistan would indeed have a president, a bicameral legislature, and no prime minister, you don't need to be an expert in the Federalist Papers to realize that there is rather more to the U.S. Constitution than these structures. It's not quite the American model to declare "no law can be contrary to the sacred religion of Islam" (Article 3) or that "provisions of adherence to the fundamentals of the sacred religion of Islam . . . cannot be amended" (Article 149). Supreme court justices, like the president and cabinet members, must take an oath to "support justice and righteousness in accord with the provisions of the sacred religion of Islam." The *New York Times* wrongly stated that the draft had "no mention of Shariah, a legal code based on the Koran," a claim echoed by the Associated Press. In fact, Article 130 of the constitution says that, in the absence of an explicit statute or constitutional limit, the supreme court should decide "in accord with Hanafi jurisprudence," one of the four main Sunni schools of shari'a.[23]

On October 13, 2006, *Newsweek* published an article entitled "Caliwho? Why Is President Bush Talking about an Islamic Caliphate? And What Does the Word Mean?" that criticized George W. Bush's increasing use of the term "caliphate" when he described the goals of al Qaeda and like-minded groups. The article's authors, Lisa Miller and Mathew Philips, called it a "fifty-cent word" and pointed out that most Americans had no idea what it meant. They appear to have missed the fact that al Qaeda, and other groups, have consistently and repeatedly asserted that their long-term goal is the restoration of the caliphate, and therefore, if we want to understand al Qaeda's goals we must understand its vision of the caliphate. The authors compound this oversight by claiming that the caliphate ended in Baghdad in 1258, something that would no doubt be a great surprise to the Ottoman caliphs who ruled from Istanbul for centuries until Atatürk abolished the institution. The fact that most Americans do not know this is surely a good reason not to ignore it; rather, it is essential that the president, or any other government official, or any journalist, inform them of its importance.[24]

These accumulated omissions and misconceptions illustrate journalists' religious blind spots, but they also frequently lead to the misreporting of particular events and trends in terrorism. This can be shown in the coverage of the bombings of nightclubs in Bali and the UN headquarters in Iraq, repeated attacks on Christians in Pakistan, and terrorism in Saudi Arabia.

The United Nations, Indonesia, and Iraq

The October 12, 2002, bombings of two nightclubs in Bali, which killed some two hundred people, were described by the media as directed at "the West," with little mention of the fact that they occurred in Indonesia's only Hindu-majority territory and coincided exactly with bombings on the Philippine consulate in Manado, a Christian area hundreds of miles away. Before these bombings, al Qaeda affiliates in Indonesia had already orchestrated the bombing of dozens of Christian schools and churches on Christmas Eve 2000, while their Laskar Jihad allies had massacred thousands of Christians in eastern Indonesia.[25]

Imam Samudra, the bombers' field commander, tied his efforts not only to Middle Eastern politics but to local Indonesian issues and said he was partly driven by "Australia's . . . aggression against East Timor that removed it from Indonesia." In his confession early in 2003, he stressed the religious dimension that "Australia has taken part in efforts to separate East Timor from Indonesia" as part of an "international conspiracy by followers of the Cross."

Bin Laden himself had earlier voiced exactly the same grievance. His November 3, 2001, statement asserted, "Let us examine the stand of the West and the United Nations in the developments in Indonesia. . . . The crusader Australian forces . . . landed to separate East Timor, which is part of the Islamic world."[26] He reiterated this complaint a month after the Bali bombings: "We warned Australia not to join in [the war] in Afghanistan, and [against] its despicable effort to separate East Timor. It ignored the warning until it woke up to the sound of explosions in Bali."[27] Most analysts ignored this statement about East Timor. The *Washington Post* even printed the relevant paragraph with the reference to East Timor missing, and with no ellipses to indicate its absence. Its version read: "We had warned Australia about its participation in Afghanistan. It ignored the warning until it woke up to the sound of explosions in Bali."[28]

The role of the United Nations in Indonesia and East Timor spilled over into the bombing of the United Nations compound in Baghdad on August 19, 2003. To avoid being attacked in Iraq, the UN had taken great pains to distance itself from America. Secretary General Kofi Annan instructed Sergio Vieira de Mello, the head of the UN mission in Baghdad, to keep a careful distance from U.S. forces and avoid all appearance of taking sides. De Mello did so, even refusing American protection for the compound, thus making its bombing much easier.

After the carnage, pundits worried that perhaps the UN had not sufficiently distanced itself from the United States and so been caught in what was really anti-American crossfire. Such an analysis was, of course, predicated on the assumption that Islamist terrorists could not possibly hate the UN itself, even for its actions in East Timor. However, the al Qaeda Web site where the organization claimed responsibility for the bombing was quite clear about the perpetrators' hatred not only of the United States but of international organizations. It asked, "So why the United Nations? Number one, the United Nations is against Islam. . . . This issue does not need to be proved. It is clear like the light of the sun at midday."

Abu Farida, the Egyptian militant who drove the truck that blew up the compound, and a former top hockey player in Italy, said he had a dream that

"God will give me the head of a Christian" (before going to Iraq he had been attacking "filthy Coptic Christians" in Egypt). The videotape describing Farida's intentions said his dream had finally come true with the killing of the Christian de Mello and also said that de Mello was specifically targeted because he "had been used like a surgeon's scalpel to cut East Timor from Indonesia and cut up Yugoslavia, and the [UN] wanted to cut Iraq into pieces also."[29] De Mello had headed the UN mission in East Timor, and had also figured prominently in UN actions in the Balkans; those who killed him emphasized that this had made him a target.

This, too, echoes bin Laden's views. His November 2001 videotape, justifying his attacks on America, declared: "Those who . . . continue to appeal to the United Nations have disavowed what was revealed to Prophet Muhammad. . . . Under no circumstances should any Muslim or sane person resort to the United Nations. The United Nations is nothing but a tool of crime." In 2006 he called it an "infidel" body used to implement "crusader–Zionist" schemes against Muslims: "The UN is an organization of unbelief and he who is pleased with its laws is an unbeliever, and it is a tool used to implement the Zionist/Crusader resolutions, including the declarations of war against us and the division and occupations of our lands."[30]

Massacres in Pakistan

On September 25, 2002, gunmen entered the offices of a Christian charity in Karachi, separated the Christians from the Muslim workers, then bound and gagged the Christians and methodically shot them in the head at point-blank range. Although this was the sixth in a series of attacks aimed at Christian targets in Pakistan—including one in October 2001 in which masked gunmen fired on congregants at a Protestant church service in Bahawalpur, killing fifteen Christians and a Muslim guard, and a March 17, 2002, grenade attack on a Protestant church in Islamabad's diplomatic quarter that killed at least thirty-six people and wounded a hundred—much of the media played down the clear religious dimension in favor of a more secular storyline.[31]

The *New York Times* described the killings as ending a lull in assaults on "Western targets" and quoted a police official saying that the attack was designed to drive away "Western business." Agence France-Presse quoted a human rights worker arguing that the violence was directed not against Christians but against those "striving for a tolerant society." However, the Institute for Peace and Justice, where those killed were employed, has both Christian and Muslim staff, and has worked for thirty years with the poor and human rights groups. Consequently, the Muslims there, who worked for a Christian organization, can be assumed to be as committed as anyone to a tolerant society, but they were spared simply because they were Muslims. The killers did not kill "tolerant" people: they explicitly selected, separated, targeted, and killed Christian tolerant people and spared Muslim tolerant people. CNN International contented itself with the opinion that there was "no indication of a motive."[32] Would it have said the same if armed men had invaded a multiracial center, separated the black people from the white people, then methodically killed all the blacks and spared all the whites?

This refusal to acknowledge a clear religious dimension to an explicitly religious massacre, and the decision to instead substitute a nebulous geographical term, "the West," was unfortunately all too typical in reports of slaughters in Pakistan. After the killings at a Christian school on August 5, 2002, Reuters headlined its story "Pakistan Attack Seen Aimed at West, Not Christians," while the BBC said it was "aimed at Western interests, rather than Pakistan's Christian minority." The Associated Press termed it the "latest attack against Western interests" and maintained that Westerners were the apparent target, describing it as "the sixth attack against Westerners or Western interests in Pakistan this year." The *Times* (London) also labeled it "the sixth attack this year against Westerners or Western interests." The *Los Angeles Times,* using wire services, reported that "Pakistani officials said the raid on the school appeared to be aimed at the foreign community rather than at a minority faith in Muslim-majority Pakistan."[33]

Four days after the attack in Karachi, there was yet another attack on a Christian institution, this time a hospital in Taxila. Three men threw grenades as nurses, doctors, and hospital workers left the chapel at the end of a service. As the *Daily Telegraph* pointed out, the militants timed their attack to ensure that it was Christian worshippers who were killed and injured. Taxila, like the other supposed "Western targets," in fact had few links to "the West," amounting to some funding and one Swedish nurse. Nevertheless, the *Financial Times* reported, "Although the victims were all Pakistanis, senior officials said the attack on the Christian community represented a growing threat to Western interests."[34]

In fact, Taxila has major significance to Pakistan's Christian community precisely because it is *not* associated with the West. None of the major media reported that this site was where, in 1953, the "Taxila cross" was discovered. This cross, with four arms of equal length, is believed to date from the second century and is valued by Pakistan's Christians as archaeological proof of the church's presence in the country many centuries before Islam, and a millennium and a half before British colonialism. This is why, at its inauguration on November 1, 1970, the Church of Pakistan adopted the Taxila cross as its symbol. For the news media to miss this fact is somewhat like missing the possible religious significance of an attack on, say, the Vatican.

Agence France-Presse did try to explore one religious angle, correctly pointing out that Taxila is also "an ancient Buddhist town" and that "some 30 Buddhist peace marchers from Japan, Central Asia and Russia are currently staying" there. But it is not entirely clear why they thought this relevant to an attack on a Christian hospital lying at the symbolic heart of Pakistan's Church.[35]

As it is, the people widely believed to be behind the attacks made their motives plain. Members of Lashkar-e-Jhangvi, the terrorist group claiming responsibility for the massacre in Bahawalpur, said that "they planned to kill Christians" in revenge for Muslim deaths in Afghanistan. The men who claimed responsibility for the school attack announced that they "killed the nonbelievers." Similarly, Daniel Pearl, the *Wall Street Journal* reporter kidnapped in Pakistan in January 2002, was killed not only because he was a Westerner but also because he was Jewish, as his murderers made quite explicit.

Slaughters in Saudi Arabia

On November 8, 2003, a Lebanese Christian neighborhood in Riyadh was bombed.[36] Of the seven publicly identified Lebanese victims, six were Christian, and that country's newspapers were replete with photographs of Maronite Catholic and Greek Orthodox victims. Following the attack, *Daleel al Mojahid*, an al Qaeda–linked Web page, praised this killing of "non-Muslims." In his justification of the assault, Abu Salma al Hijazi, an al Qaeda commander, took great pains to emphasize that the attack was not on Muslims: "This place was under surveillance for many months. . . . [T]here were at least 300 Americans and a large group of Lebanese Christians who had tortured Muslims there, in Lebanon, during the civil war. . . . [I]t was appropriate to attack this place and destroy it. . . . As a result, praise Allah, at least 40 Americans were killed, as well as 27 Christians from Lebanon."[37]

While the terrorists again used religious categories to describe their targets and victims, much of the media focused instead on a very insular American concern, ethnicity, and emphasized that the victims were Arabs. CNN pointed out: "Most of the dead and the wounded were Arab." ABC Evening News asserted "the victims were Arabs, not Westerners." The *Washington Post* said the compound was "home primarily to foreign workers, particularly Arabs." UPI referred to an "apparently deliberate attack on a mainly Arab-inhabited compound." Associated Press added, "At least 13 of the 17 killed Saturday were Arabs, including seven from Lebanon and others from Egypt and Sudan." Some added a category to "Arab": The BBC asserted that the "bombing killed Arabs and Muslims."[38]

While perhaps literally correct, since all the victims were indeed Arabs or Muslims, the BBC's circumlocution "Arab and Muslim" failed to note the key point that most of the victims were *Arab non-Muslims*. It hid the fact that large numbers of Christian Arabs from Egypt, Lebanon, and elsewhere, including India and Ethiopia, work in Saudi Arabia and other Gulf countries, and have long been targeted by Islamic extremists as well as by the Saudi government. (Indeed, at the time of the bombing, two Egyptian Christians, Sabry Gayed and Guirguis Eskander, were incarcerated in a Riyadh prison for the crime of holding a worship service.)

Perhaps because of a tendency to equate ethnicity and religion, and so to think of Arabs as exclusively Muslims, many journalists compounded the error by implying that the attack was, in fact, on Muslims. CNN said that "businessmen, like expatriate Jordanian pharmacist Haldoun and his friends . . . now worry Muslims are also al Qaeda's targets." Reuters and the Associated Press described the bombing as against "fellow Muslims," the *Washington Times* called the victims "innocent Muslims," and the *New York Times* termed them "expatriates from other Muslim countries."[39]

Saudi spokesmen reinforced this error by being studiously vague about the bombings' targets. While avoiding outright falsehood, their careful phrases hid the true nature of the attack. Saleh bin Abdul-Aziz, the Islamic Affairs minister, described it as "flagrant aggression . . . against Islam, the people of Islam, in the land of Islam." CNN quoted Adel Al-Jubeir, adviser to Crown Prince Abdullah, saying he was convinced al Qaeda was purposely attacking fellow Muslims. Later, when asked in three separate CNN interviews about the targets of the bombing, he each time switched the topic to a bomb factory uncovered in Mecca, complete with booby-trapped Qur'ans, saying, "These Korans were intended for Muslims." None of the three interviewers challenged him on this, and so the implication that the targets of the Riyadh bombing were Muslims was allowed to stand. (The Saudis almost certainly knew who the actual targets were because, three months before the bombing, the *mutaween* (religious police), headed by a Saudi cabinet minister, had raided the compound, not for the first time, because of an "un-Islamic" party in progress).[40]

Similarly, media coverage of the October 4, 2003, suicide attack on Maxim, a restaurant in Haifa, Israel, noted that one co-owner was Jewish but described the other simply as "Arab." Commentators then wondered, as in Saudi Arabia, why Palestinian terrorists were killing "Arabs." But the second co-owner was actually a Lebanese Catholic, as were many of those killed. The term "Arab," while playing into America's obsession with ethnicity, hides the religious dimension that is central to the worldview of al Qaeda, and of Hamas and Zarqawi's network in Iraq. Their view of the world is centered not on Arab/non-Arab, but on Muslim/infidel.

A Global War

In Riyadh and Khobar, al Qaeda targeted "infidels," killing Christians and Hindus, and also those Muslims, who—because they lived in a gated compound with swimming pools and alcohol, mixed with infidels, and allowed women to go unveiled—were seen by the terrorists as apostates from Islam and therefore worse than infidels and deserving of death. In Riyadh, al Qaeda and its confreres explained why their targets were chosen: to further its aims, the terror network will kill or subdue all "infidels," Muslim or non-Muslim, who stand in the way of its goal of restoring a worldwide caliphate governed, Taliban-style, by the strictest, narrowest interpretation of Islamic law. The killings in Bali, Manado, Baghdad, Haifa, Bahawalpur, Karachi, and Taxila were justified in the same way.

Bin Laden and his cohorts are indeed concerned about the United States, Israel, the Palestinians, Iraq, and Afghanistan. But they have an explicit and highly developed religious worldview and so are especially concerned about Saudi Arabia and the Al-Aqsa mosque, and continually point to attacks by infidels in Lebanon, Tajikistan, Burma, Kashmir, Assam, the Philippines, Fatani, Ogadin, Somalia, Eritrea, Chechnya, Bosnia, Bokhara, Bangladesh, Turkey, Chad, Mauritania, South Sudan, Darfur, Algeria, the Philippines, Yemen, Tashkent, Indonesia, and East Timor.

Clearly, religious beliefs and ideology are not the only things we need to know in order to understand al Qaeda's goals. But, equally clearly, we cannot understand these unless we take their religious beliefs seriously. Yet too many Western journalists seem limited to the more familiar categories of first world/third world, globalization, ethnicity, the "West," and Middle Eastern nationalism, and thus miss the nature of these terrorists' strategy, tactics, justifications, and goals. Hence, to the degree that our views of the nature and goals of Islamist terrorism are shaped by the media, we are consistently being misinformed about the nature of our enemies and the nature of the conflicts we are in.

3

Three Decades of Misreporting Iran and Iraq

Michael Rubin

War is always a hot story for journalists. Walter Cronkite, Morley
Safer, and Christiane Amanpour rose to national prominence as
war correspondents. First in 1991 and again in 2003, hundreds of
journalists flooded into Kuwait and Iraq to cover the U.S. military.
For many of them, war was a sexy story; religion was not. Ignoring
religion, though, is a mistake. Particularly in the Middle East, war,
politics, and religion can be so intertwined as to be inseparable. In
any story the devil is often in the details, and as journalists rush to
produce seven-hundred-word copy, they can seldom address theology
in detail, but failure to understand the nuances of religion can lead
to misanalysis and an artificial emphasis on political and diplomatic
motivations.

It would be an exaggeration to say that correspondents in the
Middle East always ignore religion. Few miss the religious angle
to the Arab-Israeli conflict or the Lebanese civil war (1975–1990).
Journalists described the sectarian nature of protests against the
Sunni ruling family in majority Shiite Bahrain in 1995 and 1996,
although only after years of ignoring such tension. The general rule
for Western correspondents in the Muslim world, though, is to report
violence and political intrigue, but ignore underlying religious tension. This is especially true when disagreements involve doctrinal
disputes *within* sects rather than fighting *between* sects or religions.
As a result, the Western media often gets the Middle East wrong.

Ignoring Theological Debate: Getting
the Islamic Revolution Wrong

Nowhere has the media's disregard for Islamic doctrinal dispute eroded the accuracy of its coverage more than in its reporting of Iran and Iraq, the two countries with the largest Shiite populations in the Middle East. The 1979 Islamic Revolution in Iran surprised Western correspondents. They had chronicled the rise and victory of Ayatollah Ruhollah Khomeini, but, while they had followed his fight against the shah and the subsequent seizure of the U.S. embassy, few paid attention to his doctrinal heterodoxy, which culminated in a system not of the Islamic democracy about which he often spoke, but rather of clerical rule. A quarter century later, the problem is reversed: Having witnessed revolution and the imposition of a Shiite-inspired theocracy, many journalists, commentators, and even government officials now accept the Iranian experience as representative of normal, mainstream Shiism. It is not. As a result of misunderstanding Shiite doctrine, the Western press misreads Iraqi politics.

Doctrinal debates within Islam often have their roots in early Muslim history; the dispute among Shiite thinkers relates to the succession dispute that followed the death of the Prophet Muhammad (569–632). At that time leadership of the Muslim community passed to Abū Bakr (573–634), a companion of the Prophet. But one faction—which would later become the Shiites—believed that leadership belonged instead in the hands of 'Ali Abu Talib (600–661), the Prophet's cousin and son-in-law. The term Shiite derives from the Arabic phrase shi'at 'Ali, literally, partisans of 'Ali.

Understanding early Islamic history is important because Islamic practice rests not only upon the Qu'ran, which Muslims believe to be the immutable word of God, but also upon the hadith, examples from the Prophet's life. Because of the importance of precedent in religious debate, these differences have been magnified over time to influence theology well beyond questions of the Prophet's succession. Sunnis' and Shiites' many differences play out politically across the Middle East, but, when layers of distrust and dispute are peeled away, the two sects differ over the veracity of certain hadith.

'Ali eventually did become caliph, although an assassin's knife cut short his stewardship. His death worsened the schism within the Islamic world. The Shiites believed that members of the Prophet's family should hold the mantle of leadership. Those who became Shiites placed their allegiance in a line of imams whom they traced from 'Ali through several generations to Muhammad al-Mahdī (b. 868), the twelfth imam, whom believers say did not die but rather went into occultation. Some journalists have described imams as saints, an analogy resented by many Shiites because of the prohibition of saint worship in Islam.[1] In contrast, those who became the Sunnis accepted the leadership of the Umayyad caliphs who were descended from an elite tribe of pre-Islamic Mecca.

The 'hidden imam' or mahdī, plays a key role in Shiite doctrine as a messianic figure. Shiites believe that upon his return he will rid the world of evil and injustice. By extension, therefore, traditional Shiism teaches that any temporal authority holding power before the return of the mahdī is to some degree unjust and corrupt. Such a belief has become the basis of a loose separation between mosque and state in Shiite societies whereby religious authorities might advise kings and pashas, or issue fatwas (religious rulings) when rulers pursued policies that contravened religious sensibilities.

While Ayatollah Ruhollah Khomeini (1901–1989) accepted Shiism's traditional separation between spiritual and temporal rule in his early years, his views shifted with time. Journalists, academics, and diplomats got Khomeini wrong by failing to understand how heterodox his theological interpretations had become. Initially, he adhered to the separation doctrine. "We do not say the government must be in the hands of the *faqih* [jurisprudent]," he argued in 1943, "rather we say the government must be run in accordance with God's rule."[2] In the 1960s, as the shah accelerated his modernization program, antagonizing more-traditional segments of Iranian society, Khomeini became a figurehead for the opposition, culminating in his arrest and exile. In 1970 six years into his Iraqi exile, Khomeini delivered a series of lectures that were published the following year in a book, *Hukumat-i Islami* (Islamic Government),[3] which outlined his concept of *vilayat-i faqih* (guardianship of the jurisprudent). In practice, this amounted to theocratic rule by clerics.

While *Hukumat-i Islami* was vague in its practicalities, Khomeini's subsequent declarations hinted at his ultimate goals. "How is it that now, when it is the turn of the present generation of religious scholars to speak out, we invest excuses and say that it is 'incompatible' with our status to speak out?" he asked in 1971.[4] The following year, he exhorted students to "devote greater attention to planning the foundations of an Islamic state and studying the problems involved."[5] In February 1978 Khomeini preached that Qom—a religious-seminary town in Iran—would supplant the traditional holy city of Najaf, in southern Iraq, as the center for Shiite thought.[6] This pronouncement was symbolically important, for it signaled an end to the theological supremacy of Najaf, whose resident ayatollahs supported the traditional separation of religious and temporal authority.

A newspaper article or sixty-second television report is obviously no place to get into the vagaries of Shiite jurisprudence, but it is the journalists' job to be familiar enough with it to report news accurately. Yet, in the run-up to the Islamic Revolution, too many Western reporters ignored religion. They spoke of the ayatollah's agitation but failed to mention his philosophy toward Islamic government. In 1978, having moved to France from Iraq, Khomeini granted a number of interviews to the press. He denied any personal political ambition. "Personally, I can't accept any special role or responsibility [for governance],"[7] he told Le Journal. To Le Monde, he declared, "I will not become a president nor accept any other leadership role."[8] Journalists accepted his statements at face value. With few exceptions, they failed to mention the Shiite concept of taqiya (dissimulation), which allows figures to lie to those they deem enemies.[9] By getting religion wrong, journalists became vessels of Khomeini's propaganda rather than chroniclers of news.

In December 1978, as Khomeini commanded the masses to rise, the Washington Post suggested that Khomeini's "Islamic democracy" might resemble "parliamentary democracy along Western lines."[10] A few days later, its editorial page featured a commentary by an American University professor who wrote, "Iran is hardly prone to turn toward Islamic revival . . . or to reject an alignment with the West."[11] Steven Erlanger, at the time an assistant national editor at the Boston Globe—and now a Middle East correspondent for the New York Times—predicted at the height of the Islamic Revolution that clerical rule could not last.[12] Had Western commentators traced Khomeini's evolution, they might not have downplayed the import of the ayatollah's actions. The rest is history.

On February 1, 1979, Khomeini arrived in Tehran, triumphant after fifteen years of exile. Alluding to the mystical mahdī, Iranian newspaper headlines announced "Imam Amad" ("The Imam Came").[13] Once in Iran, Khomeini maneuvered to eliminate rivals and consolidate autocratic control. The Islamic Revolution redefined concepts of political evolution and modernity.

Misunderstanding the Leadership Struggle: Getting Iraq Wrong

Twenty-five years later, Shiite debates about the role of the clergy in politics continue. When the U.S. military poured into Iraq, several hundred journalists accompanied the troops.[14] Few knew much about Iraq, and fewer still about Shiism. The Washington Post, for example, sought volunteers from its metro-beat bureau. Many of the journalists were in their thirties and forties. They grew up with images of Iranian hostage-takers seizing the American embassy in Tehran. A generation of Americans saw televised images of Khomeini's ally, Ayatollah Sadiq Khalkhali, the hanging judge of the Islamic Revolution, abusing the corpses of American servicemen killed in the aborted hostage rescue attempt of 1980.[15] Meanwhile, political cartoonists adopted the scowling, turbaned and bearded Khomeini as the symbol of Islamist challenge.[16] His caricature expanded in the public mind to encompass all Shiites.

On April 4, 2003, as more than a hundred thousand coalition troops converged on Baghdad, the *New York Times* made its first mention of Grand Ayatollah 'Ali Sistani, the most influential Shiite cleric in Iraq.[17] Sistani's existence was a revelation for the paper's audience because, for months before the war, the paper had ignored the theological schisms within mainstream Shiism.[18] In one example, Tehran-based correspondent Nazila Fathi published a profile of Ayatollah Muhammad Baqir al-Hakim, the leader of the pro-clerical rule Supreme Council for Islamic Revolution in Iraq, reporting simply, "The Ayatollah, 63, is popular in Iraq."[19] She might have tried to gauge his popularity by, for example, questioning religious Iraqis about to which ayatollahs they paid their religious alms. However, she did not, perhaps out of ignorance of the question or perhaps because she deemed the topic too sensitive for the Islamic Revolution. Either way, she dropped the ball by accepting blindly the word of Iranian authorities who had an interest in promoting a pro-clerical rule ayatollah over the mainstream, anti-clerical rule ayatollahs dominant in Iraq. The subsequent subordination of Hakim to Sistani indicated the earlier failure of the *New York Times* and other newspapers to understand, let alone explain, the nature of Shiite leadership and the contrasting claims to leadership.

By conflating political and religious popularity, the *New York Times* underlined their confusion about the intra-Shiite dispute regarding the political role of the clergy. For traditional Shiite clerics, such as those that predominate in Iraq, political popularity is irrelevant. What matters is who Shiites follow as their *marja' at-taqlid* (source of emulation). The Shiite clergy are hierarchical but, unlike in Catholicism, where the pope is elected by the college of cardinals and accepted as the undisputed head of the Catholic Church, Shiism does not require universal recognition of leadership. Local mosques may have mullahs, many with little more than a rudimentary education. A *mujtahid* or *'alim* who continues his studies in a religious seminary in Najaf, Karbala, or Qom may become a *hojjat ol-Islam* (proof of Islam), *ayatollah* (sign of God) or, after decades of research and teaching, an *ayatollah al-uzma* (grand ayatollah).[20] Individual Shiites adhere to the teachings of a living *marja' at-taqlid* but may choose which individual source of emulation is best for them. They might study their source of emulation's writings, and even address questions to him, but, ultimately, their allegiance to any particular religious figure is voluntary. The figure to whom most Iraqi Shiites turn is Sistani, but he is by no means the only *marja' at-taqlid*. There are approximately a dozen grand ayatollahs alive today, all of whom have their own followers.

Contemporary theological disputes have made consensus on a single source of emulation impossible.[21] While most Iraqis pledge their religious allegiance to Sistani, other Iraqis follow Ayatollah Sayyid Taqi al-Modarresi or Grand Ayatollah Sayyid Sadiq Husayni Shirazi. National boundaries do not necessarily correlate to religious loyalty. A small number of Iraqi Shiites follow the Iranian-based cleric, Grand Ayatollah Kazim al-Haeri, and some may even follow Ayatollah 'Ali Khamene'i, the supreme leader of the Islamic Republic of Iran. A minority influenced by Lebanese Hezbollah pay heed to Grand Ayatollah Muhammad Husayn Fadhlullah, that movement's spiritual leader.

There has always been a component of Najaf-Karbala rivalry between some religious figures resident in Iraq, with a resurgent Qom complicating matters further. While the State Department and the Pentagon scrambled to reach out to various Shiite religious leaders influential in if not resident in Iraq, the Western media became aware of some of the more serious rivalries only shortly after allied forces occupied Baghdad when followers of Muqtada al-Sadr, a follower of pro-clerical rule Haeri, hacked to death Abdul Majid al-Khoei, a well-respected traditional cleric and son of the late grand ayatollah Abul Qasim al-Khoei.[22] Again, it might not be the job of journalists to report the nitty-gritty of internal Shiite religious differences, but their belated attention to the subject increased the chasm between prewar reportage and prewar planning. Journalists-turned-authors such as *New Yorker* correspondent George Packer and *Washington Post* reporter Thomas Ricks preserved this gap in their attempt to write a first draft of history.[23]

While Shiite history is replete with leadership disputes, Khomeini's introduction of the concept of clerical rule into the mix complicated the debate. While traditional ayatollahs like Sistani and Shirazi welcomed differences of interpretation, political clerics who have followed Khomeini's line shun them. When ayatollahs are not only religious models but also political leaders, any alternate source of authority undermines their legitimacy. Because Khomeini and, subsequently, Khamene'i, claimed ultimate authority in Iran, any sign that Iranians followed other clerics became not a sign of traditional doctrinal diversity, but rather of outright insubordination. The presence of rival sources of emulation, like Sistani in Iraq, continues to strain Iranian social fabric today. Iranian authorities have sought to silence potential religious rivals on their own territory; for example, keeping Grand Ayatollah Husayn Ali Montazeri under house arrest and banning publication of his memoirs.[24] They have not, however, been able to impose their will on rival religious figures in Iraq, though they have tried.

In 1994 Grand Ayatollah 'Ali Araki died in Tehran, reputedly at the age of 105 or 106. He had been a traditional cleric who wielded great influence on theological questions, but, despite the Islamic revolution, had remained aloof from politics.[25] Many Shiites, both inside and outside Iran, looked to Araki as their spiritual guide, but, according to the tenets of Shiism, on his death they would need to shift their allegiance to a living guide. Araki's death was thus a moment for which Iran's revolutionary ayatollahs had been waiting. The Iranian government argued that its supreme leader, Khamene'i, who had acceded to the Islamic Republic's top position following Khomeini's 1989 death, should be "the first *marja'* of the Shiite world."[26]

However, the Iranian attempt to assert its political authority upon the Shiite world fell flat. Simply put, to the majority of the Shiite world, Khamene'i had neither the learning nor the charisma to be their spiritual guide. The rejection of Khamene'i's claim highlighted the legitimacy problem that continues to be the Islamic Republic's Achilles' heel.[27] The vulnerability of the Iranian hierarchy was mitigated by Saddam Hussein's regime, which kept Iraq's population under rigid control.

For years, this tension was not apparent to Western audiences, in part because of the failure of journalists to engage in religious issues. Iraqi president Saddam Hussein kept a tight lid on the Iraq-based clergy, effectively silencing those who most opposed Khomeini's theological deviation.[28] At the same time, the Iranian regime limited access for any Western journalists who might spotlight dissident voices who opposed the clerical regime. In February 2001, for example, Reuters bureau chief Jonathan Lyons and his wife, *International Herald Tribune* correspondent Geneive Abdo, both left Iran involuntarily after they covered subjects that displeased the regime.[29] Particularly infuriating to the authorities was a January 31 interview Lyons conducted with a disaffected former Iranian intelligence official who had exposed the Iranian government's domestic death squads.

The *New York Times*'s decision to suggest a close ideological relationship between the traditional Shiism espoused by Sistani and the theocracy promoted by Khomeini and his successors was inaccurate and ahistorical.[30] As late as July 2004, the paper implied unity between Iraqi Shiites and the Iranian theocracy. Correspondent Edward Wong explained, "Iraqis are torn between religious and national loyalties. Just how much sway Iran will exert over a new Iraq is far from clear. But some warn that Iran, the world's dominant seat of Shiite Islam, could be the silent power broker."[31] The reality was that Iraqis who expressed Shiism as their paramount identity still voiced disdain for Iranians, whom many Iraqis see as arrogant and whom others distrust for their pre-Islamic legacy and their non-Arab ethnicity. Iraqi Shiites often quip that "if you break the bones of an Iranian, shit oozes out."

By presenting the Islamic Republic of Iran as representative of Shiite orthodoxy, the Western press got the story backward. It was not Khamene'i that threatened the allegiance of Iraqi Shiites, but rather Iraqi clerics who under-mined loyalties to their Iranian counterparts. This was encapsulated by an episode ignored in the Western press but which had profound consequences in Iran:[32] Islamic months begin with the sighting of the new moon. Because Khamene'i claims ultimate political and spiritual authority in Iran, he reserves the right to make the final decision on when months begin and end. In order to exert authority and highlight religious differences, he often declares months to begin the day after religious authorities in other countries do. In 2003 most Shiite clerics declared the end of Ramadan to be on November 25; Khamene'i decreed its end to be the following day. However, Iranian journal-ists had already interviewed Sistani and published his answer. While innocu-ous to a Western audience, Sistani's direct contradiction of Khamene'i shook the political establishment in Iran. How could Khamene'i be the supreme leader if numerous Iranians looked toward Sistani for guidance? Exposing their authoritarian nature and insecurity, the Iranian government responded with a crackdown on the journalists.

Only in the aftermath of Iraq's first democratic elections did the Western press get a clearer perspective on the Islamic Republic's vulnerability.[33] The Iranian leadership's awareness of its theological vulnerability shapes its strat-egy in Iraq, and it responds by supporting several militias, including the Badr Corps and the Jaysh al-Mahdi. Militias exist to impose through force of arms values to which society might not otherwise adhere; hence, by supporting mili-tias, Tehran hopes to intimidate and silence independent-minded Shiite clergy. Journalists may describe the symptoms, but they miss the cause.

The January 30, 2005, Iraqi elections underlined the theological differences between Sistani and Khamene'i. Despite some media alarmism about clerical interference, Sistani remained aloof from the political process. Although he urged his followers to vote, and called for Shiite unity, he neither explicitly told his supporters for whom to vote nor became involved in the pre-election cam-paign or in the post-election jockeying for position.[34]

The experience of the Islamic Republic of Iran stands in sharp contrast. The Constitution of the Islamic Republic restricts candidacy to those who believe in "the system of the Islamic Republic,"[35] thereby mandating belief in clerical dominance in politics and excluding the vast majority of traditional Shi-ites. An unelected Guardian Council, half of which is selected by the supreme leader,[36] vets candidates to eliminate those deemed too liberal or those whose views diverge from the supreme leader's. The resulting parliament, itself repre-sentative of only a tiny segment of the population, selects the other half of the Governing Council, thereby completing the clerical grip on power.

The Governing Council has not hesitated to wield its power. While the media celebrated the so-called reformist Mohammad Khatami's 1997 election victory, with headlines such as "A New Chapter,"[37] and "Iranian Youth Celebrate Khatami's Clear Mandate for Social Change,"[38] few journalists noted that the Guardian Council disqualified 234 out of 238 candidates. In 2005 the Guardian Council's slash-and-burn against potential candidates went further: Only eight of more than a thousand candidates passed muster. Far from remaining aloof from politics, Khamene'i has sought to manipulate all levers at his disposal in order to shape it.

Contrary to the earlier musings of journalists, the tension between Iran and Iraq has become one of the dominant features of post-Saddam Iraqi politics. But, by casting the tension in terms of religiosity, Western media have shown a bias that confuses fervor with radicalism. Shiites commemorate both the martyrdom of Husayn, the third imam, and *arba'in*, the anniversary of the fortieth day after his death, which marks the end of the traditional period of mourning.

On the first *arba'in* after Saddam's fall, major newspapers suggested that Shiites might use the commemoration's traditional processions—long banned under Saddam—to push for Iranian-style theocratic rule.[39] This analysis revealed an inability to discern the differences between the Shiism espoused by Iranian officials and that practiced by most Iraqis. Journalists may claim neutrality, and often seek it, but they frequently use man-on-the-street quotes to shape articles according to their biases. In one extreme example, a journalist for the *Guardian*, a leading left-of-center British broadsheet, wrote stories first and then sent an Iraqi assistant out to find quotes to fit. Knight Ridder newspaper correspondents, whose work is published in newspapers like the *Philadelphia Inquirer* and *Miami Herald,* did likewise.

In the run-up to *arba'in*, pro-Iranian Shiite firebrands in Karbala had little trouble swaying the *San Francisco Chronicle,* whose staff had already taken an editorial stance against the U.S. invasion of Iraq, to an alarmist interpretation. Its Iraq correspondent, Robert Collier, demonstrated ignorance when he warned ominously of a "groundswell" in support of an Iranian-style Islamic Republic. "The Shiite sect has inspired resistance movements for centuries," he explained. "The 1979 Iranian Revolution created a Shiite theocracy in that country, and the Hizbullah organization has institutionalized Shiite militancy in Lebanon."[40]

Collier's explanations are inaccurate in several ways. Firstly, they ignore the majority quietist strain in Shiism. Hezbollah may have institutionalized militancy among some in Lebanon, but the organization's roots have been far from spontaneous and are more the product of direct Iranian aid and assistance. More seriously, the statement that Shiism had contributed more to modern Middle Eastern resistance than Sunnism is simply untrue. The basis of far bloodier resistance and terrorism in both Egypt and Algeria was Sunni, as are Islamist movements operating in the Palestinian territories. Al Qaeda, which stylizes itself as a movement resisting foreign influences in the Islamic world, is also Sunni. In sharp contrast to Collier's alarmism, Sunni Arabs have become the base of the insurgency in Iraq, while the Shiite leaders have been the driving force for elections. Likewise, despite media alarmism about Shiite radicalism, Sunni groups, not their Shiite counterparts, were long the driving anti-secular, anti-liberal force in Iraq.

The newfound religiosity of some Iraqi Shiites was a shot across the bow of the Iranian leadership. While the millions commemorating *arba'in* were Iraqi, many of the ayatollahs resident in Najaf and Karbala are Iranian. This is not a new phenomenon. Meir Litvak, the leading historian of the Iraqi shrine cities, has documented the migration of Iranian scholars into Najaf. In the second half of the nineteenth century, Iranian migrants outnumbered native scholars four to one.[41] The continuation of this pattern has underlined Iran's vulnerability, since the fact that the holiest Shiite shrines—those containing the tombs of Imam 'Ali and his son Husayn—have fallen under political control independent of the Iranian supreme leader weakens the Islamic Republic's claim to represent Shia worldwide.

Except during the Ba'athist interlude, Iranian clerics have always used their presence in Najaf and Karbala to maintain independence from Iranian despots. During the nineteenth century, Iranian scholars used their relative freedom in the shrine cities, then in Ottoman territory, as a safe haven from which to criticize the Iranian shah's policies. In the early twentieth century, they used their base in Najaf and Karbala to encourage constitutionalists fighting to end the absolute and spurious quality of Iran's monarchy. In the 1960s and 1970s, Khomeini used his time in Najaf to agitate against the shah, just as quietist clerics now use their Iraqi safe haven to undermine the dictatorship that Khomeini ushered into their homeland.

Many journalists missed this historic pattern when, in the months after the invasion, they began to question Sistani's citizenship, implying that his Iranian birth made him an advocate for theocracy. One Associated Press reporter encapsulated the question when he asked, "How did someone gain such power even though he's an Iranian?"[42] But, while, of the four grand ayatollahs resident in Najaf, only Sistani held Iranian citizenship, several of the others had different foreign origins. Muhammad Sa'id al-Hakim at-Tabataba'i was Iraqi, but Muhammad Ishaq Fayadh was an Afghan and Bashir Najafi carried a Pakistani passport. All were quietist; they did not mirror the politics of their countries of birth. *Washington Post* correspondent Anthony Shadid put facts in perspective. "Of Najaf's four grand ayatollahs," he wrote, "all are students of the most quiet tradition in Shiite Islam, which traditionally confines the role of clergy to spiritual [rather than political] matters."[43]

Once insurgent violence accelerated in Iraq, many journalists became trapped in a cycle of reporting various car bombs and explosions. Several, such as Dan Murphy at the *Christian Science Monitor,* asked analysts like University of Michigan professor Juan Cole to interpret the roots of violence. Cole, who had never been to Iraq, viewed the violence through the lens of anti-colonialism: Bombs exploded because Iraqis disliked occupation.

Iraqis point to a more complex reality. On August 29, 2003, a car bomb killed Ayatollah Muhammad Baqir al-Hakim as he left the holiest Shiite shrine in Iraq. Many journalists suspected that Sunni insurgents or Sunni al Qaeda members might be behind the car bombing[44] and, indeed, several were subsequently detained. While Iraqis did not dispute that insurgents had planted the bomb, many speculated that Iranian authorities had reason either to kill the cleric or to lend support through proxies to those who actually carried out the operation.

While al-Hakim had taken a line close to that espoused by Khomeini and Khamene'i during his exile in Iran, after returning to Iraq his teachings had shifted back to the quietist, anti-clerical rule positions espoused by most traditional Shiites. Politicians from al-Hakim's Supreme Council for Islamic Revolution in Iraq have privately suggested that they believe Iranian intelligence knew in advance of the plot but chose to let it proceed because of disappointment over Muhammad Baqir al-Hakim's growing theological and political independence; his brother, Abdul 'Aziz al-Hakim, to whom the mantle of leadership passed, has followed the Iranian line more closely.

Along similar lines, there has never been evidence to support the conventional wisdom voiced in the *New York Times*[45] and elsewhere that Sunni Islamists in groups like al Qaeda and Shiite Iranians could not overcome sectarian differences to cooperate. Iranian authorities founded the Sunni terrorist group Palestinian Islamic Jihad. The 9-11 Commission subsequently traced Iranian cooperation with al Qaeda.[46]

Getting Iraqi Politics Wrong

Knowledge of religion is important to understand not only the big divides in Iraqi society, but also the country's daily politics. Once Western journalists discovered Sistani, they sought to convey his opinions and bolster their stories with statements from his followers and associates, covering the elderly grand ayatollah as perhaps they felt they should have treated Khomeini a quarter century before. But, many covered Sistani's representatives as if they were McSistani franchises, failing to understand the nature of the religious bureaucracy.

In December 2003, for example, Knight Ridder's Maureen Fan wrote that "Sistani's agents have insisted that Iraq's judges be drawn from the Hawza, the religious council of scholars over whom he presides."[47] In March 2004 the *Chicago Tribune* ran a story citing Shaykh Abdul Mahdi al-Karbala'i, "al-Sistani's representative in Baghdad," who declared the municipal council to be illegitimate "because it was the work of the occupation forces."[48] In the wake of the Iraqi election, the *Christian Science Monitor*'s Dan Murphy quoted 'Ali al-Wa'idh, "Sistani's representative in the Baghdad district of Khadimiya," as saying "The Koran should be the main basis for writing the constitution."[49] When gunmen assassinated Sistani's representative in the town of Salman Pak, the *Los Angeles Times* placed the story on the front page.[50]

All of these stories fall short. They misrepresent the structure of Sistani's office. The grand ayatollah maintains two types of representatives: *vakil al-'ahm* (general representative) and *vakil al-hasbiyah* (certified representative). The former can represent Sistani on almost all matters, be they religious, policy, or financial. He has only two general representatives, one in Qom and the other in Europe.

In contrast, Sistani employs many certified representatives, each of whom is limited to specific functions. Most are financial agents, collecting religious taxes and alms. Their authority does not extend to policy. When Western journalists quoted Sistani's representatives about policy, the representatives spoke as individuals, not as Sistani's spokesmen.[51] This would be analogous to Iraqi journalists visiting Washington and treating Internal Revenue Service tax collectors as spokesmen for the White House.

The Western media's failure to understand the Shiite religious hierarchy's financial system has undercut their reporting of both Iraqi and Iranian politics. The *New York Times* raised alarm about transfers of money from Iran to Sistani's office,[52] even though there was nothing nefarious about individual donations. All Shiites are obligated to pay religious taxes to their source of emulation. The fact that Iranians are donating money to Sistani rather than Khamene'i suggests that the religious claims of the Islamic Republic's hierarchy holds little legitimacy for ordinary Iranians.

Collection of religious taxes also played an important role in another postwar episode largely missed by the media. In both April 2004 and again four months later, Shiite irregulars and militiamen loyal to firebrand cleric Muqtada

al-Sadr rose up in rebellion. Muqtada al-Sadr was the fourth son of Grand Ayatollah Mohammad Sadeq al-Sadr who was, between 1992 and 1999, one of the
most renowned scholars in Najaf, holding a position of public esteem not too
different from that which Sistani enjoys today. Upon his father's death, Muqtada
al-Sadr had to shift his religious loyalties to a living source of emulation. He
turned to Ayatollah Haeri, who conformed to Khomeini's ideology more than
to the quietist tradition espoused by Sistani.

Many journalists and columnists missed the religious angle. They sought
to portray Muqtada al-Sadr's uprising as having its roots in anti-Americanism
or nationalist, anti-occupation sentiment. For example, Knight Ridder described
Sadr as having "built his following on armed resistance against the U.S.-led
occupation and Iraqi government."[53] In an analysis of Muqtada al-Sadr, *USA
Today* focused on his resistance to occupation and oppression.[54] In reality it had
just as much to do with the interplay of intra-Shiite religious disputes and a
desire to control religious taxes. In each uprising, much of the internecine fighting between militias commanded by Muqtada al-Sadr and those loyal to Sistani
was centered on control of the lucrative shrines in Najaf and Karbala to which
Shiites donate money during pilgrimages. Control over pilgrimage income
would translate into greater disbursement, patronage, and political power.[55]

Ignoring religion has also undercut the coverage of some Iraqi politicians.
In the aftermath of the Iraq War, journalists and diplomats often reinforced
each other's preconceived notions and consistently misread the political scene.
The most acute example has been coverage of Ahmed Chalabi. The scion of
a political family under Iraq's monarchy, Chalabi was the son of a former
president of the Iraqi senate. The 1958 revolution forced his family into exile,
where Chalabi completed his education in Great Britain and Lebanon and
became a banker and businessman. He returned to Iraq in 1992 as head of
the umbrella Iraqi National Congress. As an advocate for both regime change
and democratization, he became a lightning rod for criticism and the subject of
interdepartmental battles within the U.S. government. Angered with Chalabi's
unwillingness to follow their orders strictly, both the State Department and the
Central Intelligence Agency turned on their former client. They badmouthed
him to the press, which echoed these agencies' concerns about his political
impotence. But, while journalists like the *Independent*'s Patrick Cockburn and
the *Los Angeles Times*' Alissa Rubin labeled Chalabi "unpopular" among Iraqis,
neither addressed his religious connections.[56]

Chalabi makes no claims to be a populist politician. But every U.S. government attempt to knock him out of contention has failed, largely because U.S.
officials underestimate his religious connections.[57] Although having a secular outlook, Chalabi has had more than a dozen audiences with Sistani and

maintains close connections with a variety of other Shiite religious and political figures both inside Iraq and abroad. How could Chalabi be so unpopular and yet remain in the good graces of Iraq's highest religious authorities? The answer lies with his connections to the Kadhimayn Shrine in Baghdad. The resting place of both the seventh and ninth imams, Kadhimayn is, after Najaf and Karbala, the holiest pilgrimage site in Iraq. Its proximity to Baghdad—and eventual absorption into the city—made Kadhimayn a focal point of Shiite-Sunni sociopolitical and religious interaction.[58]

The Chalabis had lived in Kadhimayn for generations, and the family used their business and political connections to establish a powerful network of contacts.[59] Chalabi's father had also financed Kadhimayn's renovation. Of the twenty-five Governing Council members, Chalabi was the only one to return to his family's property, a small villa near the shrine. Not only did this underline Chalabi's roots in Iraq despite years of exile, but it also signaled a continued connection to the shrine. Chalabi may not have enjoyed popular support—more than a decade of Iraqi state television vitriol took its toll on his reputation as did the abuse of power of many in his entourage—but his religious ties proved more important than transient political opinion.

Getting the Sunnis Wrong

It was not just Shiism that the media got wrong, but Sunnism as well. Despite its diversity, many journalists sought to portray Iraq's Sunni community as monolithic, often conflating Sunnism with Arabism. Knight Ridder correspondents repeatedly failed to acknowledge that perhaps half of Iraq's Sunni community is non-Arab. Half of Iraq's ethnic Turkmen and 90 percent of Iraqi Kurds are Sunni. On February 14, 2005, for example, its correspondents wrote, "But as the Shiites and Kurds celebrated victories, the fifth of the nation that is Sunni Muslim faced the reality that only one predominantly Sunni ticket, that of interim president Ghazi al-Yawer, will have seats in the assembly."[60]

Accentuating the problem has been the assumption that, in Iraq, sectarian identity was paramount. Former *New York Times* editor and Council on Foreign Relations president Leslie Gelb contributed to this perception.[61] Despite terrorist provocations such as the bombings of the Shiite shrine in Samarra and a tendency by the Coalition Provisional Authority and the U.S. embassy to treat Iraqi politicians as representatives of specific ethnic or sectarian communities, Iraqis have not rallied so readily into unified ethnic or religious groups. Both Sunnis and Shiites lack cohesive political leadership.

Take the insurgency: Although many of the insurgents may have been Sunnis, so too were their victims. That Sunnis were targeting other Sunnis suggests a political struggle within a community and, by extension, diversity of thought. Likewise, while Sistani might be the most prominent religious figure among Iraqi and, for that matter, Iranian Shiites, Iraqi Shiites have been unable to coalesce around a single political leader. Although Supreme Council for Islamic Revolution in Iraq leader Abdul 'Aziz al-Hakim proposed that Iraq's southern nine provinces coalesce into a single Shiite federal unit, political dissension and rivalry within this diverse region shelved his plans.

A tendency to simplify religious identity can undercut reporters' accuracy in other ways. Due to their highlighting and exaggerating sectarian polarization, few journalists noted that one-in-seven members of the "Sistani-endorsed"[62] United Iraqi Alliance were actually Arab Sunnis, a representation in proportion to the Arab Sunni component of the general population. The Los Angeles Times omitted mention of the United Iraqi Alliance's Sunni component, even when discussing how "Members of the United Iraqi Alliance . . . are thinking about how to include some Sunnis in the government."[63] The New York Times chose not to cover a January 9, 2005, United Iraqi Alliance rally in Najaf that featured Mudhar Shawkat and Sheikh Fawaz al-Gerba, two Arab Sunnis campaigning on the so-called Sistani list. Correspondent Dexter Filkins visited the rally, but did not highlight such sectarian cooperation.

Several reporters sought artificially to construct a Sunni hierarchy to complement the Shiite one. For many, the Association of Muslim Scholars fits the role. Founded soon after Iraqi liberation by Shaykh Ahmad al-Kubaysi, a radical cleric who spent his exile in the United Arab Emirates, al-Kubaysi assembled the group with money supplied by wealthy Persian Gulf donors.[64] Rather than build a wide-ranging umbrella organization, he patched together a membership composed of former regime officials and Salafis who practice a radical interpretation of Islam subsidized by Saudi authorities.

Salafis aspire to recreate Islamic practice as they believe it existed at the time of Muhammad. Many seek to implement strict Islamic law and reject cultural imports from the West. Although the Association of Muslim Scholars claimed to speak on behalf of Iraq's [Arab] Sunnis; in reality, they spoke only for the most radical fringe. Nevertheless, Associated Press writer Mariam Fam cited the group's spokesman for comments on behalf of Sunnis in a February 12, 2004, article examining disputes over election timing.[65] The New York Times was slightly more careful when it described the group as "claim[ing] to speak for as many as 3,000 Sunni mosques," and later said that "it is increasingly understood here [in Baghdad] as the voice of the insurgency."[66] Analysis such as that which appeared in the *Financial Times*, discussing competing Sunni trends, was a rarity in the Western press.[67]

A byproduct of the Western media's inclination to consolidate communities into a single voice is the tendency to stereotype religious communities, especially the Sunni Arab community. Journalists and editorialists have conflated religion with ideology by implying that Sunnis are naturally sympathetic to Ba'athism. For example, the Cleveland *Plain Dealer* blamed the Sunni insurgency on "vindictive fiats barring non-criminal Ba'athists from positions of power."[68] Not only is this factually wrong, but it addresses neither the myriad Sunni Arabs who have opposed both Ba'athism and the insurgency nor the fact that within the senior ranks of the Ba'ath Party were a number of Kurds, Turkmen, and Shia. The *Chicago Tribune* likewise lumped Sunnism with Ba'athism.[69] The *Washington Post* also fell into this trap.[70]

This stereotyping of Iraqi Sunnis undercut both the accuracy of journalists' stories and the relevance of their analysis. The Association of Muslim Scholars promoted only one theological strain, and its Salafism is not representative of the Iraqi Sunni community; not only does such radicalism emerge from a school of Islamic jurisprudence not dominant in Iraq, but there is also an influential Sufi presence that spans Iraq's ethnic mosaic.

Sufis embrace a mystical and spiritual interpretation of the Qu'ran that directly challenges the Salafis' literal approach. In some ways, the dichotomy between Salafi and Sufi implied a struggle within the Sunni community between foreigner and native, a phenomenon played out on the larger scale within the insurgency. Consequently, the Sufis became the chief targets of Salafi Sunnis. Long before the Western media reported the insurgents' seizure and decapitation of Western hostages, Islamist insurgents targeted the Sufis.[71] Shortly after Baghdad's fall, Salafi gangs began a campaign of intimidation and murder of Sufi clerics, taking over neighborhood congregations in Baghdad by force.

While scores of journalists descended upon the restive city of Fallujah, only the *Financial Times* mentioned that the largely Sunni city had one hundred Sufi lodges, in addition to two hundred mosques. As its correspondent Nicolas Pelham suggested, "Who wins this theological battle for the Sufi lodges will largely determine the US's future in Iraq."[72]

Perhaps nowhere is the moderation encouraged by Sufism more apparent than in Kirkuk, an oil-rich town in northern Iraq contested by Iraq's three major groups. Even before the war began, some journalists were highlighting Kirkuk—which under Saddam's regime was the site of a brutal ethnic-cleansing campaign conducted by Arabs against Kurds and Turkmen—as a potential flashpoint.[73] The *New Republic*, for example, called the city "the one Iraqi obstacle you haven't heard of."[74] In October 2003 more than six months after coalition troops occupied the city, Agence France-Presse described Kirkuk as "unstable."[75] In the wake of the 2005 Iraqi elections, the *Boston Globe* labeled the city "volatile."[76]

Although Kirkuk has been tense and there have been occasional acts of violence and terrorism, the fact that the fabric of the city has held despite doomsday predictions is perhaps due to religion more than to any other factor: Kirkuk is home to a number of Sufi *takiya*. Membership in these Sufi lodges spans ethnicity; these institutions encourage unity in a city otherwise susceptible to the centripetal force of ethnic nationalism. Arabs, Kurds, and Turkmen meet in Kirkuk's takiya to study, pray, talk, and socialize.

Many journalists have ignored the takiya and, indeed, Coalition Provisional Authority political officers stationed in Kirkuk did not bother to visit the important sites. Since they did not have parallel institutions in their own lives, both journalists and diplomats remained largely unaware of their presence. Only Nibras Kazemi, himself an Iraqi Shiite, wrote about the importance of Kirkuk's takiyas.[77] Much of the Western press is unaware that Jalal Talabani, the newly appointed president of Iraq, derives his political legitimacy not only from his position as leader of the Patriotic Union of Kurdistan, but also his association with Kirkuk's Talabani takiya, where most of his ancestors are buried.

Conclusions

After Saddam's regime fell, reporters took over the Sheraton and Palestine hotels in downtown Baghdad. Others rented mansions in posh neighborhoods adjacent to the homes of Iraqi political leaders. The *Washington Post*, for example, established their bureau in a house down the street from Iraqi president Jalal Talabani's fortified compound. Subsequently, few reporters left their secure compounds.[78] Some Iraqis, taking advantage of their new freedom to watch foreign channels via satellite, joked that they should hang a banner on the 14th of Ramadan Mosque—across the street from the two hotels—urging reporters to find a new backdrop.

Many journalists grew reliant on the same fixers (local assistants) to whom they were once assigned by Iraqi president Saddam Hussein's Ministry of Information.[79] These fixers—most of whom were Sunni Arabs who had led privileged lives under Saddam's regime—relayed their ideological and sectarian biases, many of which became reflected in mainstream reporting. The general ignorance of religion among Western journalists caused many to miss the opportunity to ask pertinent questions, and others to be led by fixers who viewed them as gullible. As a result, even skilled and veteran journalists misinterpreted events, transmitted faulty analysis, and generally undercut the quality of their reporting. Analysis without an awareness of religion will always be faulty.

Religion need not and should be the central focus of reporting, but Middle East political and diplomatic reporting devoid of religious context is apt to be inaccurate. Many American and European journalists are decidedly secular. Reporters may have grown up in a society separating religion from politics, and journalists may separate religion from their daily life, but not all people do so. Downplaying or ignoring religion in the Middle East sacrifices accuracy and understanding. To convey conflicts, politics, and diplomacy accurately, Western correspondents must steep themselves in religious debates in order to understand the who, what, where, and why of the events they seek to describe. Theology need not shape journalists' work, but an understanding of it should.

4

The Faith-Based
Human Rights Quest:
Missing the Story

Allen D. Hertzke

The mainstream press largely missed one of the great foreign policy
and human rights surprises in recent decades. Beginning in the
mid-1990s, a new movement burst unexpectedly onto the international stage—a faith-based quest devoted to advancing human rights
through the machinery of American foreign policy. A movement of
unlikely allies passed a series of landmark congressional initiatives,
each of which faced fierce opposition. They are:

> The International Religious Freedom Act of 1998
> The Trafficking Victims Protection Act of 2000
> The Sudan Peace Act of 2002
> The North Korean Human Rights Act of 2004

These laws literally built a new infrastructure into U.S. government that makes possible greater advances in human rights around
the globe. And movement activists continue to press for aggressive enforcement, often engaging in pitched battles to overcome
bureaucratic intransigence or inertia in implementation. As I argue
in *Freeing God's Children*, this movement is filling a void in human
rights advocacy, raising issues previously slighted—or insufficiently
pressed—by secular groups, the foreign policy establishment, and
the mainstream press.[1] We can see this by taking a brief look at the
movement's achievements.

Before 1998 religious freedom was the stepchild of human
rights. Human rights groups slighted or sometimes even dismissed

reports of religious persecution, especially against Christians, and American diplomats were often ignorant of religious communities in their countries.[2] That situation has changed through the scaffolding built by the International Religious Freedom Act (IRFA). Promotion of religious freedom is now a basic aim of American foreign policy. Our foreign service must now investigate and report on the status of religious freedom in every country, shining a light on abuses and advancing policies to ameliorate them.

The interfaith movement also publicized the tragedy of Sudan, which had failed to garner international concern. Long before the crisis in Darfur, Christian solidarity activists and their Jewish allies were attempting to draw attention to the nature of the Khartoum regime, whose racial and religious ideology led to a twenty-year war on the African civilization of southern Sudan, with two million dead and five million displaced. In a stunning development, pressure brought by the Sudan Peace Act and the movement led the government of Sudan to sign a peace treaty with southern rebel groups, ending Africa's bloodiest civil war. Religious advocates are now bringing similar pressure to bear to end the regime's atrocities against the people of the western province of Darfur.

To take another previously underreported issue, the trafficking of women and children for sexual exploitation and sweatshop labor metastasized during the freewheeling globalization of the 1990s. Yet the response by governments, and even some human rights groups, was often complacent, until the religious community engaged the issue. Now, because of the new Trafficking Victims Protection Act, many countries are changing laws and practices, crime syndicates are being broken up, and more protective norms are emerging. Women and children are literally being set free.

Finally and most recently, the faith-based alliance has focused attention on the North Korean regime of Kim Jong Il, whose abysmal human rights record includes a vast system of brutal gulags, wide-scale arrests, torture, and killings, in addition to engineered starvation, in which the authorities literally decide who eats and who doesn't. North Korean refugees who flee this hell are subject to rampant exploitation in China, or are sent back to face concentration camps or execution, especially if they are suspected of being Christians. In response, the North Korean Human Rights Act expands protection for refugees, conditions U.S. humanitarian aid to North Korea on transparent improvements in access for people in need, and calls for the inclusion of human rights considerations in all negotiations with the regime.

Any one of these initiatives is a major story, but together they represent the most important human rights movement since the end of the cold war, a movement that is shaping international relations in ways unimaginable a decade ago. Yet do readers of mainstream newspapers and consumers of the mass media know this? Not likely, because journalists—although they have some-times reported on individual initiatives—have not produced a record commen-surate with the importance of this new force in foreign policy.

Why is this so? After following these initiatives for nearly a decade, I have come to a simple overriding conclusion: because evangelicals provide crucial grassroots muscle for the movement, reportage often miscasts the story in the time-worn stereotypes of "Christian Right" politics, thereby missing the broader interfaith coalition and its impact. Heretofore associated with domes-tic skirmishes in the culture wars, evangelicals increasingly engage in inter-national humanitarian and human rights causes—an engagement that flows from globalization of the faith. This facilitates their joining into unlikely alli-ances to promote global human rights, alliances that do not fit the common storyline of "Christian Right opposed by mainline churches" (or Jews or femi-nists or liberals). Indeed, in various campaigns I watched conservative evan-gelicals team up with liberal Jewish groups, the Catholic Church, Episcopal leaders, Tibetan Buddhists, Baha'is, secular human rights groups, feminists, labor unions, and the Congressional Black Caucus. To understand how news outlets often missed the impact of these unlikely alliances—but also to credit worthy exceptions—we must examine coverage of both the individual initia-tives and the wider movement.

A Word about Method

To capture mainstream coverage of the individual initiatives, I surveyed, in detail, all news stories from the *New York Times, Washington Post, Wall Street Journal,* and *Los Angeles Times* a month before and after passage of each initia-tive in each house of Congress, and signature by the president. In cases where initiatives went through a lengthy gestation time in Congress (major-committee consideration, etc.), I also surveyed relevant news stories over a much longer duration. I do not include explicitly religious presses, which often provided fuller coverage, because my objective in this chapter is to understand how *secu-lar* blinders affect coverage of *overtly faith-based* initiatives.[3]

The *New York Times* will feature heavily in this chapter, for three reasons. First, despite recent blows to its reputation, the gray lady remains the "news-paper of record," often guiding coverage in other print outlets and media broad-casts. Its reporting, or lack thereof, looms large in shaping how a phenomenon is understood among policymakers. Second, the *Times* stood out in provid-ing some of the most vivid examples of distorted or slighted coverage. Third, the *Times* also provided, in opinion columns and exceptional cases, laudable contrasts to its overall coverage, illustrating how secular journalists, by taking religion seriously, do their readers a service.

In my analysis I draw a distinction between regular news coverage and opinion columns. This makes sense in part because the very purpose of this book is to analyze how regular news reporting missed significant stories. But drawing this distinction serves another, rather ironic purpose, because opinion columns often captured the issues and dynamics of the new faith-based quest better than regular reporting did, especially at the *New York Times*. Indeed, columns by Abe Rosenthal, Michael Horowitz, Nina Shea, Paul Marshall, Charles Jacobs, Eric Reeves, and Nicholas Kristof serve as one of the most valuable documentary records of the issues examined in this chapter.[4] These columns illustrate how taking religion seriously, and understanding its complexities, enhances a story's accuracy, depth, and significance.

The Campaign for Religious Freedom

The religious-freedom campaign galvanized grassroots constituencies and forged the unlikely alliances that fueled later initiatives. Press coverage for the campaign varied by outlet, but some distinct features emerged. First, decent coverage of the situation in China, which flowed from the high-stakes politics of summits and trade status, was not matched by coverage of the broader religious-freedom campaign. Second, coverage of the anti-persecution movement especially veered off in accuracy when reporters overstressed the "Christian Right" angle. Third, mainstream coverage of evangelical backing for the cause was sometimes patronizing in ways that would have been unimaginable with regard to other constituencies. Fourth, when reporters failed to grasp the full religious dimensions to the stories, coverage was simply off base or, in one case, embarrassingly wrong.

Given the length of the campaign, I surveyed papers over a full three-year period, beginning in 1996, when agitation for legislation against persecution began in earnest, and continuing through the end of 1998, when the International Religious Freedom Act (IRFA) passed. During this period we witnessed a flurry of activity, from unprecedented congressional hearings on the persecution of Christians and other religious minorities, to State Department reports, to the introduction of competing House and Senate bills.

Nonetheless, the greatest coverage of religious persecution concerned China. High-level summits, along with the annual process of renewing normal trade relations with the United States (which ended in 2000, when most favored nation status was made permanent), gave leverage to critics of China's poor record on religious freedom. Because of this unique context, journalists did a better job of covering the lack of religious freedom in China—and the budding alliances to combat it—than they did covering the broader campaign. A number of stories, for example, noted the harsh repression of Buddhists in Tibet, Muslim Uyghurs in Xinjiang, or underground Protestants and Catholics. Other articles noted how conservative Christians joined with unlikely allies, such as "liberal-leaning unions and human rights groups," in demanding tough measures to combat widespread persecution.[5]

One of the most notable pieces, penned by Laurie Goodstein of the *New York Times,* reported on a petition on human rights in China signed by persons who "rarely appear on the same page." These signatories included "two Roman Catholic cardinals and a dozen bishops, a spokesman for the Church of Scientology, Reform and Orthodox rabbis, evangelical Christian ministers and broadcasters, Muslims, Tibetan Buddhists, Southern Baptists, Methodists, Presbyterians, African-American religious leaders and Orthodox Christians."[6]

What is striking about this coverage is that it failed to translate into an understanding of similar alliances for the broader anti-persecution campaign. As we will see, Goodstein and others at the *New York Times* failed to capture equally broad alliances on religious-freedom legislation, instead heavily emphasizing the "Christian Right" angle in the battle for IRFA, often to the exclusion of other major players.

Other news outlets fared a bit better. As an inside-the-beltway newspaper, the *Washington Post* positively profiled such movement champions as Congressmen Chris Smith, a Catholic whom it described as a human rights "hero," and Frank Wolf, whose born-again conscience leads him to tell fellow citizens "how bad things are in countries they seldom hear about." The *Post* also captured how evangelical groups reached out for "collaborative convergence" with the U.S. Catholic Conference, the Union of American Hebrew Congregations, and the Campaign for Tibet. But like the *New York Times,* the *Post* also lapsed into typecasting the legislation as the pet project of the religious Right.[7]

Given its location and heavy immigrant readership, the *Los Angeles Times* provided distinct coverage of the plight of Asian minorities, particularly the repression of Buddhists. Characteristic was a piece describing "the largest celebration" of Buddha's birthday in the United States, in which some twenty thousand Vietnamese Americans used the occasion to protest persecution of Buddhist monks in Vietnam.[8] Such deep community connections probably helped the *Times* provide relatively extensive and straightforward coverage of the cause of religious freedom and the budding alliances championing it.[9]

This brings us to the illustrative case of the *New York Times.* What emerges from its reportage is a decidedly inconsistent pattern, where a straightforward story is followed by a slanted one, an account of broader alliances by a story that exhibits a distorted Christian Right angle.

We see this in accounts of the legislative battles surrounding the movement for religious freedom. Ironically, some of the *Times*'s best treatment occurred in the early phases of the movement. This owed in large part to the astute coverage of veteran religion reporter Peter Steinfels, who happens to be a noted Catholic author and scholar.[10] Before retiring from the *Times*, he produced three pieces in 1996 charting the evolution of the nascent campaign. In one he described how evangelical advocates compared their campaign "to the Jewish community's efforts for Soviet Jews in the 1980s," noting that much of the persecution against Christians "arises in the remaining Communist regimes or in nations under militant Islamic governments." Another piece reported on the International Day of Prayer for the Persecuted Church, which involved thousands of U.S. congregations "primed with booklets, videotapes, model sermons, relevant Bible passages and practical tips on making contact with government officials." Steinfels quoted key leaders of the evangelical community joining in the battle: Charles Colson of Prison Fellowship, Richard Land of the Southern Baptist Convention, and Richard Cizik of the National Association of Evangelicals. This reportage provided an informative accounting of the looming movement and its issues, illustrating how important journalistic sensitivity to religious issues can be. In other words, reporters matter, and their backgrounds matter.[11]

In subsequent reporting, however, the *Times* seemed to struggle to make sense of the legislative maneuvers, often relying on a narrative hook that defines the issue as the cause célèbre of the "Christian Right." Even as the legislation was modified and diverse new groups came on board, the *Times* often failed to take these developments into account. Nowhere, for example, did it report that the legislation was endorsed by the U.S. Conference of Catholic Bishops, the Union of American Hebrew Congregations, and the Campaign for Tibet.[12] In a sense the *Times*'s preoccupation with the "Christian Right" seriously deprecated the vigorous efforts of Catholics, Jews, Episcopalians, Baha'is, Tibetan Buddhists, and others on behalf of the religious-freedom cause.

Evidence that reporters for the *Times* hooked their stories on the Christian Right theme can be found by looking at which groups they featured. Throughout the 1998 legislative battle, the only conservative Christian group mentioned by name was the Christian Coalition—the organization most clearly tied to hardball politics. Even though the Christian Coalition was a declining organization and not a central player in the alliance for the legislation, it remained on the Rolodexes of news organizations and served as a convenient synecdoche for the dreaded religious Right. Nowhere was there mention of Land, Colson, and

Cizik, or a variety of moderate evangelical groups. Thus, even the *Times*'s treatment of evangelicals was skewed toward emphasizing the hard-Right theme. In stories we learn that "social conservatives like the Christian Coalition" are pitted against "moderates, encouraged by the chamber of Commerce." Passage of the House bill is depicted as "a major victory for the Christian Coalition," while the vote for Senate legislation is described as the triumph of "the Christian Coalition and other conservative groups." Minimal interviewing of congressional sponsors and activists would have revealed many others who claimed and contributed to the victory equally.

Another indication of the *Times*'s preoccupation with the Christian Right occurred when it gave its most prominent coverage of the actual legislative battle. That occurred on July 24, 1998, when it declared the legislation *dead,* on the front page of the newspaper, *above the fold.* In recounting that action two days later, a *Times* editorial said that the Senate had "killed a bill dear to social conservatives," leaving out entirely those others equally devoted to its passage. The premature prediction of the bill's demise, which activists felt was almost gleeful, appeared three months before the bill was passed unanimously by both houses of Congress. A check for bias and a better grasp of the potent and diverse religious forces backing the legislation might have led the *Times* to qualify such embarrassingly wrong reportage.[13]

Ironically, readers of the *Times*'s opinion columns would often have been better informed of the issues involved in the religious-freedom campaign—and the legislative attempts to address them—than would readers of the paper's regular reporting. This is entirely due to former executive editor and columnist Abe Rosenthal, who penned no fewer than twenty columns dealing with religious persecution and the campaign against it.[14] Rosenthal's columns were widely syndicated in religious outlets, reprinted in denominational newsletters, mentioned in religious broadcasts, and referenced in actual worship services. Thus, they not only raised public awareness of the issue, but, as a letter nominating Rosenthal for a Pulitzer noted, "enhanced the institutional credibility" of the *Times* "with many religious believers who had seen the mainline press as patronizing if not hostile."[15]

Reportage on the issue that sparked the movement—concern for persecuted Christians abroad—was equally inconsistent. Steinfels's reportage suggested that the problem was real and had been slighted. That reportage was followed by straightforward pieces summarizing the State Department report on global persecution, which provided vivid highlights of the treatment of Christians in some seventy-eight countries. Later that year, a major *New York Times Magazine* story featured an account of the growing movement for persecuted Christians. While not uncritical, the piece reported on the brutalization of Christians in Sudan and oppression in such countries as China, Cuba, and Saudi Arabia.[16]

Most of the time, however, the *Times* seemed religiously tone-deaf, leading to slighted or distorted reportage. A year after Steinfels wrote a report about the annual day that Christian parishioners especially remember and pray for fellow believers abroad—and just as the campaign for legislation was heating up—the *Times* ignored the International Day of Prayer for the Persecuted Church. This absence of mainstream coverage did not go unnoticed. *New York Times* columnist Abe Rosenthal took his fellow journalists and colleagues to task. Is it a story, he asked pointedly, that "on Sunday, November 16, about eight million Americans gathered in about 50,000 Protestant and Roman Catholic churches across the country" to offer their voices for religious freedom? For the *Times* and others, the answer was clearly no. His colleagues ignored the story, Rosenthal argued, because they failed to pay "attention to what led up to it," the striking "conservative-liberal" alliance against global persecution.[17]

Ignoring the cause of persecuted Christians was one thing, but the *Times* also veered off by minimizing the problem and negatively stereotyping evangelical backers of legislation to ameliorate it. In an extended November 1998 piece, Laurie Goodstein depicted evangelical advocates for fellow believers in patronizing terms as neophytes who oversimplify complex issues. Thus, abusive treatment of Christians abroad was labeled "persecution"—in quotation marks. A grassroots group was described as gathering to pray for "what it calls" Christian martyrs, as if there were doubt about the authenticity of such martyrdom. Movement backers were described as focusing on "what they call" the persecuted church. Those who seek release of prisoners were described as engaged in letter writing to countries "whose names they cannot pronounce." And so it went. The piece also implicitly discounted the actual problem of religious repression by stating that "what outside observers often label Christian persecution is often a complex brew of racial, economic, political, tribal, and religious rivalries." This conclusion, however, was not backed by actual reportage from the countries in question, nor did it cite the easily available and massive State Department report on widespread abuse of Christian minorities, nor did it even draw upon the *Times*'s and even the reporter's own previous reportage.[18] Finally, the piece conflated the campaign for persecuted Christians with the wider movement for religious freedom, ignoring the diverse religious groups that backed IRFA and leading to the distorted implication that the new law focused primarily or exclusively on abuse of Christian minorities.[19]

In a stunning contrast to this kind of coverage, the *Portland Oregonian* produced a Pulitzer-caliber, five-part series on the persecution of Christians around the world—a series published just two weeks before Goodstein's piece. In

October 1998 the newspaper sent veteran reporter Mark O'Keefe to the field to investigate conditions for Christian minorities in five nations: Pakistan, Burma, Sudan, Egypt, and China. Those stories illustrate journalism at its best: on-the-ground reportage of vivid specific cases placed in wider documentary context.

The story on Pakistan, for example, depicted what was (at the time[20]) a weak and impoverished Christian minority under siege—subject to mob violence, injustice, intimidation, threats, abductions of women and children, killings for "blasphemy," and burned churches. In one instance, three girls were seized from their Christian parents in full view of police escorts, the justification being that the girls had supposedly converted to Islam. The Muslim lawyer who represented the parents received death threats, while the city magistrate decided against them for fear of causing a riot. As the judge admitted, the law was on the side of the parents, but the mob would react like the American KKK and lynch him if he returned the girls.[21]

Other articles were equally compelling. The piece on Burma showed how a military dictatorship harassed religious communities and manipulated them against each other. Especially targeted are Christian Karen (an ethnic group), who have faced "destruction of their churches and restrictions on their worship, attacks on their villages as well as stints of forced labor," all apparently designed to "terrify and demoralize" believers. Soldiers who march into villages and refugee camps routinely ask whether people are Christians to single them out for threats or violence.[22] In Egypt the report painted a picture of discrimination, harassment, and terror visited on Christians, and the same for Muslims who convert.[23] On China the article offered a sophisticated analysis of the differential treatment of official versus unregistered churches, with underground Christians subject to harassment, arrest, and imprisonment in "reeducation-through-labor" camps.[24]

The story on Sudan featured the most afflicted Christian community on earth at the time, and O'Keefe's piece remains far superior in detail, depth, documentation, and analysis to anything I have yet found in the mainstream press. He captured the undeniably religious dimension of the attacks on Africans in southern Sudan—interviewing abducted children who were given Muslim names and forced to convert as slaves, documenting church burnings, and reporting the killings of catechists. He also catalogued the massive scale of scorched-earth policies and attendant denial of food aid to starving people, which Khartoum employed to subdue its Christian and animist population. He described the process of slave redemption, noting the efforts by redeemers to avoid creating a market for slaves. Reading this piece more than six years since publication remains highly informative.[25] While other mainstream outlets treated the persecution of Christian minorities more straightforwardly than did the *Times,* none surpassed the *Oregonian* in the depth of field reportage and documentation.

To sum up, inconsistent mainstream coverage of the religious-freedom campaign flowed from the inability of some journalists to capture the complex religious dynamics behind the campaign. This resulted in overall reportage that failed to convey the full scope, significance, and potential of the new human rights movement. The passage of the International Religious Freedom Act, however, did mark an improvement in regular reporting on this phenomenon. Several news outlets covered the bill's passage, some in depth and others in perfunctory fashion.[26] And as the new law was implemented, news about religious persecution, and U.S. efforts to combat it, percolated up, just as advocates had hoped it would. Mandated State Department reports, hearings by the U.S. Commission on International Religious Freedom, and designations of "countries of concern" for their egregious denial of religious freedom, kept the issue in the press. But the full story *behind these policies* was still often missed.

Ending a War in Sudan

The Sudan campaign was a direct extension of the religious-freedom campaign, so I analyze it here, even though it culminated several years later. The twenty-year civil war in southern Sudan, and the successful campaign to end it, remains the most underappreciated story of modern times. This becomes clear when we think of it in the abstract. Imagine an event akin to the fall of apartheid, a human rights breakthrough that for millions of black Africans means an end to massacres, ethnic cleansing, man-made famine, and literal enslavement by a despotic regime. Imagine, too, that this triumph was gained through an American grassroots campaign of exposure and pressure that led the regime to relent. Repeated front-page news, one would think; feature stories on the nightly broadcasts. Yet the story earned mostly perfunctory treatment in the mainstream press, nothing like the related and more recent crisis in Darfur. More than this, coverage was, at times, simply off base.

The scale and significance of this story was missed because it involved religious dimensions both within Sudan and in the protest campaign that seemed to stymie clear and forceful reporting. To begin with, until the last few years, press and media coverage of the civil war in southern Sudan was remarkably skimpy; indeed, the conflict continued to be dubbed "Africa's forgotten civil war" as late as 2001.[27] What early reporting did occur on Sudan tended to slight the specific devastation of animist and Christian minorities. This was the unintentional consequence of characterizing the war as another intractable "ethnic conflict" in Africa, a depiction hardly designed to elicit a strong Western response.[28] Often missing, in other words, was the religious dimension that explained the historic import of what was happening—that Islamist militancy was driving the conflict. Indeed, it was the effort by Khartoum in 1983 to impose militant *shari'a* (Islamic law) across Sudan that shattered a decade-long peace and ushered in the twenty-year conflict. And the blame for mass civilian deaths rested largely on the deliberate tactics of the government of Sudan to Islamicize, subdue, or wipe out non-Muslims.[29] But with the exception of opinion columns and a few notable pieces,[30] this dominant feature of the conflict was slighted in the mainstream press until reporting on the Sudan Peace Act kicked in.

In 1998, for example, a famine spread across southern Sudan and the response of Khartoum was to ban relief flights, in effect seizing the opportunity to manufacture starvation. But as Nina Shea noted, few at the time were writing about that. Instead, the conflict was depicted as ethnic, or as a battle over pastureland or water rights—concerns that would fail to elicit as much reaction as a potential religious genocide.[31] It was not until the push for the Sudan Peace Act kicked into high gear that most press reports began to recognize this crucial religious dimension, but even so the virulence of Khartoum's campaign was often either underplayed or cast in coverage stressing "complexities" that religious activists, especially evangelicals, purportedly failed to grasp. Not only did this result in distorted coverage of the scale of the Sudanese catastrophe, it ironically slighted the work of Jewish groups, black churches, and many others in the cause that the mainstream press might have been more sympathetic in treating.[32]

This feature was evident in several instances of *New York Times* coverage. In November 1999 the Sudan campaign gained passage of a congressional initiative designed to get food aid to southern areas cut off by Khartoum. Though backed by a wide array of religious groups, academics, and the U.S. Commission on International Religious Freedom, the initiative was framed in a "Christian Right" subtext by Jane Perlez of the *Times*. More specifically, it was cast as a dispute between seemingly unbiased food aid groups concerned about unintended consequences of the measure—who were fulsomely quoted—and conservative Christians never mentioned by name, who were depicted as opposing a Muslim (rather than militant Islamist) regime. None of the diverse religious leaders backing the measure were cited. Nor did the article place the issue in the wider context of the existing manipulation of food aid by Khartoum that gave rise to the initiative in the first place.[33]

Similarly, when word leaked on May 30, 2001, that the Bush administration was considering Chester Crocker as special envoy to Sudan, Perlez cast the story as the effort by Secretary Colin Powell to "keep the Christian right at bay." Once again, going with the Christian Right storyline grossly oversimplified the story. Observing that conservative Christians were urging the administration to back "Christian rebels against the Islamic government," Perlez depicted Crocker as "seasoned" and even-handed, someone who would not tilt "too heavily toward the Christians" in the conflict. Crocker was quoted as saying he wanted to be insulated from "conservative views" at the White House, as if championing the cause of the southern Sudanese was solely a conservative position. The article noted, however, that African American lawmakers were also pressing for aggressive support for the southern Sudanese, which hinted at the broader coalition involved in the campaign but left out entirely the wide religious alliance involved. The article's passing nod to African Americans and silence about the broader coalition left the reader confused. Ironically, the story acted as a lightning rod for the coalition, making Crocker unacceptable and leading to the appointment as special envoy of former senator John Danforth, who ultimately helped negotiate the peace treaty.

The treatment of slavery in Sudan also illustrates how a press emphasis on the Christian Right angle could slant coverage. The abduction of thousands of southern Sudanese women and children into slavery for Arab masters had been used for years as a tool by the National Islamic Front to subjugate its African population. The existence and brutality of the practice—beatings, maiming, rape, concubinage, and genital mutilation—have been widely documented. Yet in the story on Crocker, Perlez wrote this: "The conflict has become a lightning rod for Christian advocates and for black lawmakers because of *what they call* [emphasis mine] the Sudan government's policy of allowing Christian black Sudanese to be abducted and sent into slavery in the Islamic north." Dismissing the Sudanese government's complicity in massive slavery as nothing more than a claim by advocates undermined the *Times*'s credibility. As Richard John Neuhaus caustically put it: "What do you suppose the *New York Times* knows that the U.S. State Department, Freedom House, Human Rights Watch, the *Atlantic Monthly,* the *Baltimore Sun,* and others do not know?"[34] And we might add, how did the *Times* remain unaware of what the *Portland Oregonian* had documented?

One response to Sudanese slavery involved systematic redemption efforts, in which Western groups work with Arab intermediaries to purchase the freedom of slaves and return them to their homes. The practice was controversial among Christian advocates, but the largest of the redemption groups, Christian Solidarity International (CSI), undertook extensive safeguards against fraud.[35] Still, rather than report on slaving itself, some press accounts went out of their way to highlight alleged widespread abuses and cast redeemers as manipulated Western Christians.

Most dramatic was Karl Vick's front-page *Washington Post* article, "Ripping Off Slave Redeemers."[36] Vick depicted slave redemption as "rife with corruption," involving stage-managed transactions in which "slaves weren't slaves at all but people gathered locally and instructed to pretend they were returning from bondage." Redemption activists, such as John Eibner of CSI, were depicted as well meaning but naive, and readers were left with the clear impression that most redemption efforts were hoaxes and scams. One consequence of the story: the mind-bending reality of violent slaving could hardly have been depicted in a manner more consciously designed to induce complacency in the West, much to the benefit of the Sudanese regime.[37] Illustrating the power of one report, the story "ricocheted around the world." CBS's *60 Minutes II* with Dan Rather ran with it in a broadcast "slanted toward 'fake' slave redemptions." Other news organizations circulated the same account, much to the chagrin of human rights leaders on the ground in Sudan.[38]

A flurry of responses to Vick's Nairobi-based research revealed that he "never witnessed any slave-redemption," "never interviewed any redeemed slaves or slave retrievers," "never produced a single false slave from the 60,000 plus slaves CSI has redeemed," "relied almost exclusively on remote sources who never witnessed CSI activity but who had political axes to grind," and ignored investigators who had traveled to document redemption efforts.[39]

An independent journalist came to a similar conclusion about the tendentious nature of Vick's account. Tony Norman, a columnist for the *Pittsburgh Post-Gazette*, originally took the *Post* story at face value in a column titled "Turning a Profit on the Price of Freedom." In the column Norman concluded that the "Sudanese slave scam is an example of how cynicism distorts even missions of mercy." Challenged by Charles Jacobs of the American Anti-Slavery Group to investigate the issue thoroughly on his own, Norman concluded that the *Post* story was a "hatchet job." Referring to his earlier column, Norman wrote that "if there ever was a column I wish I could retract, it's that one."[40]

The *Post* was not alone in dismissive coverage of the redemption issue. Jane Perlez of the *New York Times* depicted church groups as financing "redemption" missions in which Americans pay money to "free" abductees. Putting these words in quotation marks, of course, implied that naive American Christians were being duped or used, and seemed to put the *Times* in the Olympian position of saying that people held captive for years were not actually being freed when restored to their families. Ironically, the negative tenor of this coverage was matched only by official Sudanese government press releases, which also put "slave redemption" in quotation marks.[41]

Such patronizing coverage—unimaginable with other constituencies—was not uncommon. In a story on the U.S.-brokered security pact between the government of Sudan and southern rebel groups, the *New York Times* referred to the war in Sudan as a "pet cause of many American religious conservatives."[42] It is hard to imagine the *Times* describing the plight of Soviet Jewry as a "pet cause" of American Jews, or opposition to apartheid as a "pet cause" of African Americans.

Condescending coverage illustrated how the Sudan cause became "tainted" by association with evangelical Christians.[43] Also, as noted, such depictions tainted the achievement of many others in the extraordinary coalition that pressed for peace in Sudan—African American pastors and black political leaders, Jewish groups, Catholic and Episcopal bishops, students, and academics. Thus, even as coverage picked up in the wake of movement initiatives, reports on American interest in slavery or the role of oil in the conflict, while noteworthy, continued to miss the broadly interfaith nature of the alliances.[44]

By ignoring the dynamic activism in American religious communities in Sudan, journalists missed some compelling stories. Consider that former Sudanese slaves spoke at synagogues and black churches while people wept; lay evangelicals from the heartland traveled to Washington to join with civil rights leaders in demonstrations; African bishops offered dramatic testimony before Congress; and campus activists helped organized a divestment campaign that resulted in plummeting stock prices for oil companies doing business in Sudan. Practically the entire religious community in President Bush's hometown of Midland, Texas, mobilized around the cause, and local activists became citizen diplomats, communicating directly to rebel groups and Sudanese officials their unwavering commitment to end the war.

In other words, by failing to take the Sudan campaign seriously and by failing to investigate its complexities thoroughly, journalists missed many great stories of human drama. Take the example of the Sudan Peace Act, which we now know altered the trajectory of that nation's history. While negotiations between the government of Sudan and rebel groups did receive attention in the mainstream press, with particularly good coverage of religious dimensions appearing in the *Los Angeles Times* and *Wall Street Journal*,[45] the Sudan Peace Act was scarcely covered. Only the *Washington Post* ran an actual story on the signing of the act, but that coverage consisted of a mere three paragraphs in its broader "Washington in Brief" story.[46] The *New York Times*, which ran no story, included a reference to the act only in a caption of a photograph included in another story on Africa.[47]

That dry caption failed to capture the remarkable story contained in the photograph, which shows President Bush looking up to a slender young Dinka man named Francis Bok, whose tale seems biblical in its sweep. Captured at the age of seven, when Arab militia attacked his village and killed his parents, Bok was sold into slavery to work for a herder who made him sleep with the animals and beat him if any got loose. After ten years in captivity, Bok escaped, ultimately making it to the United States to become an advocate working to "free [his] people in bondage." The invitation to the White House ceremony thus capped a remarkable journey that took Bok from slavery in the Sudanese bush to the center of American power, as the president signaled the nation's resolve to help achieve Bok's dream. Capturing the poignancy of the moment, one activist observed: "This may be the first time, since the nineteenth century, an American president has met with a former slave."[48]

With the exception of the *Wall Street Journal*, which had previously published an account of how Francis Bok went from slave to "American celebrity,"[49] the mainstream press missed a golden opportunity to connect the personal vignette with the larger meaning of a global story. Spurred by pressure from the American Sudan campaign, the regime in Khartoum finally signed a historic peace agreement with rebel groups on January 9, 2005. This event, witnessed by Colin Powell, received coverage worthy of its significance. Both the *Washington Post* and the *New York Times* ran extensive articles on the signing in Nairobi.[50] But while analyses dealt clearly with the religious nature of the conflict on the ground, the movement forces that helped end the war were almost entirely ignored. The *Times* made no reference to the interfaith alliances that pressed the U.S. government to make ending the war a top foreign-policy priority, while the *Post* noted only pressure by evangelical groups. Here again, by failing to appreciate the crucial role played by other religionists in the Sudan campaign—Jews, Catholics, Anglicans, black pastors—the media missed the deeper meaning and significance of the story.

Better Coverage: Trafficking into Slavery

Of all the initiatives discussed here, the campaign against global trafficking may produce the most far-reaching impact, because it created a permanent U.S. institution charged with using the tools of American soft power to end modern-day global slavery. This initiative also produced a remarkable strange-bedfellows alliance in which feminists and born-again Christians joined forces for legislation resisted by the Clinton administration. That alliance continues to back robust enforcement of the law. Given these features, it was hard for the press to ignore the story, especially since it was a *New York Times Magazine* feature that first brought to light the wrenching reality of the global sex trafficking of vulnerable women and children.[51]

The *New York Times, Washington Post,* and *Los Angeles Times* all ran numerous solid stories in October 2000 as the final bill passed Congress on the way to the president.[52] Though most did not cover the religious–feminist alliances involved, the coverage lacked the kind of patronizing taint we saw on religious freedom and Sudan, instead providing straightforward treatment of the trafficking problem and provisions of the new law to combat it.

One of the most notable treatments—which proves how incorporating religion completes a story—came from the *Los Angeles Times,* which published long, detailed, and well-informed pieces that outlined the global problem of trafficking, in addition to its ties to California and other areas of the United States. One article in particular did not mince words, noting that a "dramatic increase in sex trafficking" moved Congress to pass "a measure designed to protect women and children smuggled into the United States and forced into prostitution and other forms of slave labor." It cited figures provided by a local antislavery activist, which stated that as many as ten thousand Asian women work in underground brothels in Southern California alone. The article also documented the unlikely allies who fought for the legislation—members of Congress on opposite sides of the ideological spectrum, and feminist leaders and conservative Christians. Readers were left with a greater awareness of the problem itself, along with a sense that people of goodwill and conviction were tackling this terrible affront to human dignity.[53]

The trafficking issue also garnered that most rare commodity: broadcast-media attention to faith-based human rights work. That coverage highlighted the work of the International Justice Mission (IJM), led by Gary Haugen, whose global Christian ministry employs direct intervention by investigators and lawyers on behalf of victims of gross injustice. Operating in a dangerous milieu in which organized crime syndicates run trafficking operations, IJM had investigators pose as potential customers and videotape conversations and transactions. This kind of dramatic footage not only provided the basis for several media features on the horrors of trafficking, especially of children, some of whom were as young as six, but also aided in crackdowns on child-prostitution rings in Asia.[54]

Better coverage, however, did not prevent media biases or blinders from occasionally showing, nor did it ensure that the breadth of the religious alliances at work would always be captured. For example, when in January 1999 there was a crucial battle over negotiations of a United Nations treaty on sex trafficking, the *New York Times* completely ignored the vital role of religious constituencies.[55] At issue was whether treaty wording would refer only to "forced prostitution," or to trafficking more generally, as sexual exploitation. Clinton administration negotiators were backing the narrower definition, while an alliance of faith-based groups and U.S. feminists argued that referring only to "forced" prostitution diluted the treaty, minimized the extent to which coercion was present in all trafficking, and played into the hands of organized-crime syndicates that run the operations.[56]

In reporting on this challenge to the Clinton administration, the *Times* reporter portrayed feminist groups as *leading* an "unusual" alliance that *included* "conservative Republicans" and "leaders of the Heritage Foundation and other politically conservative groups."[57] Not only did this article completely ignore the broad alliance of evangelicals, Jews, and Catholics that coalesced against sex trafficking, it also conflated such groups with secular conservatives, as if the global ministries of Campus Crusade for Christ or the Southern Baptist Convention were mere think tanks like the Heritage Foundation or policy arms of the Republican Party. This distorted interpretation probably reflected both an ignorance of the distinctiveness of faith commitments (lumping them together with secular conservatism) and a reluctance to feature evangelicals in a favorable light. The real story was that such evangelical figures as Chuck Colson, Richard Land, Bill Bright, Diane Knippers, and Kay Coles James (a fellow *at* Heritage[58]) were joining forces with Gloria Steinem of *Ms.* magazine, Patricia Ireland of NOW, Eleanor Smeal of the Feminist Majority, Gloria Feldt of Planned Parenthood, and Jessica Neuwirth of Equality Now in the fight on behalf of trafficking victims.[59]

North Korea: Failing to Connect the Dots

While previous sections dealt with particular stories, coverage of the North Korean initiative showed how the press largely failed to connect the dots between them. This resulted in scant coverage of what may turn out to be a momentous international story.

The vast human rights tragedy of North Korea has largely been placed on the back burner in favor of press coverage of nuclear arms talks. From a "realist" perspective, this prioritizing makes sense, given the monumental danger the regime of Kim Jong Il poses to the peninsula and the region. But the work of the interfaith coalition, through the North Korean Human Rights Act, will in fact influence those high-level nuclear talks. This possibility has not been well appreciated because the press has yet to make the connection between the prior initiatives and the North Korean campaign.

The North Korean Human Rights Act of 2004 is best understood as the latest in a string of legislative successes by the new human rights movement. Because this dimension was largely ignored, the significance of the North Korean initiative—with the exception of an early reference in the *Wall Street Journal*[60]—has so far been missed. The act is envisioned by activists as analogous to the Helsinki accords, in which human rights leverage on the Soviet Union opened fissures that ultimately brought the downfall of the Communist empire. Remarkably, none of the four newspapers ran a story at all on the passage of the act.

If they had connected the act to prior initiatives, reporters would have captured the broader import of the legislation. Moreover, an appreciation of its effect would have enabled reporters to discern similar features between the North Korean initiative and previous campaigns. Like earlier initiatives, for example, the act faced formidable opposition, and foreign governments were shocked by its passage. As with the Sudan Act, the North Korean legislation requires the appointment of a high-level special envoy on human rights. Like IRFA, it is designed to expose diplomatic efforts to bargain away human rights concerns for strategic concessions, in this case compromises on nuclear arms. As with all of the initiatives, movement activists are poised to monitor implementation of the act and fight against any attempt to undermine it.

Crucial here is another fascinating story of great news value in its own right. The North Korean campaign galvanized the predominately Christian Korean American community. Dynamic pastors forged a new association, the Korean-American Church Coalition, which held its first annual convention in Los Angeles on the eve of Senate deliberations on the North Korean Human Rights Act in the fall of 2004.[61] Though some senators were threatening to filibuster the legislation, that opposition melted when word began to filter into district offices that fiercely patriotic Korean Americans, linked with other faith-based activists, were closely monitoring action in Washington. The fascinating story of an ethnic group beginning to flex its muscles on the global stage thus eluded the press. Now well integrated into the broader alliance of religious groups, Korean American Christians intend to scrutinize U.S. actions and ensure that the plight of their brothers and sisters in North Korea remains part of the geopolitical calculus.

In sum, it is hard to imagine a different movement's triumph receiving such scant coverage, especially after its demonstrations of formidable clout. Missing the interfaith alliance on North Korea helps explain this.

Capturing the Broader Movement

We have seen how slighting or misapprehending religion results in slanted or incomplete news coverage. We have also observed that to capture the new politics of global human rights, the press must incorporate a sophisticated understanding of faith-based dynamics. To see how "getting religion right" enhances the depth and accuracy of coverage, I will show some outstanding examples of how reporters did just that. To a certain extent, better coverage flowed as events overtook initial biases. But given that reportage on the movement remains modest at best, good coverage happened when reporters took religion seriously, which many still do not. It was field travel to probe human rights and humanitarian problems around the world that led *New York Times* columnist Nicholas Kristof to take a fresh look at the global engagement of evangelicalism. Though Kristof is not a reporter in the strict sense, this put him in touch with a variety of Christian groups operating in some of the most hostile places on earth.

Taking up the mantle of the retired Abe Rosenthal, Kristof not only featured issues tackled by the faith-based movement but offered a sympathetic, though not uncritical, portrait of born-again activism on these issues. As he wrote in one column, "America's evangelicals have become the newest internationalists . . . fighting sexual trafficking in Eastern Europe and slavery in Sudan." He also linked successful backing of IRFA with evangelicals' triumph on trafficking legislation, and he applauded their push for increased AIDS funding for Africa. In another column he lauded the work of evangelical missions in building orphanages, schools, clinics, and hospitals in Africa. In a third column, he used the humanitarian leadership of Senator Sam Brownback (a Republican from Kansas) to highlight how "the Christian Right" has "staked out" ground on human rights with which Democrats ought to be sympathetic. Employing Brownback as his exemplar (though sometimes backhandedly), Kristof lauded conservative Christian activism against atrocities in Darfur, Uganda, and North Korea, and challenged liberals not to shun it.[62] Ironically, Kristof's challenge to liberals could as well have been made to his own newspaper.

The *Wall Street Journal* also made a major contribution to better understanding of the movement in a piece that did exactly what was so often lacking in mainstream coverage: connect the initiatives. Authored by Peter Waldman, the long article observed how "evangelical groups, once among America's staunchest isolationists, are making a mark on U.S. foreign policy." Citing activism by evangelicals on religious freedom, trafficking, Sudan, and North Korea, the article offered a balanced account of the pros and cons of such activism, including possible unintended consequences. The piece showed how the new engagement is rooted in the growth of foreign missions and overseas trips, in which "record numbers of evangelicals have fanned out across the globe . . . often returning acutely aware of oppression and poverty." The article also noted diverse alliances, though its emphasis on neoconservative Jewish backing underplayed somewhat the breadth of those religious alliances.[63]

This brings us to the fascinating case of the *New York Times*. While its regular overall coverage of evangelical engagement in the faith-based movement has been particularly slight, inaccurate, or biased, it nevertheless provided the single best story on the same phenomenon. That piece appeared on the front page of the October 26, 2003, Sunday newspaper, with the headline, "Evangelicals Sway White House on Human Rights Issues Abroad."[64] What sparked that singular coverage was a story that seemed to hit reporters in the face. In a major address to the UN General Assembly, on September 23, 2003, President George W. Bush challenged the nations of the world to tackle human trafficking, which he characterized as a spreading "humanitarian crisis." Describing the specter of women and children being "bought, sold or forced across the worlds' borders" to live subject to "brutality and lonely fear," the president announced aggressive actions by his administration to implement the nation's trafficking law. This reference left governments and reporters scrambling to find out what was behind the president's posture, and Elisabeth Bumiller of the *Times* was the one who got the story right by interviewing the key born-again leaders (and others) who helped influence the president's action. That inquiry led her to write a broader piece about global evangelical engagement and to note the unlikely alliances evangelicals forged with liberals on a range of issues.

Bumiller linked evangelical concern for the "persecuted church" with subsequent activism on trafficking and Sudan, and she documented the pragmatic willingness of evangelical leaders to work with Jews, Catholics, and feminists on such issues. She also observed the movement's influence within the White House and noted how its evangelical component represented a kind of conservative human rights conscience. Finally, she captured one of the most frequently missed features of the new faith-based movement: the remarkably enduring alliances forged between evangelicals and Jews (and not just neoconservative ones). Bumiller reported on how Charles Colson, the conservative founder of Prison Fellowship, and Rabbi David Saperstein, the liberal leader of the Union of American Hebrew Congregations, met with top Bush aide Karl Rove to press the case for the administration's intervention to end the civil war in Sudan. She quoted Saperstein at length about his work in the coalition "on issues below the radar screen that are of deep concern to the evangelical community."[65] This piece—though unfortunately not followed up by the *Times*—brought together the strands of the movement in a particularly sophisticated and informative way. Given previous regular coverage by the *Times*, that was indeed "real news."

Subsequent coverage of various issues championed by the movement revealed modestly growing press awareness of the new global engagement of evangelicals, and occasionally the unusual alliances they have forged.[66] But with the exception of a single piece by Susan Page in *USA Today*,[67] nothing has appeared with the comprehensiveness of Bumiller's account, suggesting that the ongoing interfaith quest for human rights remains underreported in mainstream outlets.

A lesson here goes to the heart of the mission of a free press. Missing or misapprehending crucial stories, especially by the mainstream press, damages the credibility of journalism as a profession, because as we have seen, laypeople *are* reading these accounts of faith-based activism in religious magazines, bulletins, and alternative news outlets. The disconnect between what they are experiencing as citizens and what the mainstream press reports becomes glaring. Getting the story right, as Bumiller and Page did, gains precious credibility for the press. But, of course, it also serves the broader goal of a free press: better informed citizens and policymakers.

5

"Misunderestimating" Religion in the 2004 Presidential Campaign

C. Danielle Vinson and James L. Guth

Following the 2004 presidential election, journalists and political pundits seized upon religion and concerns about moral values to explain George W. Bush's somewhat surprising victory. While much of the "Wednesday morning" analysis oversimplified the factors influencing voters, there is no doubt that religion played an important role in that 2004 election, one that the media sensed but often struggled to grasp.

That is not to say that journalists failed to cover religion in the campaign. They reported at length on the candidates' faith, religious rhetoric, and appeals to religious voters. They discussed "moral issues" such as gay marriage, stem cell research, and abortion. But the coverage, to borrow from President Bush's lexicon, "misunderestimated" the impact of religion. Journalists underestimated the critical importance of the candidates' own religious beliefs and comfort with religious questions, and they misunderstood religious voters and the full significance of church-based mobilization.

We begin our analysis by examining some barriers to good journalism on religion's role in American elections. Then we look at the way the media (primarily major national newspapers) handled three topics of interest in 2004. First, we examine stories on the candidates' own religion, where journalists and opinion writers often reached different conclusions about the importance to voters of the candidates' beliefs. Second, we evaluate reporting on "religious" voters, specific issues, and the efforts by George W. Bush and John Kerry to mobilize religious groups and churches. Finally, we examine some data on religion's impact and assess the adequacy of the coverage.

Barriers to Understanding

Covering religion's role in American elections poses distinct challenges to journalists. As we can attest personally from years of experience, the most significant problem is not media bias but media ignorance. When discussing religious politics with fellow reporters, we usually begin with a brief version of "Religion 101." As a host of surveys has shown, most political reporters have weak religious ties, if any (see, for example, Robert Lichter's *The Media Elite*).[1] Indeed, to many, the world of religion is unfamiliar and, sometimes, exotic. Daniel Okrent, former "public editor" of the *New York Times,* has observed that *Times* reporters see devout Catholics and Orthodox Jews (among others) as "strange objects to be examined on a laboratory slide."[2]

Religious complexity compounds the effects of reportorial secularism: American religion is extremely diverse, making sweeping generalizations problematic. The great variety of faith traditions, the internal divisions within each, and other nuances of religion itself make good reporting difficult. Thus, reporters are often at a loss even to identify their target. Some focus on historic religious traditions: "Protestants, "Catholics," "Jews," or, more recently, "Muslims." The more sophisticated may even distinguish Protestants as "evangelical" or "mainline," but this is still surprisingly rare. For most, "evangelical" is often simply a synonym for "fundamentalist," meaning "an abnormally religious Protestant"—although *Time* did include two Catholics among its "Twenty-Five Most Influential Evangelicals"![3]

Other reporters favor ideological categories, such as "religious conservatives" and "religious liberals," usually without informing the reader whether the "conservatism" and "liberalism" are religious or political, or explaining what makes believers one or the other. And, as Louis Bolce and Gerald De Maio have pointed out, until recently the media have ignored "the secularist factor in American politics," despite the critical political role played by such voters and activists, especially in the Democratic Party.[4] The storyline of "religious conservatives" versus "religious liberals" has some merit, especially if the labels are defined theologically and "seculars" are included, but more often these rubrics substitute for rigorous analysis.

Although stories focused on specific religious traditions or on generic ideological alliances were not impossible to find in 2004, most reporters seized upon "religiosity" as the dominant motif, often cast as "the God gap" or "the religion gap." On this accounting the basic religious split was between the "religious" from all traditions and the "less religious" or even "secular," with religiosity translating to "frequency of religious observance." A host of stories reported on churchgoers' preferring the Republicans, while the less faithful gravitated toward the Democrats.

Altogether, then, the media had three competing frameworks for understanding the political role of religion, and journalists slid between a focus on historic traditions, ideological alliances, or simple religiosity with little effort—or thought. Such confusion was reinforced by the failure of most polling organizations to ask thoughtfully worded questions on religion when assessing political behavior. For example, the exit polls sponsored by the major news networks were still addicted to notoriously crude categories of religious tradition, such as "Protestant," "Catholic," "Jewish," "Other Christian," and "Something Else," sometimes supplemented by questions on church attendance or "born-again" status.

The Pew Research Center for the People and the Press, another widely used source, does somewhat better, dividing "Protestants" into "evangelical" and "mainline" traditions, although on the basis of "born-again" status rather than denominational affiliation. The center sometimes inquires about church attendance but rarely asks theological questions to identify, say, "religious conservatives" or "religious liberals." Even where more sophisticated religious measures are available, reporters cannot usually make good use of such information on short deadlines.

Thus, reporting on religion in electoral campaigns suffers from several persistent problems: the unfamiliarity of reporters with the religious landscape, the complexity of American religion itself, and the absence of good sources of up-to-date information on religious voters. Despite these limitations, the media devoted a great deal of coverage to three aspects of the 2004 campaign: the religion of the candidates themselves, the nature of religious mobilization during the campaign, and the factors influencing religious voters. What main themes emerged from all this coverage, and how well, on balance, did the media do in its coverage?

The Candidates: Irrational Faith versus Intellectual Reason

From the very start of the campaign, there were obvious religious contrasts between George W. Bush and John Kerry. Bush was an evangelical Methodist comfortable discussing faith and using religious language. Kerry was Catholic by upbringing, inclined to keep his religious beliefs private, and often inarticulate on how his faith influenced his public duties. How did journalists handle these distinctions?

We found that the media often went far beyond reporting to offer rank speculation about religion's influence on each man. Journalists and pundits made it clear that Bush's religion was troubling and its impact on his policies dangerous, whereas Kerry's willingness to separate his faith from his policy was regarded as a triumph of rationality. The public, however, did not agree, as the media underestimated the importance of the candidates' faith to most voters.

Religious Rhetoric

As wordsmiths themselves, journalists were especially attentive to religious rhetoric. *New York Times* reporters Jodi Wilgoren and Bill Keller claimed that "Mr. Bush uses the language of faith, not only to mobilize conservative Catholics and evangelicals, but also to underscore his sense of purpose and to justify an unwavering certitude."[5] Articles routinely quoted lines from Bush's stump speech that signaled his conservative stances on abortion and gay marriage— "We stand for a culture of life. . . . We stand for marriage and family."[6] The *New York Times*'s David Sanger noted similarities between Bush's "talk about 'the transformational power of liberty' . . . [and] the power of religion to transform the soul."[7] Perhaps the president's most-quoted line involved the administration's pledge to spread democracy: "Freedom is not America's gift to the world, it is the Almighty God's gift to each man and woman in the world."[8] When Bush briefly omitted the statement from speeches late in the campaign, journalists immediately concluded that he was "toning down" his religious rhetoric.

In contrast, Kerry's religious rhetoric was usually ignored, largely because he used little of it outside African American churches until polls revealed that people wanted to hear more about his faith—and he was prodded by the *New York Times* to respond.[9] When he did use religious terms, the media noticed. In a *New York Times* article by David Halbfinger and David Sanger, Kerry quoted the Bible to criticize Bush's tactics and policies: "The Scripture teaches us—John says, 'let not your heart be troubled, neither let it be afraid.' . . . What these folks [Bush] want you to do is be afraid. Everything that they're trying to do is scare America."[10] The *Washington Post, Los Angeles Times,* and *Washington Times* all remarked upon Kerry's discovery of religious rhetoric and quoted him using biblical passages to explain the problems he would address as president. In addition, the media reported Kerry's claim that "faith affects everything I do."[11] Although reporters saw that Kerry's new use of religious rhetoric was designed to reassure voters, very few suggested it was insincere or a cynical ploy to win votes, and none that we encountered viewed his new language with suspicion or concern—in stark contrast with their coverage of Bush.

Faith and Policy

A continuing theme of the media, especially on editorial pages, was that Bush's decisions were dominated by his faith, whereas Kerry was driven by intellect and reason. At the end of the Republican Convention, the *New York Times* quoted conservative commentator Bruce Bartlett: "The key to understanding George W. Bush is to understand that he is a deeply religious man in a fundamentalist sense. . . . He truly believes there is good and evil in the world and that his job is to be on the side of good."[12]

If articles and op-eds often saw a link between Bush's faith and his policies, most writers were at least uncomfortable with, and more often hostile to, that connection. During the summer, journalists widely reported separate comments by Ron Reagan Jr. and Bill Clinton that raised questions about the propriety of a politician's faith influencing his policy decisions. These reports often seemed to be rebukes to Bush. Sheryl Gay Stolberg, for example, reported in a June 15 *New York Times* campaign story that at former president Ronald Reagan's funeral, "Ron Reagan [his son] delivered a eulogy that castigated politicians who use religion 'to gain political advantage,' a comment that was being interpreted in Washington as a not-so-subtle slap at Mr. Bush."[13]

These concerns became louder and more direct during the fall campaign. In a widely quoted column, historian Arthur Schlesinger Jr. lamented the advent of "the first faith-based presidency in U.S. history," asserting that Bush was "unique among presidents in his extensive application of religious tests to secular issues" such as stem cell research. Schlesinger also cited Bob Woodward's *Plan of Attack* to prove that Bush saw the Iraq War as part of "God's master plan."[14] *New York Times* columnist Maureen Dowd echoed this theme, claiming that the president's foreign policy issued from his questionable beliefs: "W.'s willful blindness comes from mistakenly assuming that his desires are God's, as if he knows where God stands on everything from democracy in Iraq to capital gains tax cuts."[15]

Few voices challenged such views. A *New York Times* op-ed by Grove City College political scientist Paul Kengor was a rare exception, arguing that Bush's faith did affect his foreign policy, but not in the sense "that the Almighty told him to send in the marines." For Kengor, the president's policy reflected his belief that "God has implanted a desire for freedom in all human hearts," reiterating the Founders' belief that liberty was an unalienable right given by the

Creator.[16] A perceptive *New York Times* article by Laurie Goodstein went even further in dismissing simplistic interpretations. She noted that Bush was not "doctrinally dogmatic" and might even be a little "out of sync with the conservative evangelical Christians who make up his political base," citing his claim that Christians and Muslims worship the same God and his frequent attendance at a liberal Episcopal church.[17] But such nuanced understanding of the president's faith was rare in the elite press.

Kerry's own faith was covered from two angles—his dissent from the Catholic Church's stance on abortion and, in the waning days of the campaign, his attempts to explain the role of faith in his life. The first angle dominated coverage: From the time the senator became the frontrunner for the Democratic nomination, articles proliferated on his differences with the Catholic hierarchy. Journalists reported at length on the announcement of several bishops that they would deny the Eucharist to pro-choice Catholic politicians. Indeed, reporters attached to the Kerry campaign began a weekend "wafer watch" to see if Kerry challenged the policy by attending Mass in parishes in the dioceses where bishops had issued such warnings. (He did not.)

Reporters noted frequently that Kerry was "personally opposed" to abortion despite his pro-choice voting record. But a *Washington Post* article on June 3, 2004, quoted a Kerry spokesperson explaining that "John Kerry's personal feelings about church doctrine are a private matter. He's made it clear that he's committed to upholding a woman's right to privacy."[18] The *Washington Times* reported Kerry's response to queries about his Catholic faith, "My task, as I see it . . . is not to write every doctrine into law. . . . But my faith does give me values to live by and apply to the decisions I make."[19] Most reports were neutral or even sympathetic to Kerry in his quarrel with the Church and supportive of his willingness to separate his personal beliefs from policy decisions. For example, a *New York Times* article by Pam Belluck reported that even the Vatican had rejected the idea that Kerry's abortion stance was heresy or warranted excommunication.[20] And in most of this coverage, Kerry's differences with his church were secondary to questions of whether the bishops had overstepped their bounds.

Occasionally, though, a more negative note sounded. The Associated Press reported on an "open letter" newspaper ad in battleground states that took Kerry to task, saying his pro-choice "stand contradicts both [his] faith and reason."[21] And a *New York Times* op-ed by Denver archbishop Charles J. Chaput claimed that "religious believers [who] do not advance their convictions about public morality in public debate . . . are demonstrating not tolerance but cowardice." But even this article by a leading critic of pro-choice Catholic politicians failed to mention Kerry by name.[22]

Aside from Kerry's conflict with the Catholic Church (or at least some militant pro-life bishops), most coverage of his beliefs followed his own belated and sometimes tortured attempts to clarify the role of religion in his personal and public life. *New York Times*'s Jodi Wilgoren and Bill Keller quoted Kerry, "I was an altar boy, you know. . . . I got through a war. I wore a rosary every day of battle. I know what faith is. I've tested it and struggled with it like anybody who has faith and worked through it."[23] Many articles explained that Kerry's religion led him to a social justice perspective that would guide his policies in office, especially on poverty and health care. Most were implicitly supportive; indeed, we discovered no stories about Kerry that worried about the candidate's faith influencing policies in the way that coverage of Bush often did.

Faith versus Reason

Stories also persistently pitted Bush's blind faith against Kerry's intellectual rationality with a clear assumption that religion and reason do not coexist. As a *New York Times* headline on October 24 proclaimed, "Ardent Faith Squares Off Against Earnest Reflection." In the story itself, Roger Cohen contrasted Bush's "faith in faith" and unwillingness to question his decisions with Kerry's promise "to put 'common sense' back in the White House." Cohen quoted a Kerry supporter who wanted a president "who reads and reflects . . . not someone who just goes with his gut and then prays to God he's right."[24]

As the campaign wore on, articles with this theme seemed to multiply. In a *New York Times* op-ed on October 28, Robert Wright ruminated about Bush's choice of Scottish theologian Oswald Chambers for his daily devotional readings. Wright described Chambers as "abandoning rational analysis and critical re-evaluation for ineffable intuition and iron certainty" and wondered "whether Chambers' worldview, as mediated by Mr. Bush, should help shape the world's future."[25] In the same vein, *Newsweek*'s Eleanor Clift criticized Bush for converting his religious beliefs into policy, while praising Kerry for "put[ting] his faith in rational decision-making."[26] And on October 7 the *New York Times* contrasted Bush's and Kerry's approaches to stem cell research: Bush had consulted clergy and "prayed over" the issue, while Kerry "framed it as a matter of clinical science" and "portray[ed] himself as the champion of human reason and scientific progress."[27]

Although articles frequently compared Bush's "faith-based" approach unfavorably with Kerry's rational one, others ignored Kerry altogether, simply blaming Bush's faith for his propensity not to question his own decisions and to discourage challenges from others. Maureen Dowd wrote in the *New York Times*, "The president's certitude—the idea that he can see into people's souls and that

God tells him what is right . . .—is disturbing. It equates disagreeing with him to disagreeing with Him."[28] Dowd pressed on: "People who live by religious certainties don't have to waste time with recalcitrant facts or moral doubts."[29] And in a *New York Times Magazine* article entitled "Without a Doubt," Ron Suskind quoted approvingly Bruce Bartlett's assessment that "absolute faith like that [of Bush] overwhelms a need for analysis. The whole thing about faith is to believe things for which there is no empirical evidence. . . . But you can't run the world on faith."[30]

Coverage repeatedly questioned the desirability, propriety, and even constitutionality of Bush's faith influencing his decisions. In some cases, editorial writers expressed concern, but news articles also repeatedly cited sources critical of the public expression and presumed influence of the president's religious beliefs, often without offering competing opinions. For example, a *New York Times* article reported Kerry's charge that "Bush had politicized faith to an unacceptable degree, used religion to divide and breached the boundary between church and state by promoting government aid to 'faith based' organizations."[31] We found no editorial or news article, however, that questioned Kerry's religious rhetoric or his claim that his own faith would influence his decisions, or that the social gospel would guide policy. Rather, Kerry was praised for the other occasions when he insisted that his religion was quite separate from his policy.

The media clearly valued intellect and reason over faith and implied that the two were incompatible. Election results, however, suggested that journalists may have misjudged the importance of the candidates' religion to voters. *New York Times* columnist David Brooks recognized this early on, chiding his colleagues in a June 22 column: "Many people just want to know that their leader, like them, is in the fellowship of believers. Their president . . . does have to be engaged, as they are, in a personal voyage toward God." Brooks noted that less than 10 percent of the public saw Kerry as a man of strong faith, and he cautioned that "unless more people get a sense of Kerry's faith, they will feel no bond with him and they will be loath to trust him with their vote."[32] Most of the mainstream press ignored the evidence Brooks cited until later in the campaign when they reported that polls had prompted Kerry's increased reliance on religious talk and rhetorical use of Scripture.

Indeed, whatever the elite media thought, most voters were not put off by religious language and appeals. On August 24 the Pew Research Center for the People and the Press reported that 72 percent of the public wanted a president with "strong religious beliefs." Only 24 percent thought Bush talked about religion too much, and a mere 10 percent said the same about Kerry. And only 15 percent thought the president relied too much on faith in making decisions, despite repeated warnings from the media.[33] The 2004 Survey on Religion and Politics, conducted by the University of Akron and cosponsored by the Pew Forum on Religion and Public Life, produced almost identical results on similar questions asked during the campaign. After the election, the same poll found only 29 percent of respondents saying that there had been too much discussion of religion in the campaign, while a slightly smaller number (20 percent) thought, to the contrary, that there had been too little.[34] The voters were not nearly as discomfited by religious language as most reporters and editorial writers were.

Moving the Churches

A second major focus in 2004 was on religious mobilization. As an October 13 Associated Press report put it succinctly, "Religious involvement has intensified this year."[35] And the media correctly recognized that activating religious voters might be critical to the outcome. But journalists did not view Republican and Democratic tactics through the same lens: The Bush campaign in evangelical churches was portrayed as unusual and certainly questionable, whereas Kerry's outreach through black churches was seen as routine, usually mentioned only in passing as part of a larger story. Attempts by both parties to mobilize other religious groups were usually missed altogether.

Coverage of the GOP's wooing of religious voters began early in the general election campaign and immediately fell into a common theme: Would political involvement jeopardize churches' tax-exempt status? As a June 3 *Washington Post* headline read, "Bush Push May Cost Churches Tax Breaks." The *Post* reported on an e-mail sent by the Bush campaign to Pennsylvania churches, recruiting supporters to coordinate the distribution of information and voter-registration materials to congregations.[36] Although campaign officials quickly clarified that the missive was aimed at individuals, not churches, critics saw it as an unacceptable politicization of religious institutions. A month later the *Washington Post* described the campaign's attempts to obtain church directories and volunteers to distribute issue guides.[37] Kerry supporters immediately attacked the GOP for encouraging partisan activity in churches. The *New York Times* chimed in on July 2: "Bush Appeal to Churches for Help Raises Doubts."[38]

In the fall, coverage expanded to include Bush's wooing of religious groups usually allied with the Democrats. The *New York Times* discovered that Republicans had staged national convention events especially for Catholics and Jews.[39] Late in October the *Times* saw Bush's rallies with Catholic audiences and a meeting with the archbishop of Philadelphia as further evidence of a campaign to mobilize Catholics, warning that such appeals would create hostility between secular and religious voters.[40] Journalists also covered Bush's outreach to African American Christians through his talks with black pastors, often quoting critics who doubted the GOP's commitment to civil rights or saw the mobilization as "an effort to neutralize the black church."[41] Although few picked up on the obvious implication that the black church had not previously been "neutral," pundits attacked Bush's "use of churches for political purposes," calling it "alarming."[42]

Only very careful readers would notice that Kerry was also pursuing religious voters: Most references to his frequent church appearances were embedded in stories on other issues, such as African American turnout or social security. For example, a long New York Times piece about the determination of African Americans to make their ballots count in 2004 mentioned that Kerry had attended two black churches, along with Rev. Al Sharpton and Rev. Jesse Jackson, to encourage black voters.[43]

Another New York Times article on social security reported that Kerry, speaking in a black church, had criticized Bush's plan. That article also had a picture of vice-presidential candidate John Edwards "campaigning in Daytona Beach, Fla."[44] If not for the cross on the pulpit in front of Edwards, the reader would not have known that the "campaigning" was in a church. Under a headline on the "search for black votes," Times reporters Jim Dwyer and Jodi Wilgoren reported a week later that Al Gore had "sprinted across six pulpits," criticizing Bush and encouraging black turnout. The same article noted that it was the fourth straight Sunday that Kerry had attended a black church, and quoted a pastor comparing Kerry to "Moses leading the children of Israel to the Promised Land."[45]

Seldom was the Democrats' religious "campaign" the main focus of such stories. Bill Clinton was covered visiting a Jewish temple in Florida, reassuring worshippers that Kerry would support Israel.[46] And the Washington Times ran an Associated Press article reporting that the Bush campaign had criticized the Democratic National Committee's Web site for encouraging people to distribute a DNC chart comparing Kerry and Bush on values in churches, a tactic for which the Democrats had lambasted Bush and his religious allies.[47]

Remarkably, there was little criticism of the Democratic campaign in churches, even when the events were blatantly partisan. Any questions raised were in general articles voicing concern about intermingling churches and politics. Many mainstream newspapers carried at least one story—usually from the perspective of pastors—on the delicate balance clergy had to strike between legitimate voter education and the political endorsements that would prompt IRS investigations.[48] A rare explicit criticism of Kerry's use of churches appeared in a *New York Times* report by David Kirkpatrick that Americans United for Separation of Church and State would file an IRS complaint against a black church where Kerry spoke because the program included "all Democratic speakers, and a pastor got up and endorsed Kerry from the pulpit."[49]

Most reporters seemed to think that what Republicans were doing in evangelical churches was somehow different from what Democrats were doing in black churches. A Kerry spokesman made this point explicitly: "Speaking to a church is well within the limits of the tax code and it is quite different from the way the Bush campaign has aggressively pushed to use churches to distribute their campaign material and treated them as an arm of its reelection effort."[50] There were indeed differences between the activities of churches and pastors on behalf of Bush and those on behalf of Kerry, though it is not clear that the IRS would find all the objectionable practices on the Republican side. What is evident is that reporters did not address the contrasts (or, for that matter, the similarities) in political activities between white evangelical and black churches—even when covering activities in both.

A *Washington Post* story by Paul Farhi and Vanessa Williams vividly illustrates this point. In describing the Republican mobilization, the authors concluded that one evangelical pastor's sermon led to the *"unstated* conclusion" (emphasis added) that Democrats were on the wrong side of Christian issues. In addition, they mentioned that "volunteers handed out [Christian Coalition] voter guides . . . [that did] not endorse a candidate" but did compare their records in a way that favored Bush. The same *Post* reporters also covered Democratic church visits, watching as Senator Ted Kennedy *"campaigned* for Kerry" (emphasis added) in black churches, as did the candidates themselves. In contrast to the "unstated" preferences of the evangelical pastor, the message in black churches was explicit: Not only did Kennedy praise Kerry, but the pastors explicitly endorsed him, and in one church "ushers passed out Kerry-Edwards fans."[51] Even after watching such events, few journalists puzzled about the failure of Bush or Cheney to campaign in churches on Sunday morning.

The role of churches was certainly an important story in the 2004 campaign. But the media left this debate unbalanced, focusing on "questionable" activities in white evangelical churches and raising substantially fewer questions about the open and institutionally partisan messages in black churches. Despite the evidence in their own stories, journalists either did not notice or did not care to comment on the relative political involvement of white conservative and African American pastors and churches.

Perhaps this neglect was due to the novelty of open political activity of evangelical churches compared to the historically high activism of many African American pastors and congregations. Of course, that would suggest yet another story that the media missed: What caused the conservative churches to "catch up" with African American churches in 2004? Rather than seeing that evangelical churches were doing what black churches have done for decades, the coverage portrayed their activity as unusual and suspicious. Since much of the academic evidence available shows that electoral activities in black churches—usually on behalf of Democrats—are more extensive than those in evangelical congregations, this is a serious failure.

To illustrate this point, we can compare the church-based political activities reported by white evangelical and African American Protestants in the 2004 Survey on Religion and Politics, cited earlier. On most political activity, the balance favored black Protestant over evangelical churches: Political information was more often available in church (24% vs. 13%), and pastors more often sought to mobilize their congregations to vote (60% vs. 53%), although the rate of reported candidate endorsements was identical but low (8%). Similarly, most campaign issues received more attention from the pulpit in black churches, such as the war in Iraq (37% vs. 34%), hunger and poverty (40% vs. 28%), education (43% vs. 24%), and environmental policies (22% vs. 11%). Only on same-sex marriage and abortion did evangelical pastors "outpreach" their black counterparts (38% vs. 27% and 36% vs. 21%, respectively).[52] Determining whether the media missed this part of the story because of a bias against evangelicals or a longstanding neglect of African Americans is beyond the scope of our analysis. Whatever the reason, the coverage missed important aspects of the mobilization of evangelical and black churches.

The media also largely omitted the way the campaign played out in other religious traditions. Discussion of the political activities of mainline Protestant churches and their leaders was almost totally absent, and the competing campaigns to mobilize Catholic traditionalists and liberals by religious and political leaders—a very interesting story indeed—were covered in depth only by the Catholic press. In addition, Bush's successful outreach to Hispanic Protestant clergy and congregations was missed almost entirely.

That electoral politics is not confined to evangelical and black churches is evident from poll data. The National Survey of Religion and Politics found that Catholics (especially Hispanic Catholics) were actually more likely to find voter guides at their parish churches than evangelicals were (14% for white Catholics, 31% for Hispanics) and that Catholic priests were more likely to endorse a candidate (usually Bush) than were clergy in any other tradition (14%). White Catholic pastors topped the list in preaching about abortion (38%), but came close to the top on hunger and poverty as well (38%). And although mainline Protestants were less likely to be in church in the weeks before the election, the data show that there was a good deal of "politicking" in liberal white churches as well. All this suggests that reporters need to move beyond thinking that campaigning in religious venues occurs only as a new and scary development in evangelical churches or as an ancient and understandable routine in black congregations.

What Makes Religious Voters Tick?

In addition to reporting on the candidates' faith and their attempts to mobilize religious voters, the national media devoted some coverage to religious voters and the moral or cultural issues assumed to matter to them. But we discovered that coverage was often oversimplified and prone to stereotyping. As a result, reporters missed some important voting trends and misunderstood how issues affected religious voters.

As we noted earlier, some campaign coverage focused on voters defined by religious tradition. Many articles focused on which candidate each tradition was likely to support and whether or not this was a departure from the group's past behavior—"Arab and Jewish Votes" (*New York Times*), "Muslims Seen Abandoning Bush" (*Washington Post*), "Bush Makes Significant Gains in Two Polls of Catholic Voters" (*Washington Times*), and "How the Evangelicals and Catholics Joined Forces" (*New York Times*).[53]

A handful of stories recognized the inadequacy of these broad categories based on religious traditions. Almost all of these were based on the pre-election National Survey of Religion and Politics, directed by University of Akron political scientist John Green. Both the *Economist* and the *New York Times* explained that religious traditions were often divided by members' attitudes toward historic doctrines, yielding factional divisions between traditionalists, centrists, and modernists. These articles pointed out that traditionalists in very different religious groups often have more in common politically with each other than they do with modernists in their own faith.[54] Jane Lampman argued insightfully that these distinctions showed where Kerry might find added religious support in the last days of his campaign.[55] Peter Beinert also recognized such religious complexity when he declared the "end of the 'Jewish vote,'" predicting that Orthodox Jews would likely behave like traditionalist Christians and vote for Bush.[56]

New York Times religion writer Peter Steinfels conceded that some journalists would object that the divisions produced by Green's study were too complex to manage, but he mocked such claims, pointing out that there are "30 professional baseball teams in two leagues and six divisions" and "millions of semiliterate 13-year-olds who manage to keep all that straight."[57] Nevertheless, despite a brief flurry of stories on the Akron study, most campaign reporting remained focused on one of the simpler, if inadequate, religious classifications, usually "religiosity."

Beyond the question of which candidate these blocs of religious voters would support, coverage also focused on the issues concerning them. Some of this coverage was stereotypical, tying religious support for the Republicans, especially from evangelicals and Catholics, to "family values" and "culture war" questions such as abortion, same-sex marriage, and stem cell research. For example, *New York Times* articles about two battleground states—Missouri and West Virginia—attributed Kerry's declining support there to the worries of evangelical Christians over Kerry's positions on abortion, same-sex marriage, and gun control.[58] Cultural issues also played prominently in articles about the mobilization of religious voters. The *Washington Post* reported that evangelical leaders were using a rally against same-sex marriage to encourage turnout, while the Southern Baptist Convention had set up an Internet voter guide on "iVoteValues.com."[59] Many other articles speculated that gay-marriage initiatives in eleven states could boost turnout among conservative religious groups.[60] These articles often painted religious voters as one dimensional in their interests.

In contrast, some reporters and editorial writers intimated that religious voters might have a broader agenda than "moral" issues and that their interest in the economy or the Iraq war might reveal conflicting values. This was particularly true in coverage of Catholics, who were attracted to Bush's stances on abortion, gay marriage, and stem cell research but would find more in common with the Democrats on Iraq, health care, the environment, welfare policy, and taxes—at least according to op-ed writer Mark Roche.[61] Such stories emphasized that Catholics were "wrestling" with the moral questions of whether Iraq was a "just war" and how to achieve social justice in domestic policies.[62]

Reporters also occasionally looked at the cross-pressures faced by evangelicals, but less often in the form of conflicting policy values than in terms of the supposed tension between religious faith and economic class. A *New York Times* review of a CNN documentary on evangelicals argued that the program missed the real story when it failed to explore the statement that evangelicals who agreed with Bush on cultural issues were "more inclined to agree with Mr. Kerry on questions of economic policy and international relations."[63]

A few other articles echoed this claim—some even citing polling data[64]—but such articles generally lacked much empirical warrant. One reporter did cite contradictory data provided by GOP strategists, who claimed that evangelicals were not voting against their economic preferences to support Bush but rather believed that tax cuts and deregulation policies would benefit the middle class.[65] Although the available evidence from the National Survey on Religion and Politics tended to support this latter argument, there was little discussion along those lines.

For those who saw religious groups cross-pressured by moral and secular issues, there was little agreement on which issues or values would prevail in the voting booth. One op-ed claimed that "neither region nor religion can override class divide" and that "most poorer Americans of every faith—including evangelical Christians—vote for Democrats," but provided no evidence.[66] Meanwhile, other articles asserted that "cultural issues will trump economic issues."[67] Still others maintained that evangelicals would decide that "other issues are secondary to what they see as 'life' issues" whereas African American Christians would rely on their sense of social justice and the obligation of "lifting up the poor and protecting the outcasts."[68]

With a few exceptions, however, most stories did not consider that differing religious perspectives might produce distinctive views on policy matters far beyond the stereotypical "moral" issues. Perhaps economic policy, the war on terrorism, the Iraq War, the Middle East, the environment, and many other issues might be understood in a religious frame of reference, not as "secular" issues. Nor did they consider that a religious group's predominant stance on each of several issues might often point them in the same political direction. To cite one important example, the Akron survey showed that most evangelical Protestants were not only strongly conservative on "cultural issues," such as abortion and same-sex marriage, but also took more conservative stances on tax cuts and government spending and were most supportive of the "Bush Doctrine" in foreign policy. This pattern was hardly new, but appeared during the 2000 and 2002 presidential and congressional elections.[69] Thus, some "cross-pressures" or conflicts blithely posited by journalists did not exist, or at least did not take the form suggested.

If voters were looking to news coverage for a clear explanation of the moral or cultural issues or a detailed comparison of the candidates' positions to help them decide which issues to consider in voting, they were usually disappointed. Three issues with obvious religious or moral elements received extensive attention—gay marriage, abortion, and stem cell research. However, most coverage evaluated how the candidates and others used (or abused) the issues to advance their campaigns with little focus on the issues themselves or the candidates' positions.

Of the three moral issues, gay marriage received the most attention. It was usually portrayed as a "wedge issue" designed to separate socially conservative Democrats, especially African Americans, from Kerry and to energize religious traditionalists. For example, articles in all the major newspapers reported that House Republicans brought the gay marriage amendment to a vote to force conservative Democrats to choose between their party and their constituents.[70] Journalists also devoted much space to the gay marriage initiatives in eleven states and their likely impact on turnout.

Another prominent vehicle for media coverage of gay marriage was Kerry's reference to Dick Cheney's lesbian daughter during the final debate. In addition to the news coverage, op-eds, like "Play It Straight" by William Rubenstein,[71] questioned the wisdom of Kerry's strategy in invoking Mary Cheney's name. Most such articles barely mentioned Kerry's stance on gay marriage, though they often brought up Bush's position, if for no other reason than to highlight disagreement with his vice-president. Only a few articles included a substantive comparison of the candidates' positions on gay marriage.[72]

Abortion emerged as an issue in three different storylines. First, it was part of most articles discussing the GOP platform, with some attention to the party's moderates, who seemed resigned to include a pro-life plank. It was also highlighted in stories about Bush's references to a "culture of life," which many saw as code for his opposition to abortion and expanded stem cell research, appealing to religious traditionalists. Most often, of course, abortion came up in the context of Kerry's position as a pro-choice Catholic and the subsequent conflict with Catholic bishops who wanted to deny him communion over the issue.

Finally, stem cell research was covered more substantively than were the other two issues but was still portrayed primarily in terms of political strategy. Media attention was drawn to the issue by the death of actor Christopher Reeves, an activist for stem cell research, by Kerry's decision to emphasize the issue to appeal to moderate Republicans and independents in the final weeks of the campaign, and by a stem cell research initiative on the California ballot. Stories frequently mentioned Kerry's support for expanded government-funded research and his hope that this would win undecided voters.

Reporting on Bush's position was less clear. Most articles that mentioned his position accurately noted that Bush had permitted federal funding of research only on a limited number of stem cell lines, but others often left the impression that Bush had restricted all stem cell research, not just what was federally funded. For example, a *New York Times* article by Laurie Goodstein mentioned that in his attempt to appeal to pro-life voters, Bush "imposed limits on embryonic stem cell research."[73] Other articles included Kerry's claim that scientific research leading to new treatments was impossible or being delayed because of Bush's "stem cell ban," though many of these pointed out the inaccuracy of Kerry's claim. [74] At least one article reported Republican senators saying Bush might change his position in a second term, allowing additional stem cell research.[75] Few stories, mostly op-eds like one by Leon Kass in the *Washington Post,*[76] sought to explain Bush's moral or ethical concerns about additional federal funding. Depending on what they read, then, voters may have come away with conflicting views of Bush's position, but most could not help but notice that the issue was used by both candidates for strategic purposes.

After the election the media jumped on the emerging debate over the role of "moral" issues in the outcome. This controversy was fueled by exit poll results showing that 22 percent of the electorate cited moral values as the issue that mattered most in their vote decision and that 80 percent of those voters chose Bush. Although the economy and jobs mattered most for 20 percent, with terrorism (19%) and Iraq (15%) close behind, both Christian Right leaders and centrist Democrats latched on to the first category as the main explanation for Bush's victory. Although liberal commentators soon minimized the importance of faith and morals in the outcome, the impression that both played a part remained predominant.

Obviously, the role played by religion, by "moral" and other issues, and by factors such as social class will be analyzed in great depth by political scientists in coming years. However, a look at preliminary findings in the National Survey on Religion and Politics allows us to assess some approaches used by journalists during the campaign. Certainly, the pervasive theme of the "God gap" in partisan choices finds clear support: Those attending church more than once a week gave Bush 64 percent of the two-party vote (exit polls estimated 65%), while those never attending services favored Kerry with 76 percent of the vote.

The historic religious traditions also differed, with evangelical Protestants choosing Bush by a 78 to 22 percent margin, white Catholics splitting in the president's favor by 53 to 47 percent, and mainline Protestants dividing evenly. This marked the first time in history that a Democratic presidential candidate has mustered a break-even performance among what was once the primary GOP religious constituency. This result received little notice in the press. For that matter, neither did Bush's remarkable success among Hispanic Protestants, a group he carried with 63 percent, although their Catholic brethren went for Kerry by an even larger margin. In the same category of important tendencies ignored, Mormons voted almost unanimously for Bush, and members of non-Christian religions gave three quarters of their ballots to Kerry. Thus, there were clearly massive political divisions by religious tradition, and by religious observance.

Nevertheless, even the focus on religious traditions or observance does not capture the most significant electoral developments. Within the large Christian traditions, the voter's theological position was just as important as membership in the tradition. Those who were most theologically orthodox in each tradition were also most Republican. Thus, "traditionalists" gave Bush more voters than "modernists" among evangelicals (88% vs. 48%), Catholics (72% vs. 31%), and mainline Protestants (68% vs. 22%). Similar, if weaker, theological divisions appeared among Jews, Hispanic Protestants, and Catholics, and even among black Protestants.[77] Thus, neither observance nor religious tradition alone is an adequate basis for analysis. Clearly, Peter Steinfels was right: journalists must grapple with religious complexity if they hope to understand the nexus between faith and electoral politics.

Similarly, the role of issues was much more complex than usually portrayed during the campaign or in the later struggle for control of the "meaning" of the election. Moral issues, Iraq, terrorism, and the economy all mattered to most voters, but in ways that clearly varied by religious group: Evangelicals (especially the traditionalists) saw moral issues as most important to their vote, Catholics and mainline Protestants (especially centrists and modernists) viewed foreign policy as most vital, and secular voters were moved most by the economy. And, in a clear refutation of some media predictions, social class made remarkably little difference among white voters: Religious characteristics were much better predictors of the vote.

Conclusion

During the 2004 election, journalists rightly sensed that religion would play an important part in determining the outcome. They were less clear on how to understand the relevant facets of religion or how those might affect the results. The extensive coverage focused on relatively few topics: the candidates' faith and policy implications, the activities of religious conservatives, and the impact of a few "moral issues." In each instance, coverage suffered from some clear defects: The religious traits of Bush and Kerry (and their campaign activities) were not subjected to the same standards for analysis and criticism; the coverage of religious groups was spotty, with a disproportionate focus on evangelicals and the Catholic hierarchy; and the emphasis on "religious" issues was narrowly confined to the "moral" issues. In each instance, as we have shown, these tendencies produced misleading analyses and resulted in the neglect of topics vital to understanding the role of religious faith.

What can be done to improve coverage? It is perhaps encouraging that some major papers, such as the *New York Times*, have since recognized the inadequacies in their coverage of religion, and are promising to do better.[78] One could hope that political journalists might become more knowledgeable about American religion; unfortunately, recruitment and assignment patterns make it unlikely that most reporters will come from personal or educational backgrounds that foster such familiarity. Indeed, some of the best work on religion in the campaign was done by religion editors, such as Peter Steinfels of the *New York Times,* or reporters with the *Christian Science Monitor,* with its historic interest in religion. Other good coverage came from groups such as alumni of the Ethics and Public Policy Center's educational seminars for journalists, ventures that should be encouraged. In the meantime, academic and other specialists on religion and politics can make a contribution by continuing their own conversations with journalists.

6

The Popes

Amy Welborn

Countless events have been described as "made for television," but the drama that unfolded in Vatican City during late March and April 2005 overshadowed most other claimants. Although the world knew that Pope John Paul II was gravely ill, and major news outlets had been preparing for his eventual demise for years, the breadth of the coverage in electronic and print media was nevertheless impressive. Each hospitalization was covered in real time, the cable news networks often featuring split screens, with the quiet front of Gemelli Hospital in Rome juxtaposed with the news of the day.

Once John Paul actually passed away, coverage kicked into even higher gear. Between the pope's death on April 2, and April 8, the date of his funeral, pilgrims massed in Rome and stood in line for hours, even days, to file past the pope's body lying in state. Heads of state and representatives of many of the world's religions attended the funeral. Things then quieted down a little for a week, since only so much speculation on a new pope is possible, given the secrecy of the process. But when the cardinals finally gathered on April 17, interest heightened once again, assisted by a media novelty: never before had cameras been present at the opening ceremonies of the conclave, following the cardinals as they prayed, listened to the homily by Cardinal Ratzinger, the dean of the college of cardinals, and then processed into the Sistine Chapel, the doors swinging shut behind them.

For the next two days, the news networks again used the split screen, this time honing in on a single pipe jutting out from a roof in

Vatican City, the smallest country in the world. "Chimney cam," it was called. The curious could also pull it up on their Web browsers via a number of news Web sites. At about 5:50 p.m. Rome time on April 19 (late morning in the United States), smoke rose from the chimney for the fourth time. Observers were uncertain of the color. White? Gray? Black? Ten minutes after the smoke began, the innovation introduced by Pope John Paul II to overcome any such ambiguity—bells—began to ring out, and crowds poured into St. Peter's Square from all over Rome.

"Habemus Papam!" declared Cardinal Jorge Arturo Medina Estevez, and a few minutes later, to the roar of the crowds and the surprise of many commentators, out stepped Joseph Cardinal Ratzinger—Benedict XVI. He was installed the following Sunday, April 24. After this the visuals may have lost their intensity, but interest in the new pope did not, as the media sought to answer the big questions: Who is Benedict XVI and what will his papacy mean to the Roman Catholic Church?

During that April the coverage and discussion of Catholicism in the electronic and print media couldn't be faulted for breadth. So much time and space was devoted to this coverage that it sometimes seemed like All Catholic, All the Time. But what of depth? In the thousands of hours and column inches devoted to this story, how could it even be possible to miss any point of interest, any angle, any dimension? Were there any areas in which the press could have done a better job?

The television coverage, in general, provided more depth and more diverse viewpoints than did print. Perhaps it was because of the hours of coverage they had to fill, but the broadcast and cable networks worked hard to present the story, not just in visuals, but in explaining what the visuals were about. They brought out a wide range of experts, many of whom did an excellent job at objectively and patiently putting the rituals and beliefs of Catholicism in context: George Weigel at NBC and its cable news division, John Allen and Delia Gallagher at CNN, and Fr. Thomas Reese, S.J., almost everywhere (unlike some experts, Reese did not sign an exclusive contract with any one network) were notable among many. Nonetheless, in retrospect, some elements of this very big story were missed by both the electronic and the print media.

The Catholic Church is complex. It is a two-thousand-year old global institution. The utterances of its leaders—especially those of profound intellect such as John Paul II and Benedict XVI—emerge from a densely woven theological, philosophical, spiritual, and even legal matrix, the fruit of millennia of intellectual development. The practices and expressions of Catholicism, while shaped by contemporary sensibilities, originate in moments or events that may have occurred hundreds of years ago. When popes speak and act, they are doing so in a way that is sensitive to the deep reaches of the past and to the diversity of a global church.

Examining the coverage of the death of John Paul II, the election of Benedict XVI, and the first two years of Benedict's papacy reveals that secular media coverage of these events is hampered primarily by two factors: reporters' lack of knowledge of and long-term immersion in the subject, and the reliance on a template for reporting that almost reflexively sets the events covered or words spoken in contemporary political categories. Three areas in particular reveal these weaknesses, areas in which gaps in knowledge and the application of a contemporary political template led to thin coverage. Examining these gaps might assist journalists covering similar stories in the future. The three main areas in which such gaps appeared were:

1. What was John Paul II's impact on Catholicism?
2. What is the relationship among papal authority, Church teaching, and Church administration?
3. Who is Benedict XVI?

The Effect of John Paul II on the Roman Catholic Church

The media story began, of course, well before April 2, and had been in preparation for a long time. After all, this was the third-longest papal reign in history. The major U.S. dailies and weekly news magazines ran lengthy evaluations, some by staff journalists (e.g., Hanna Rosin for the *Washington Post*) and less frequently, by veteran religion journalists (e.g., Kenneth Woodward for *Newsweek*), in addition to many op-eds—the *New York Times* ran such pieces by death penalty activist Sister Helen Prejean, Eastern Orthodox historian Jaroslav Pelikan, and popular historian Thomas Cahill.[1] These articles, excluding the op-eds, which are not our subject, usually settled on a few themes: John Paul II as a great communicator, his travels, his emphasis on evangelism, his role in the defeat of Eastern European Communism, his emphasis on human dignity, and his purported authoritarian style.

The *Los Angeles Times* reporter Richard Boudreaux's April 3 division of the pope's life into three categories was typical: The Evangelical Papacy; The Christian Humanist; The Authority Figure.[2] Most legacy pieces followed similar themes, noting that John Paul II used his bully pulpit to vigorously spread a strong message about human dignity and Catholic Church doctrine. Boudreaux brought it together in the *Los Angeles Times*:

> He also set out to convert the world to a radical brand of Christian humanism. He insisted on a single standard—the dignity of each human—as the moral foundation for any free society. That message

transcended ideological labels: He preached against communism
and unbridled capitalism, abortion and the death penalty, population
control and degradation of Earth's environment.[3]

Bob Keeler in *Newsday* gave voice to this focus in his April 3 piece: "Like few
other leaders, religious or secular, Pope John Paul II took the last quarter of the
20th century in his strong Polish hands and shook it, laboring to retain doctrinal discipline in his church and helping to plant the seeds of the movement that
liberated his native land from communism."[4] Journalists stressed a fundamental connection between the pope's central commitment to the dignity of human
life and all the issues and causes they cited, noting, as Boudreaux did, the way
in which this commitment confounds secular ideological expectations.

From the central theme of a vigorous pope dedicated to spreading the
Gospel—which they defined mostly in terms of human rights, rather than particular theological teachings of the Catholic Church—the secular media also
gave him credit for affirming, both in word and deed, the changing relationship between the Church and Judaism and for ecumenical efforts with other
non-Christian religions. John Paul's role as a peacemaker—particularly relevant in the context of the U.S. war in Iraq—and promoter of justice was also
highlighted. U2 singer Bono, who met with John Paul in 1999 over the issue
of global debt relief, made frequent appearances in articles and photographic
montages. The pope's personal witness to the value of suffering and human
dignity in his declining years was mentioned as well.

But what of the pope's impact on the Roman Catholic Church itself? While
the coverage of John Paul's involvement in global human rights issues was usually neutral or positive, coverage of his impact within the Church veered into
language in which judgment was implicit: "disciplinarian" was often used, as
was "authoritarian" and even "monarchical,"[5] and there were frequent allusions
to a supposed tightening of Vatican control over the Church on the ground,
often highlighting actions taken in relation to dissenting theologians and the
appointment of purportedly rigid, conforming bishops. Michael Paulson of the
Boston Globe wrote in his almost five-thousand-word profile: "Even as he tried
to reach across religious divides, John Paul displayed little interest in making
peace within his own house. His conservative positions alienated many gays,
women, and other Catholics who believed John Paul regarded lay people, particularly in highly educated nations, as children needing discipline rather than
adults deserving respect."[6]

Such a lengthy papacy will take decades to analyze, and as time moves on,
today's evaluations will undoubtedly shift and deepen. John Paul traveled more
than any other pope; he canonized more saints than the all the popes during

the previous five centuries combined, and appointed all but two of the voting cardinals in the college of cardinals, in addition to hundreds of bishops. He was a busy man and his impact will be felt within the Church he served for decades. For that reason, it is almost a hopeless cause for anyone—journalist, scholar, or mere observer—to definitively "assess" twenty-six years of a very active, intellectual papacy, especially in the days and weeks after the end of that reign. The fruit of intellectual efforts takes decades to ripen, if it indeed ever does. But on the occasion of the death of a towering, influential figure, it is impossible *not* to attempt such an assessment. There would be virtually nothing to cover otherwise.

The problem, though, was that in attempting to assess the pope's impact on the Church he led for twenty-six years, secular journalistic treatments tended to revolve around that single prominent theme: "conservative" John Paul acting to bring the Church into line with "his" thinking, at the expense of the freedom of more "liberal" parties in the Church. Aside from considering problems of fact, which we will address in a moment, it is useful to question the use of this template—or any predetermined template—in exploring a news story, for in returning to a particular paradigm again and again (a paradigm which, in time, we may even stop examining critically), we exclude, without even knowing it, other aspects of the story worth reporting. In fact, we risk missing not only parts of the story, but the greater story.

Is it really accurate to condense the intellectual achievements of a papacy into an "us" versus "them" scenario? Does it do justice to the complexity of the issues involved? Many legacy articles noted, for example, that Pope John Paul II wrote fourteen encyclicals, but hardly any discussed their content, subjects which encompassed John Paul's widely ranging concerns, from social justice to philosophy and theology, and which included the dignity of human work (*Laborens exercens*), the value of human life (*Evangelium vitae*), the relationship between faith and reason (*Fides et ratio*), and the nature of truth (*Veritatis splendor*). Like any pope, John Paul wrote more than encyclicals: fifteen apostolic exhortations, eleven apostolic constitutions, forty-two apostolic letters, *and* twenty-six years worth of weekly Wednesday general-audience talks and the same number of Sunday Angelus talks.

Of course, no journalist—even a religion specialist—has time to pore over such a body of work in the few hours between death and deadline, not even those who had begun preparing an obituary years before. Meanwhile, conflict and drama are inherently interesting to general readers, whereas theological works are not. The impact of the former is more immediately felt; the impact of encyclicals and apostolic exhortations is more diffuse. But reducing our analysis of the pope's impact on the Church to the paradigm of conservative/liberal conflict limits the stories we can tell about the impact of his papacy. When it came to John Paul II, one can find, amid the hundreds of thousands of words authored by the pope, at least two examples of intellectual achievement for which he was either directly or indirectly responsible, which had and continue to have a profound impact on the Church, but which found little space in journalistic assessments.

John Paul's "Theology of the Body," articulated in his Wednesday general-audience addresses from 1979 to 1984, presents a way of understanding human life and purpose through the symbolic value of the human body. The proper use of the body can be discerned by meditating on the signs that the Creator has built into human life and experience, particularly concerning the relationship between the sexes. It is a way of thinking about morality that is not rules-based, and is not rooted not in abstractions but in the phenomenon of human existence. The "Theology of the Body" has affected the Catholic conversation on sexuality in surprisingly demonstrable, even quantifiable ways, as it is the subject not only of best-selling books, well-attended workshops, and college courses, but also of university graduate programs. The "Theology of the Body" was a part of many Canadian and Australian legacy pieces but went largely unmentioned in major U.S. news outlets' post-mortem assessments of John Paul II's legacy.

The treatment of the 1992 release of the *Catechism of the Catholic Church* provides another window on to the limitations of the conflict paradigms, and, like "Theology of the Body," illustrates the differences between the U.S. media and those of Canada, Australia, and England. The *Catechism* is an authoritative compendium of Church teaching, written in part by John Paul's successor, then-Cardinal Joseph Ratzinger. In the years since the Second Vatican Council, Catholic individuals and institutions have struggled to communicate effectively to the outside world, and to those within, exactly what the Church teaches on matters of dogma, doctrine, and morals. Various bishops' conferences have issued catechisms, and Catholic publishers have released their own guides to Catholic teaching, but the *Catechism* was the first to come from Rome in this post–Vatican II era. It was received enthusiastically by some, reluctantly by others, but its mere existence provided an invaluable resource for Catholics and seekers, and it led to most Catholic textbooks and catechetical materials being rewritten to accord with its presentation.

Since its release, it has been the best-selling Catholic book in the United States every year. In the U.S. press, the *Catechism* has received little more than a mention in chronological lists of the pope's achievements, with no discussion of its significance. Perhaps this is because an outsider's assumption might be that, of course, the Catholic Church would have a catechism. However, when one is familiar with the fluid intellectual and spiritual dynamic of the post–Vatican II era and then realizes that this was the first catechism produced by Rome since the sixteenth-century Council of Trent and that it necessitated the rewriting of all religious education materials—perhaps there is a story there after all, and a legacy to be considered.

Journalists and media organizations, aware of the importance of documents and other products of intellectual inquiry in Catholicism, might round out their coverage of this aspect of Catholic life by developing and nurturing expert sources. These scholars could be called upon to provide background and understanding so that a broader context can be offered as important documents are released, or on such an occasion as the death of a cardinal or pope.

It might also be useful for journalists to explore whether this kind of conversation about papal encyclicals and other documents is really "inside baseball" anymore. With the wide availability of these documents on the Internet and in published form, educated lay Catholics have easy access to them. If the popularity of the Vatican Web site is any indication, these materials will be heavily accessed, reflecting a sustained interest. Pope Benedict's first encyclical, *Deus Caritas Est,* sold 1.5 million copies in Italy in its first year, becoming the best-selling papal encyclical ever. Benedict's book *Jesus of Nazareth,* published in the United States in May 2007, was also a global bestseller. It might be worth journalists' time to explore the accessibility of papal writings in the twenty-first century, their popularity, and what that popularity indicates. One could argue that this amounts to a bigger story, with broader import, than do conflicts between academic theologians.

Another slightly more concrete expression of John Paul's impact on the Church concerned the "John Paul generation" of priests, young men who had been inspired in their vocations by his witness, who were nearly all of a more traditional bent.[7] Some of this influence was recorded in features and stories appearing in the last half of John Paul's papacy, for example Fr. Andrew Greeley's article about such priests in the *Atlantic Monthly,* titled "Young Fogeys."[8]

But there was more to John Paul II's papacy and religious vocations than a slight shift in the makeup of seminarians. During those years, when new reports on the life of men and women in the religious orders tended to focus on declining numbers, some religious orders, inspired by John Paul's call to refocus on mission and to re-adopt more traditional modes of living and spirituality, actually flourished. The best-known example of a traditional order that blooms while others wilt is Mother Theresa's Missionaries of Charity. Its establishment predated John Paul's papacy, but Mother Theresa and her order received enormous attention during his reign. The Missionaries of Charity maintain institutions engaged in traditional charitable work with the sick and dying in 133 countries.

Likewise, the Dominican Sisters of St. Cecilia wear traditional, floor-length habits and are committed to the apostolate of teaching. In contrast to some orders, which are selling off their motherhouses to support their aging populations, these Dominicans are currently in the process of building a new, larger motherhouse in Nashville that will house their constant flow of young candidates. And Fr. Benedict Groeschel's Franciscan Friars of the Renewal serve the poorest of the poor, wear traditional brown habits, and grow the long beard characteristic of the Capuchin branch of the Franciscans. They, too, are experiencing tremendous growth. A conservative/liberal discord template results in an incomplete telling of the story. Certainly, some religious figures and priests were in conflict with John Paul, but others embraced his vision—and had great success.

John Paul II also approved and encouraged the growth of what are often called the "new movements" in the Church—groups, mostly of laity, but sometimes including both lay and religious members, centered on a particular charism or style of spirituality. These groups—Opus Dei, the Legionaries of Christ, Sant'Egidio, Communion and Liberation, the NeoCatechumenate, Focolare—all enjoyed great success under this pope. These new movements are quite diverse in both style and structure. The Legionaries of Christ and Opus Dei, while different from each other, are highly structured and committed to what might be called a traditional reading of Catholic theology and traditional spiritual expression. In contrast, the NeoCatechumenate Way, a movement begun in the 1960s, is an attempt to reinvigorate parish life by imitating the life and structure of early Christianity. It includes celebrations of the Mass that are relatively informal and involve dialogue homilies between priest and congregation. Communion and Liberation, described by one member as "the New Movement for non-joiners" began as an outgrowth of the ministry to youth by an Italian priest, Fr. Luigi Giussani, in the 1950s, and is dedicated to helping believers reach full maturity in Christ in whatever way or direction they feel God's spirit is calling them.

That each of these diverse groups was encouraged by John Paul II indicates that the word "conservative" is an inadequate descriptive term for him. In fact, he was very respectful and interested in the many ways God works through human life and experience, and he demonstrated that these various ways could find unity in Christ and His Church.

Numbers always tell a tale, and reporters couldn't avoid examining the numbers of pilgrims who arrived in Rome during the pope's decline and after his death. Crowds were expected in Rome, but no one anticipated that they would be so large and so young. Assessments of this popularity attempted to go below the surface in two primary ways. First, many stories focused on the apparent dissonance between these large crowds and the very real collapse of European Catholicism when measured in church attendance and adherence to Catholic moral teaching. For example, the *Los Angeles Times* ran an article by Larry Stammer entitled, "Legacy of John Paul II; Attendance Is a Concern for Church," which article went on to say, "Despite the millions of pilgrims gathered in Rome, attendance at weekly Mass in many places has declined and many have left the flock." The *Washington Post* focused on the declining influence of the Church in Spain, and the *Denver Post* on how ideological revolutions of the 1960s had damaged the Church in Italy.[9]

In the North American context, articles discussed the choices that American Catholics have made, contrasting them with the teachings of the Church. The *New York Times* ran an article on this subject on April 11, as did the *Baltimore Sun* on April 5.[10] Television commentary and discussion mentioned it frequently. A segment of ABC's *World News Tonight* on April 3 is representative, culminating in Fr. Richard McBrien's statement: "For the vast majority of Catholics and for the vast majority of other people, the pope was just an icon, a celebrity, a figure that they could applaud, and then they could go home and do what they wanted." This is an interesting and valid angle—although one fraught with peril because of the difficulty of discovering how a billion Catholics actually feel about their faith.

However, in suggesting John Paul II was less than fully accepted or loved, the secular media focused on dissidents on the "Left," naturally enough since this was the template many seemed to be working from. Except for the dissent on the Left, then, one would be tempted to believe that all was well between John Paul II and the American Church, and that the only Catholics dissatisfied with his pontificate were those advocating women's ordination or changing Church positions on abortion or homosexuality. The reality is quite different, amounting to an intriguing and dramatic story that the secular media almost completely missed.

There were significant conservative subcultures within American Catholicism that had serious problems with Pope John Paul's ecumenical outreach, especially to non-Christians. Two images of John Paul's pontificate disturbed these critics: the almost mythical moment, reported by an attendee—a Chaldean patriarch—at a papal audience with a Muslim group in 1999, when the pope reportedly kissed a copy of the Qur'an. The second, caught on tape, was John Paul's 1986 gathering of world religious leaders in Assisi for the cause of praying for peace, at which there were Buddhists, Hindus, and (notoriously) an African pagan priest in attendance. These images and stories gained almost mythical status within some quarters, giving rise to doubts among some traditionalists about John Paul's commitment to the singular truth of Catholicism.

Mainstream conservative Catholics had their issues with John Paul II as well, ranging from his permitting bishops to allow girls to act as altar servers, to questions involving his enthusiasm for various "new movements," some of which incorporate questionable liturgical practices (the NeoCatechumenate) or structures (the Legionaries of Christ). An examination of Catholic publications and the many Internet sites devoted to Catholic discussion demonstrates that some of John Paul's policies were widely questioned by those "conservatives," a group that a political template assumes to be his natural allies.

There were also disagreements involving governance. Was John Paul II an authoritarian or was he indifferent to matters of governance? This was a thorny question among Catholics during John Paul's papacy. The "authoritarian" evaluation appeared everywhere in the secular press, such as in the *New York Times* on April 3:

> Dissident Catholic theologians were dismissed or excommunicated. Liberal cardinals and bishops were replaced. And in 1998, the pope changed canon law to put many passionately discussed issues, including euthanasia and the ordination of women, beyond the realm of debate for the faithful. He also made it almost impossible for groups like the National Conference of Catholic Bishops of the United States to make statements of doctrine or public policy that diverged from the Vatican.[11]

Note the vagueness and lack of context in this passage. By failing to cite precisely how many theologians were disciplined and exactly what that meant in the context of Catholicism, by implying that discouraging discussion of the ordination of women was a new approach, and by neglecting to give any historical context regarding the traditional role of bishops' conferences within Church structure, the writer leaves the distinct impression that John Paul's tenure was strongly marked by repression of liberal thinking, and that this was unprecedented. A *US News and World Report* piece gives a similar impression, stating: "While he championed human rights and challenged dictators, he was criticized for stifling debate within the church on issues like contraception, divorce, and the role of women."[12]

Again, easy to say, but the lack of details raises questions. Any casual observer of Catholic life in the United States, for example, will see plenty of discussions of these issues among Catholics and in Catholic institutions. This makes it difficult to agree that there was a "stifling" of debate. Further, the use of the words "he was criticized" is problematic, falling into the same category as "many believe" or "others argue." Without supporting citations and evidence, such phraseology can hide the insertion of editorial content into news stories. Consider this excerpt from *Time:*

> Catholic scholars who deviated from orthodox interpretations of the faith—often, it seemed, those who questioned papal prerogative— were silenced or deprived of their teaching positions and expected to take a kind of loyalty pledge.
>
> He was not much more open to greater collegial participation among his bishops. His papacy saw the centralization of church authority. He published a decree effectively requiring national bishops' conferences to get Vatican approval before making statements on doctrine and made episcopal appointments subject to seeming litmus tests on topics like abortion and homosexuality.[13]

The implication that *all* scholars who "deviated" were "silenced" is not accurate. The phrase "papal prerogative" is extremely problematic, for it communicates an ill-defined understanding of Church teaching, which claims to rest not on "papal prerogative," but on two thousand years of reflection on revelation and tradition. The story's statement about bishops' appointments raises another set of questions. The reader is moved to wonder if this, again, was an innovation of John Paul II, and if bishops appointed before his pontificate were not expected to assent to the Church's moral teaching.

The Relationship between Papal Authority and Church Teaching

The relationship between John Paul and theologians and bishops was far more complex than outside observers seemed to understand. And this was important because much Catholic-related news comes down, in the end, to the issue of authority. Indeed, as it played out in different stories, the authority issue became a powerful demonstration of gaps in reporting both on John Paul's death and on the election and early papacy of Benedict.

When reporters fail to understand a pope's responsibility to the teaching he is called to serve, or his relationship to bishops, theologians, and the laity, their coverage presents an inaccurate and decontextualized picture of significant events. This ignorance, combined with application of the political template of the "conservative" pope whipping the "liberal-leaning" rest of the Church into shape, results in a distorted picture.

It is true, for example, that under John Paul's papacy, the Congregation for the Doctrine of the Faith (CDF) did, as part of its centuries-old responsibility, examines the works of theologians who work as "Catholic" theologians in "Catholic" institutions. A number of these theologians lost their licenses to teach Catholic theology, but that does not equal "silence." In practice, it meant that their courses were no longer accredited to present recognized Catholic doctrine. They were still free to teach their courses but they were now listed in another part of the curriculum, and, it is important to note, free to publish, give interviews, and present speeches. Not exactly "silence."

In fact, one of John Paul's most famous "victims," Fr. Hans Kung, lost his license to teach *Catholic* theology at the University of Tubingen but continued at the very same institution teaching *ecumenical* theology. Fr. Matthew Fox, an American well known for his "creation spirituality" was investigated by CDF but actually disciplined by his own order, the Dominicans, not the Vatican. It is true that other theologians such as Leonardo Boff and Gustavo Gutiérrez were questioned and told to stop speaking and writing as Catholic theologians as their works were investigated. Still others were, like Fox, disciplined by their own religious communities. And only a very few—like Fr. Tissa Balasuriya of Sri Lanka, were excommunicated (he, as he expressed contrition, for only a year).

So, while there were theologians investigated and disciplined during the twenty-six years of John Paul's papacy, the secular media never put this in any context in their legacy pieces: no comparison to previous papacies, no explanation of the discipline, and never any specific accounts of exactly what these "creative" theologians were teaching. Such contexualization would have surely forced the question, for example, in the case of Balasuriya: Exactly why should a theologian who apparently denied the divinity of Christ be permitted to teach as a Catholic theologian in a Catholic institution?

We have alluded to the disagreements that various "conservative" elements of Catholicism had with John Paul. Hence, it is interesting that in terms of discipline and excommunication, the most famous excommunication of Pope John Paul II's papacy was not of a "liberal" or "creative" theologian, but of the deeply traditionalist archbishop Marcel Lefebvre, a story largely neglected by the media in the post-mortems. In 1988, after years of dissent and negotiation in which the traditionalist leader held fast to his belief in the serious errors of the Second Vatican Council, Lefebvre ultimately forced the pope's hand when he ordained four archbishops of his own, without permission. Such ordination without the permission of Rome is an act that automatically places a bishop in a state of excommunication because "communion" means communion with *the bishop of Rome*—the pope.

One could argue that this, rather than the silencing of Boff or the removal of Kung, was truly significant. Neither Boff nor Kung produced a movement, but Lefebvre had—a movement including hundreds of thousands, worldwide, who saw him as their beacon of truth in what they perceived as the wreckage of the post–Vatican II Church. However, the press coverage of the "disciplinary" hand of Pope John Paul II in these post-mortems stressed only dissent on the Left, neglecting this story that truly, unlike the others, had legs.

The appointment of bishops frequently came up in post-mortems, with the claim being that John Paul appointed only bishops who shared his "rigid" view of Catholicism. However, what we see in the United States is great diversity in the sensibilities and policies among bishops appointed by John Paul II. Bishop Fabian Bruskewitz of Lincoln, Nebraska, has declared that members of liberal groups that are welcomed in other dioceses, such as Call to Action, are excommunicated. Bishop Raymond Flynn of Minneapolis–St. Paul tolerates not only a seriously traditionalist parish (St. Agnes) within his diocese but also a proudly liberal one (St. Joan of Arc). Some are looser yet, like Cardinal Roger Mahoney of Los Angeles, who is the bane of many "traditionalists" for the liturgical creativity he permits in his diocese. Still others try to walk a middle line. For example, Archbishop Timothy Dolan of Milwaukee is quite orthodox theologically, but, as late as 2005, he permitted the national Call to Action conference to meet in his archdiocese. Every one of these bishops was appointed by Pope John Paul II, who, according to many quoted in the press, appointed only bishops who reflected his own views. When it comes to governance, even apart from the excommunication of Archbishop Lefebvre, the argument could be made that "conservative" Catholics were far more frustrated by the papacy of John Paul II than were liberals.

One of John Paul II's most contentious writings was the 1990 apostolic constitution *Ex Corde Ecclesia,* in which he set forth his vision of the Catholic university. Included in the document was the very specific note that all professors of theology at Catholic universities should be given a *mandatum,* a sort of license to teach Catholic theology. From the U.S. bishops' statement on *Ex Corde:* "The *mandatum* recognizes the professor's commitment and responsibility to teach authentic Catholic doctrine and to refrain from putting forth as Catholic teaching anything contrary to the Church's magisterium."

Fifteen years after the apostolic constitution, only a minority of professors had done so, and most Catholic colleges and universities in the United States ignored the apostolic constitution with no consequences from their bishops or, ultimately, from Rome. It was ironic that at the same time that the press was describing the supposed authoritarianism of John Paul II, reporters were frequently using two priest-professors from Catholic universities—Fr. John Paris of Boston College, and Fr. Kevin Wildes of Loyola in New Orleans—as sources supporting the removal of Terri Schiavo's feeding tube, a stance explicitly rejected by, for example, Cardinal Martino of the Pontifical Council for Justice and Peace. *Ex Corde Ecclesia* was, indeed, mentioned in stories about the pope as evidence of his supposed authoritarian style, but the controversy over its spotty adherence, and Rome's apparent indifference, was not.

Catholic conservatives frequently noted and decried a pattern: Rome made declarations on catechesis, liturgy, or other matters, and bishops ignored them, suffering no apparent consequences. The most contentious such issue was that of clerical sexual abuse. Especially during the second major explosion of this problem in the U.S. Church (2002–2005, beginning with the release of documents from the Archdiocese of Boston), and despite the pope's unequivocal condemnation of clerical sexual abuse, many Catholics asked why bishops, despite ignoring and even protecting clerical sexual abusers, seemed to bear no consequences for their sins. Why didn't the pope do something? The answer to this question, of course, necessarily involved the complex issue of what, exactly the pope could "do" to a bishop, anyway. Discussions among major media and on the Internet noted dissatisfaction with the way Pope John Paul II had handled this problem. The issue was given heightened coverage after the pope's death when, as dictated by custom, Cardinal Bernard Law, resigned Archbishop of Boston, played a role in the ceremonies. A passage from an April 8 *Los Angeles Times* story was typical:

> In Boston, Law's upcoming role in choosing a new pope infuriates many lay Catholics, said James Post, a Boston University management professor who is president of Voice of the Faithful, an organization born during the abuse crisis that calls for increased lay leadership. "They know that something is fundamentally wrong. It offends our moral sense of right and wrong to have him casting a vote," Post said.
>
> On the other hand, he added, "some people are saying he has been through hell and will bring the wisdom of that experience into the conclave. Some people are hoping he will speak to the need of finding a pope that will be stronger in responding to the global sex abuse issues. Personally, I think that is a stretch."[14]

Finally, after his death the media focused on the pope's reservations about the U.S.-led war in Iraq and capital punishment, but primarily as evidence of the difficulty of categorizing the pope, or in an effort to contrast his views with U.S. political culture. In fact, surveys show that many U.S. Catholics disagreed with the pope's perceived positions on both of these issues. Polling also demonstrates American Catholic indifference to the Church's teaching on birth control, another issue that engages many Catholics deeply. The Iraq War misgivings, as articulated not just by the pope but by other curial officials, prompted enormous amounts of discussion and even confusion on television and radio talk shows, op-ed pages, and the Internet. But disagreement between the pope and political conservatives was not noted in the assessments after the pope's death.

Why the omission? The template the mainstream media had been using for more than two decades was that John Paul II was a "conservative," and therefore "liberals" disagreed with him. This template did a disservice not only to John Paul himself, who was anything but a "conservative" as defined by politically obsessed Americans, but also to U.S. Catholics across the spectrum who were grateful to the pope for his strength and witness, but still had questions about some of his positions, policies, and actions.

Who Is Benedict XVI?

Any transition inspires questions of change and continuity. During the interregnum such matters were the subject of much speculation, with few ways to predict the outcome—no opinion polls, and a commitment to secrecy on the part of the electors. There are only so many stories on the conclave that one can run. Taking a cue from coverage of government electoral races, reporting during that "in-between period" and in the days immediately following Benedict's election tended to focus on "issues." Ironically, these tended to be issues in which there would not (and, in the language of some, *could* not) be change: the ordination of women, and sexual ethics.

These were raised in terms of "the role of women in the Church" or "openness to modern views on sexuality," but the real questions that were being asked were: Would the next pope allow more discussion of the ordination of women since that's the only "role" that women aren't permitted to hold in the Church? And would the Church shift its position on homosexuality, contraception, and abortion, either weakening its condemnation of them or reversing its position on any of them?

An *Atlanta Journal-Constitution* headline after the conclave was typical: "Pope's traditional views make changes unlikely." The *Baltimore Sun* reported, "Even with black or Latin pope, don't expect major change," and then reminded readers on April 20 that "Faithful in U.S. unlikely to see altered message from the Vatican"; the *Houston Chronicle* declared, "A vote for tradition; The election of a German cardinal as Pope Benedict XVI signals a continuation of his predecessor's unyielding view of Catholic doctrine."[15]

A deep understanding of the different types of Catholic teaching, practice, and proclamation is missing from these stories and headlines. They presume, instead, that an individual pope has the power or right to "change" a doctrine with the stroke of a pen, thus attributing more power to the pope than he actually has. Catholic doctrines are not contained in documents upon which successive popes vote "up" or "down." Catholic doctrine is understood to be a gift from God to humanity, rooted in revelation, developed and more clearly understood through the centuries in the Church's tradition. The role of bishops, the successors of the apostles, is to guard this inheritance and to ensure that it is accurately and clearly preached and taught. As the bishop of Rome, the pope shares in this responsibility not to innovate but to protect.

The announcement of Cardinal Joseph Ratzinger's name from the balcony in St. Peter's Square stunned observers from across the spectrum. Fr. Richard Neuhaus, editor of *First Things,* commenting for the Catholic cable network EWTN, and seen as a representative of the "conservative" side of Catholicism, murmured, "Oh, my God." On ABC, Fr. Richard McBrien of Notre Dame, often cited as a vanguard of the "liberal" end, fell silent and then said, "Well, I'm, I'm surprised."

Quickly, the media gathered itself up and attempted to tell the story of Cardinal Ratzinger. The basic storyline naturally focused on the cardinal's twenty-four-year tenure as head of the Congregation for the Doctrine of the Faith, and, more specifically, on that congregation's role in vetting and disciplining theologians. In addition, reporters looked for insights in the cardinal's homilies at both John Paul II's funeral and the Mass opening the conclave on April 18, and in Benedict, his chosen name.

In general, the story those first few days, dependent as it was on past media characterization of the cardinal, was all about discipline and hard lines. The *San Francisco Chronicle* stated that "U.S. Catholics Expect New Pope Benedict to Hew Hard Line." The *Boston Globe* headline of April 21, 2005, spoke of his "stern image" in one headline and "divisive image" in another. "New Pope Could Be Polarizing," said *USA Today* on April 21, 2005. "Questions about Pope's Conservatism," read a headline in the *New York Times* on April 20, 2005.[16]

Attempts to discuss Ratzinger in a broader context—his voluminous writings, his personal character, even the selection of his name—were described as attempts to "soften" his harsh image. The *New York Times* used the phrase "God's Rottweiler" five times between April 17 and 23.[17] Every report on the election of Benedict on any of the CBS news shows on April 19 and 20 began with reporter Mark Phillips saying, "In choosing Joseph Ratzinger, the cardinals picked the most polarizing figure in the Catholic Church"—a surprising judgment considering that, in just two days, he had been elected in an international conclave composed of the leading figures in the Church.

Before the election, on Monday, April 18, Paula Zahn of CNN summed up the mainstream media's description of Joseph Ratzinger, the one that held over the next few days:

> Since 1981, German Cardinal Joseph Ratzinger has headed one of the most important apartments in the Vatican. It's called the Congregation for the Doctrine of the Faith. It's the office that three-and-a-half centuries ago was in charge of the inquisition.
>
> Ratzinger guards the absolutes of the church, whether you're talking about theology or morality. As he argued in his sermon today, there are some truths that do not change, that can't be compromised.
>
> Over the years, he's butted heads with theologians and teachers, silencing dissent, shutting down debate over issues such as homosexuality and the ordination of women.
>
> The cardinal's critics accuse him of helping Pope John Paul II put brakes on some of the reforms undertaken at the Second Vatican Council, to which Ratzinger was an adviser. He was considered a liberal back then, but his thinking changed in the turmoil of the student revolts of the late 1960s. Cardinal Joseph Ratzinger is now described by church watchers as a conservative's conservative, and, by you, as our person of the day.

This limited view of a seventy-eight-year old man with a decades-long career as one of Europe's most eminent theologians could only last so long. Pope Benedict's own words, in the homilies and talks he gave early in his pontificate, and his demeanor, seemed to indicate a gentle, almost shy personality. This inspired the presentation of a fuller picture, as did the use of interviews with experts familiar with his writing, as opposed to those familiar only with the disciplinary actions of the CDF.

The greatest challenge in describing Pope Benedict XVI was to accurately report his understanding of Catholic theology and the mission of the Church in the world. For more than forty years, any efforts to do this have been hampered by the largely political categories in which the secular media tries to understand the Church. "Conservative," "liberal," and "progressive" persist as normative adjectives, despite their inadequacy. And, as we've seen, this primary template emphasizes conflict.

Such a narrow perspective provides little help in explaining the dynamics within Catholicism, not to mention the thinking and impact of figures like John Paul II and Benedict XVI. John Paul II was "monarchical," and millions of people travelled to Rome for his funeral. Joseph Ratzinger was supposedly a "polarizing" and "divisive" figure, but as Pope Benedict XVI he has drawn twice as many pilgrims to his regular Roman appearances as John Paul did. And his publications are best-sellers.

The First Two Years of Pope Benedict XVI

The first year of Pope Benedict's papacy was relatively uneventful. Press coverage was marked by reflections on the gap between the expectations of "God's Rottweiler" and the reality of a pope who seemed to be making his way rather gently. The headlines of articles marking the first anniversary of Benedict's election are indicative:

> "A 'Kinder, Gentler' Benedict in First Year as Pope" (*Boston Globe*, April 16, 2006)
> "New Pope Making Mark, and Surprising Observers; Benedict XVI Is Far from the 'God's Rottweiler' Some Predicted" (*Houston Chronicle*, April 2, 2006)
> "Papal Blessings; New Pope Steers Clear of Hardline Edicts" (*Grand Rapids Press*, April 22, 2006)
> "Pope's 1st Year Lacks an Ideological Edge: Centrist Approach Concerns Conservatives" (*Washington Post*, April 19, 2006)
> "Panzer Cardinal Is Dead; Long Live the Pope" (*Irish Times*, April 1, 2006)
> "Benedict's Appeal Moves beyond 'Caricature'; On First Easter as Pope, Reputation Gets a Second Look" (*USA Today*, April 17, 2006)

The first year's event that prompted this "second look" was the release, on January 25, 2006, of Benedict's first encyclical, *Deus Caritas Est* (God Is Love). *Deus Caritas Est* concerned the nature of divine love, how God's love is foundational in human life, and how human beings can faithfully live out that love. The first part of the encyclical emphasized theological and spiritual matters, while in the last section, Benedict defined two particular expressions of love—charity and justice—and explained the Church's role in relation to each.

Coverage of the encyclical tended to emphasize two points: a surprise that "love" was the subject, and the political implications of the second portion. In a *Los Angeles Times* article of January 26, 2006, Tracy Wilkinson wrote,

"Benedict's choice of topic was puzzling to some observers, who expected the former Cardinal Joseph Ratzinger, who had served for more than two decades as the church's chief doctrinal watchdog, to address a more controversial or dogmatic issue in this document."[18]

The *Times* story, reprinted in the *Boston Globe,* was the only news coverage of the encyclical published in a U.S. urban daily. The *New York Times* published an op-ed by Fr. Lorenzo Albacete on February 3. *USA Today* also published a news article.[19] The Associated Press did not note the encyclical's publication. This was in contrast to Australian, Canadian, and European press outlets, which gave ample and immediate coverage to the document in the days after its appearance.

All was mostly quiet on the papal front for much of 2006—until late summer, when Benedict gave a now-notorious speech at the University of Regensburg on September 12 during a six-day trip to Bavaria. The speech, given to the gathered faculty of the college in which he had taught decades before, was called "Faith, Reason and the University: Memories and Reflections." The speech was lengthy and professorial: an extended exploration of the relationship between faith and reason, and what Christian—particularly Catholic—faith brought to that relationship. In the middle of the speech, in just a few paragraphs, Benedict referenced a fourteenth-century Byzantine emperor. In a dialogue between the emperor and a Muslim friend, the pope quoted the emperor's negative assessment of Islam.

The earliest reporting on the speech noted the reference to Islam but emphasized the wider context of the speech. A stronger note was sounded by the Agence France-Presse in a morning headline: "Pope Enjoys Private Time after Slamming Islam."[20] During the subsequent controversy, complete with widespread critiques from Muslim scholars, violent deaths, ruined churches, and the pope burned in effigy, most stories emphasized the pope's supposed failure, since he was a former academic, to understand the dynamics of the very public pulpit he now enjoyed. Few attempted to reach back into the pope's history of speaking and writing to see what he had actually said about Islam in the past. His previous statements had been marked by appreciation of Islam's strength, even as, in recent years, as both cardinal and pope, Benedict had challenged European Muslims, in particular, to educate their own in the ways of tolerance and mutual respect.

The Regensburg incident demonstrates the challenges of papal coverage in dramatic ways. Some blamed the incident on Benedict's academic insularity, while others mentioned the July shift in the Vatican press office. Some, like Cardinal Jean-Marie Lustiger, blamed the press, calling the controversy "media-driven," and one could certainly argue that since the speech was not available in the languages of the countries in which most of the violent protests occurred, there was no way such protests could have even erupted but for what the protesters learned via the press.

An alternative way of portraying the speech is difficult, but perhaps not impossible, to imagine. Reporting on papal speeches tends, as we have noted, to emphasize the political, even if the political is a minor element of a larger address. That emphasis seems to be a given in contemporary religion reporting, for good or for ill. The press has a responsibility, however, for telling the whole story and doing its best to ensure that the full context is understood: In this case, it should be emphasized that Benedict's speech came down much harder on the West than on any Muslim individual or culture, and that Benedict had repeatedly expressed openness to dialogue with Muslims, including just a year before, to a Muslim audience in Cologne:

> Christians and Muslims, we must face together the many challenges of our time. There is no room for apathy and disengagement, and even less for partiality and sectarianism. We must not yield to fear or pessimism. Rather, we must cultivate optimism and hope.
>
> Interreligious and intercultural dialogue between Christians and Muslims cannot be reduced to an optional extra. It is in fact a vital necessity, on which in large measure our future depends.
>
> The young people from many parts of the world are here in Cologne as living witnesses of solidarity, brotherhood and love.
>
> I pray with all my heart, dear and esteemed Muslim friends, that the merciful and compassionate God may protect you, bless you and enlighten you always.[21]

Improving Coverage

The media had an enormous job on its hands in covering the death of John Paul II and the election of Benedict XVI. As a whole, it did an adequate and sometimes outstanding job, drawing a global audience into the richness of Catholic liturgical life and spirituality, often with illuminating commentary, especially from the broadcast and cable news networks. It was, at times, television news at its best. But telling those stories was a struggle for print, broadcast, and cable media, for many of the same reasons religion coverage is a struggle in general: media organizations don't prioritize or finance adequate ongoing coverage or the hiring of competent, knowledgeable full-time religion reporters.

Reporting on Catholicism has its own challenges, as we have seen, mostly due to the breadth, historical depth, and complexity of the Catholic world. Those news sources covering the Catholic Church can improve their coverage only if they deepen their knowledge of the Church. This does not mean becoming advocates or losing their objectivity. It means nurturing journalists who understand the history of Catholicism, the nature of authority, and the role of the pope and bishops in the Church. It means reporting on decisions and practices within their proper context. It means understanding the Catholic scene—what is happening on the ground and what ordinary Catholic believers say and think and do.

One primary obstacle that media organizations face in deepening their coverage is reliance on a handful of regularly used experts to "explain" the Catholic scene. This is problematic not only because of the dull and routine stories that result, in which we can be assured, for example, that we will see Fr. Thomas Reese, S.J., Fr. Richard McBrien, Fr. Richard John Neuhaus, and perhaps Bill Donohue of the Catholic League quoted. It is problematic also because it falls into the trap of letting the experts, who would like to promote a view that Catholics think a certain way, shape reality.

In fact, the views of Catholics—of all kinds—are widely available on the Internet. Discussion boards, blogs, and online publications can give journalists a clear look at some parts of the general Catholic conversation. One can easily, for example, explore the interest in a pope's decision or writing by researching book sales, Web site hits (including hits on the Vatican's own site), and blog aggregate statistics. These resources are like any other: They offer only a partial picture. But they certainly present a broader view than do the usual slate of self-interested experts.

Journalists who want to cover stories related to the Roman Catholic Church accurately and fully would do well to avoid the temptation of framing every Vatican-related story as an eternal conflict between "conservatives" and "liberals." Reporting is always improved when journalists listen to the newsmakers themselves, rather than quoting those who interpret and spin the newsmakers' words.

Finally, a good part of the responsibility for enabling good reporting on these matters rests with the Catholic Church. The Vatican, and all Catholic dioceses, have press and communications departments, but too often these offices have seen their roles primarily in terms of damage control. Catholic Church officials who would like their story more thoroughly and richly told would do well to staff their press offices with knowledgeable people who develop positive, helpful relationships with journalists.

The Catholic Church has more than one billion members. Its story cannot be adequately told by relying on the same old paradigm pushed by the same old activists. It is often said that the Catholic Church moves slowly. But, like anything else, it does move and change. Discarding past, established templates in order to see and explain present realities will result in more accurate reporting and far more interesting stories.

7

Jesus Christ, Superstar: The Passion of the Press

Jeremy Lott

Now that the fires have cooled a bit, it's probably safe to take a poker and stir the ashes of the press coverage of actor and director Mel Gibson's most controversial film, *The Passion of the Christ*. In the reaction to the movie, we can see a stark divide between traditional religious believers—those who went to see the movie en masse—and the bulk of journalists, movie reviewers, and the like, who didn't—and still don't—seem to understand the material that they were assigned to cover.

For all of the controversy surrounding its release—in part *because* of the controversy—*The Passion* was an astounding commercial success. Following the film's release on Ash Wednesday of February 2004, ticket sales for the first extended weekend topped $83 million in the United States alone. By the time the movie finished its run in theatres, it had earned more than $370 million domestically and $241 million in foreign box offices—a total of $611 million worldwide, give or take several hundred thousand dollars.[1]

The Passion easily took the February opening weekend record, out-grossing Ridley Scott's *Hannibal* by $25 million. Total ticket sales placed the movie ninth in all-time domestic box-office earnings, behind such blockbusters as *Titanic, E.T.,* and the Star Wars and Spider-Man franchises. All of the movies that out-grossed *The Passion* had better release dates, in the summer or over the Thanksgiving–Christmas holiday extravaganza. Studios reserve January and

February releases for weaker movies that aren't expected to do well domestically, because fewer people go to the movies at that time of the year. The kids are in school and the adults have to pay off credit-card debt from presents, decorations, and holiday travel.

For these reasons, the part of the press that covers entertainment can be forgiven for *some* of the incredulity over the success of director Mel Gibson's mad masterstroke. Here was a movie that was slated for a February release, starring a virtually unknown leading man, backed by a paltry budget for prime-time advertising, saddled with subtitles and an R rating (the second best-selling R-rated movie in terms of all-time domestic ticket sales is *The Matrix Reloaded* at number thirty-two; *Beverly Hills Cop* comes in third, at number fifty-two), dogged by charged of anti-Semitism, and more than two hours long. As Billy Crystal said of the heroes' chances in *The Princess Bride,* "It would take a miracle!"

Or the box-office equivalent of a miracle. Starting opening night, movie-goers from all over the country—from L.A. to Tampa Bay—crowded into theatres to eat overpriced popcorn and sip soft drinks while they watched the most uncommercial commercial success in the history of modern cinema. And that was only the first act of this independent film's success. *The Passion* set a record by selling more than four million units on its first day of its domestic DVD release in early September 2004. Gibson then released a "low-violence" version of the film in time for Easter 2005 so that the R rating would no longer be a barrier to its being viewed by the young or squeamish.

This overwhelming success came as a surprise to entertainment reporters, many of whom were positively rooting for Gibson to slip on a banana peel. The week before the movie's release, *Entertainment Weekly* ran a feature story that will live on in "Dewey Defeats Truman"–style infamy. On the cover was a painting in green tones of Mel Gibson with a pensive, faraway gaze, a crown of thorns atop his head. The caption read, "Can Mel Gibson Survive *The Passion of the Christ?*"[2]

Having been denied access to the film, *Entertainment Weekly* reporter Jeff Jensen relied on the judgment of "over two dozen industry executives and others" who had seen the film or were "close to Gibson." Jensen decided from these conversations that the movie was "deeply polarizing," though he hesitated to predict that the movie would flop. On the one hand, it was an anti-Semitic bloodbath that might repel most sane theatergoers and set Jewish–Christian relations back to, roughly, the Dark Ages. On the other: "Buoyed by advance ticket sales driven by churches and other Christian groups, *The Passion* could pull in $30 million in its first five days." Only $53 million off the mark. In fact, the movie was within a horseshoe's toss of $30 million after its first day.

Welcome to the New Dark Ages

As coverage of *The Passion* went, the *Entertainment Weekly* feature story was about average, which means that it included numerous insinuations and accusations of anti-Semitism. Jensen wrote that the movie's script was "augmented with material from extra-biblical writings long accused of containing anti-Semitic content." In a parenthetical that followed information about the schismatic pre–Vatican II Catholicism of Gibson's father, Hutton, the scribe added: "These 1962–65 Vatican II reforms also absolved Jews for the killing of Christ: Gibson hasn't said whether he rejects this as well." He also reported real "concerns" that the movie "is hopelessly mired in anti-Semitic stereotypes." One sentence began: "Even those in Hollywood who don't think Gibson is anti-Semitic. . . ."

Historians of pop culture may some day have difficulty grasping the enormity of the anti-*Passion* animus in press accounts. It was as if Gibson were about to release *Auschwitz: The Musical*. One hopes that future technology and diligent research assistants will help the professors sift through it all, but what follows is a first cut of the data. I ran several searches of the LexisNexis database, which contains a good cross-section of journalism, though by no means does it contain everything that appears in print.

This search attempt was initially frustrating because it was difficult to refine a search to the point that "Mel Gibson" and "anti-Semitism" would yield fewer than a thousand articles over any meaningful period under examination. Repeated slicing of the coverage did eventually produce results that could be added up to present more than a purely subjective approach to the topic. Searches for "Mel Gibson" and "anti-Semitism" yield the following results, sorted by month.[3]

2003	2004
January: 1	January: 227
February: 0	February: 2,011
March: 14	March: 1,144
April: 4	April: 371
May: 1	May: 64
June: 34	June: 53
July: 38	July: 34
August: 221	August: 41
September: 160	September: 52
October: 50	October: 36
November: 59	November: 15
December: 119	December: 72

And, of course, the numbers spiked again after Gibson's DUI arrest in July 2006.[4] His arrest had simply become too much a part of the story to ignore. Here you had a director who was charged with producing an anti-Semitic blockbuster, and that same director ranted against the Jews while sitting in the back of a squad car. But this analysis is much less concerned with private motivation than with public presentation. Many people will look to Gibson's indiscretion and conclude that *The Passion* is nothing more than a Jew-hating, blood-drenched mess of a movie. As we will see, that is very far from true, either of the movie itself, or of the reasons for its success.

As to the story that our numbers tell: In March 2003, which marks the first small spike in news hits, Abraham Foxman of the Anti-Defamation League (ADL) released an open letter to Gibson. Foxman told Gibson that his organization had "serious concerns" about the movie, which had just entered post-production. The ADL, Foxman wrote, "would like to be assured" that the movie would "not give rise to the old canard of charging Jews with deicide and to anti-Semitism." Foxman worried that the way in which Gibson depicted the death of Jesus would "have widespread influence on people's ideas, attitudes and behavior towards Jews today," and warned that "only teachings which promote understanding and reconciliation toward the Jewish people can represent religious truth and the word of God."[5]

Gibson's response to Foxman and to other critics was not conciliatory. He first ignored and then charged with theft a group of liberal scholars who critiqued the movie script to try to "improve" his film by placing less emphasis on the gospels. This culminated in an angry cover story by Boston College professor Paula Fredriksen that appeared in the *New Republic* magazine in late July. Fredriksen charged Gibson with deception and worse. She reported that Catholic leaders "feel even greater urgency [than do Jewish leaders] about [*The Passion*'s] anti-Semitism, because the ethical issue for them is so clear. Jews are the objects of anti-Semitism, but Catholics and other Christians, inspired by Gibson's movie, could well become its agents." She concluded: "When violence breaks out, Mel Gibson will have a much higher authority than professors and bishops to answer to."[6]

Writing on the front page of the *New York Times* Style section in August, former theater critic and op-ed columnist Frank Rich amplified Fredriksen's concerns. While he confessed it "hard to imagine the movie being anything other than a flop in America, given that it has no major Hollywood stars and that its dialogue is in Aramaic and Latin," Rich opined that the "real tinder-box effect" would likely be felt abroad, where anti-Semitism is more tolerated in polite society.[7] Many of the charges that cropped up over the next six months were articulated by Rich:

(1) Gibson was damned for his association with a pre–Vatican II splinter of Catholicism, and the question was suggested: If he rejects Vatican II, does he also reject Vatican II's forceful rejection of referring to the whole Jewish race as Christ killers? Also front-and-center was the major influence of the wild visions of Mary of Agreda and the early nineteenth-century mystic Anne Catherine Emmerich. One of Emmerich's many visions, Rich reported, had involved the historic blood libel (wherein Jews were accused of stealing and butchering gentile children to use their blood for a secret religious ritual), though he doubted Gibson would go quite so far as to endorse that accusation.

(2) The early screenings of *The Passion* that Gibson was allowing were selective and biased to include sympathetic voices—usually pastors or right-leaning media types—in the audience. Rich charged that these choices amounted to an exclusion of most Jews. When it was brought to Rich's attention that Gibson had screened the movie for some influential Jewish rabbis and writers and solicited their suggestions, Rich responded by characterizing them as sellouts. "One such is Michael Medved, who is fond of describing himself in his published *Passion* encomiums as a 'former synagogue president' betting that most of his readers will not know that this is a secular rank falling somewhere between co-op board president and aspiring Young Men's Hebrew Association camp counselor," Rich wrote in a follow-up column.[8]

(3) Rich accused Gibson of libeling Jews in his "politicized rollout of the film," suggesting that the schismatic director's "game from the start has been to foment the old-as-Hollywood canard that the 'entertainment elite' (which just happens to be Jewish) is gunning for his Christian movie." He charged "Gibson and his minions" of going to absurd lengths to "bait Jews and sow religious conflict."

Blue and Red All Over

The *Crossfire*-style political approach to covering *The Passion* worked its way down the media food chain. This enraged Gibson, which made for an entertaining—though less than civil—back-and-forth between the director and the press. Of Rich, Gibson famously told the *New Yorker* (in his best deadpan "*Mad Max* stock crazy character voice," I'm sure), "I want to kill him. I want his intestines on a stick . . . I want to kill his dog."[9]

In the same story came Gibson's intemperate response to the scholars' recommendations for revision. It is reproduced here in spite of its vulgarity so that readers can get a feel for just how, well, passionate the director was about his project. "They always dick around with it, you know? Judas is always some kind of friend of some freedom fighter named Barabbas, you know what I mean? It's horseshit. It's revisionist bullshit. And that's what these academics are into. They gave me notes on a stolen script. I couldn't believe it. It was like they were more or less saying I have no right to interpret the Gospels myself, because I don't have a bunch of letters after my name. But they are for children, these Gospels. They're for children, they're for old people, they're for everybody in between. They're not necessarily for academics. Just get an academic on board if you want to pervert something!" Gibson told the *New Yorker*.

In fact, getting an academic on board is exactly what some of the scholars were advocating. In a statement that should be noted by, and taped to the computer monitor of, anybody who studies the controversy surrounding *The Passion*, Fredriksen complained that Gibson didn't "even have a Ph.D. on his staff" to guide the movie down the narrow path. The Anti-Defamation League, the scholars, and other critics, were quick to fall back on the "we're not calling for censorship" defense, and in the strictest sense they weren't: They were not calling on the government to exercise prior restraint. But it was clear that they wanted veto power and they wanted the final form of *The Passion* to be watered down in response to their particular concerns.

How else should we construe Fredriksen's warning that Gibson would have blood on his hands, or the ADL's expressed desire to shape the movie's theological agenda, or some of the quiet "you'll never work in this town again"–type Hollywood intimidation that Gibson freely and plausibly admitted to receiving? There are nuances that my tin ear might miss, but this sounded more like blackmail than like criticism.

The Hollywood whisper campaign, especially, deserves elaboration. In the *Entertainment Weekly* cover story, one anonymous studio executive said that he would "try very hard never to work with [Gibson] again." Another warned that Gibson had "driven his career right to the edge of a cliff. One more false move, it goes right over." A third opined that the director had "stepped into a huge pile of shit" when he "decided to give his hero an antagonist." We learn that "most of the major studios" contacted by the magazine "say they never seriously entertained releasing the movie." Twentieth Century Fox, Gibson's usual distributor, was picketed by activists and refused to distribute the film. Gibson's production company Icon had to scramble to secure another distributor in time for the movie's release.

If I were teaching journalism, I would challenge my students to consider framing the story in this way: You had a Howard Hughes–like eccentric, obsessive director–financier trying to do something new and different and utterly personal, cutting and re-cutting the film right up to its release to refine the art and the message. And then you had a bluenose establishment of critics, competitors, and lobbyists, which didn't want this upstart exciting the masses or sullying a venerable art form, putting roadblocks in his path.

Many reporters took to sounding like the bluenoses. For instance, rather than use the controversy as an occasion to have a good look at how power is exercised in Hollywood, *Entertainment Weekly*'s Jensen chose to deliver a warning to Gibson: "If *The Passion* is denounced as anti-Semitic, and still becomes the most popular piece of hate-fueling cinema since *The Birth of a Nation,* his defiant, unconciliatory stance may well read as a decision to trade away Jewish concerns for Christian box-office dollars. That's something Hollywood may not be so quick to forgive or forget." Substitute "your" for "his" and the message could have been delivered by one of the anonymous studio executives that Jensen quoted.

A Very Thin Gruel

Passion watchers had to suffer through a lot of predictable, unimaginative journalism to get at anything of substance. In August 2003 we read in the *Miami Herald* that most theatres would avoid showing the film. *Hollywood Reporter* writer Martin Grove predicted that "threats of violence and pickets" would dissuade theatre owners from showing it. In fact, he estimated that "probably not more than a million people" would watch the film. For a pre-release judgment of the story, the reporter turned to no other than Paula Fredriksen, who "said she loves biblical movies but predicted this would be a dud: 'There is no plot, no character development, no subtlety. The bad guys are way bad, the good guys are way good.'"[10] Clearly, what the vulgar masses were clamoring for was more art house movies.

In September 2003 the *Boston Globe* opined that the movie was shaping up to be "a cultural, ideological, and religious wedge issue." Charges of anti-Semitism? Check. Complaints about Gibson's selective screenings? Check. Plenty of column inches devoted to quoting Gibson's ideological critics? Check. Prediction that the movie will flop? Check.[11] In October a subhead in the *San Francisco Chronicle* said that "*The Passion* according to Mel Gibson has everybody talking." However, the headline writer wondered, "Is it Gospel truth or anti-Semitism?" Answer: "Few have seen it so far, but everyone seems to have an opinion about it."[12] In November the *Los Angeles Times* wrote that someone at Twentieth Century Fox may or may not have produced a pirate copy of an early version of the film and passed it to the *New York Post.* The flap was said to touch on two of Hollywood's hottest issues: piracy and "concerns and curiosity about

The Passion itself." The *Times* explained, "Some who have seen the movie in early screenings have praised it," but there was also "widespread criticism for what some fear is its potential to fuel anti-Semitism."[13]

"Et cetera, et cetera, et cetera," as the King of Siam would have it. With a few worthy exceptions, the mainstream press offered Americans who were genuinely curious about *The Passion* a thin gruel of theologically obtuse reporting, incorporating copious charges of anti-Semitism, along with a lot of thumb-sucking commentary. This approach reduced the story to a frustrating dialectic: Mel Gibson's medieval religious mindset versus our modern tolerant norms; his literalism versus the scholars' nuance; Jewish Hollywood executives versus this "ultra-traditionalist" Catholic director; the hysterical-but-peaceful reactions of enlightened critics who hadn't seen the movie versus the pogroms that those who finally viewed the flick were likely to instigate.

Gibson also bears blame for this poor coverage because part of the problem was that journalists lacked access to him. When I last worked a regular reporting beat, I had a simple practice for dealing with cooperative versus uncooperative subjects. If the subject of a story cooperated and didn't lie to me, the coverage would be more favorable toward him or her. If the subject refused to play ball, the story would be less favorable, sometimes bordering on savage. Most journalists, either by inclination or necessity, adhere to this practice. No matter how much a reporter strives for balance, when one side in a dispute is unwilling to cooperate, then the final story is going to more closely reflect the view of the chatterbox party—in this case Frank Rich and the Anti-Defamation League, with Gibson's rare, and often over-the-top, public remarks thrown in for good measure.

The director's decision to pre-screen early versions of the movie before only audiences that he thought would be somewhat sympathetic, and only if they signed one-sided, legally dubious confidentiality agreements (as one watcher explained it to *Entertainment Weekly*, "The way I interpreted it was 'If you like the film, feel free to talk about it. And if you don't like the film, feel free to honor the confidentiality agreement.'") had definite repercussions. Christian or conservative viewers could for once feel like part of the "in" crowd. They could also rail against the movie's know-nothing critics who hadn't even seen the film: For them, it became very much "our movie."

The critics could respond that, for all they knew, Gibson could be fostering his own mystery religion in there. They continued to raise questions about the movie's purported anti-Semitism and to demand access. They asked why, if Gibson had nothing to hide, he would not let them in. Reporters, whose ethical canons wouldn't allow them sign the confidentiality pledge and then write about the movie with one hand tied behind their backs, were left outside with the critics. For the most part, they had to sort the story out with no access to the film, very little access to the director, and deadlines looming.

The resulting lousy coverage was part of a vicious cycle that nearly drove Gibson insane but led some critics to charge that he was crazy like a fox. When *Los Angeles Times* reporter Rachel Abramowitz caught up with him in mid-February 2004, she found a director at wit's end. "He might be lolling around one of the most luxurious hotels in Los Angeles," she wrote, "but he has clearly brought his personal bunker with him."[14]

Gibson appeared "alternately embattled and exhausted, angry and self-pitying." Abramowitz reported that he "barely speaks above a whisper, as if trying to keep a tight fist around his emotions." He confessed to her that he felt "subjected to religious persecution, persecution as an artist, persecution as an American, persecution as a man." Defending himself against charges that he is "some cult wacko," he explained, "All I do is go and pray. For myself. For my family. For the whole world." Gibson professed what appeared to be genuine shock that people would see in his retelling of the story of the last twelve hours of Jesus's life a message of hatred because this story had had such a profoundly positive effect on his own life.

Critics Scourge *The Passion*

Every January the online journal *Slate* hosts a moderated back-and-forth by several of the country's notable movie critics. The conversations wander all over the map, but the ostensible subject is the previous year at the movies. In January 2005 the critics turned their attention to *The Passion*, with depressingly predictable results.[15]

Salon's Charles Taylor called the movie "anti-Semitic shit" and "a disservice to the art" of moviemaking. He was responding to Christopher Kelly, movie reviewer for the *Fort Worth Star-Telegram*, who had insisted that, although he didn't like *The Passion*, and although he claimed to have received a few voice-mail death threats over his negative review of the movie, it (along with Michael Moore's *Fahrenheit 911*) had made 2004 a "wonderful, privileged year to be a film critic" because simply "*everyone*" (italics his) wanted to know what film critics had to say about the movie.

But most critics didn't have much to say about the film that didn't come off sounding like a Greek chorus. Kelly "reviled" the movie. He found it to be "bludgeoning, repetitive, and snuff-y" and wondered if it would lead to a new era of filmmaking—the era "of the Filmmaker as Bully and Pop Ideologue." Kelly then threw out the most back-handed of back-handed compliments, allowing that he preferred Gibson's "bluntness and nutjob proselytizing" to a few of the year's martial arts films. *Boston Globe* film critic Wesley Morris found the film "unwatchable, ugly, and redundant," saying it should be written off as "a discriminatory work whose literalism and single-mindedness demean its art." *L.A. Weekly* reviewer Scott Foundas huffed that "there's no overestimating the public's appetite for crass, obvious spectacle."

The movie's only defender in the forum was one Armond White, prickly critic for the alt-weekly the *New York Press*. White wrote that he found most discussion of *The Passion* to be "oppressively lopsided." He complained, as a non-Christian, that "no mainstream publication will hire a Christian movie critic," which might have helped give readers a clearer picture of what the movie was about. White had not "read a single mainstream review that sought to appreciate Gibson's basic, powerful imagery on its own terms." He asked, "Does atheism rule? Does blindness rule criticism?" He warned his fellow critics that there are "millions of readers who, understandably, feel the lack. They aren't getting from criticism what they want/need to know about art, mythology, spirituality. They're only getting objections, recriminations, and remonstrations."

He wasn't mistaken about the overall tone and tenor of the criticisms of the film. According to Rotten Tomatoes, a Web site that aggregates criticism from all over the country, in major publications reviews of *The Passion* ran 38 percent positive (or "fresh") versus 62 percent negative ("rotten"). To give some perspective, *Fahrenheit 911*'s reviews were 80 percent fresh and 20 percent rotten. Director Guillermo Del Toro's summer action flick *Hellboy* was rated 88 percent fresh and 12 percent rotten. Alexander Payne's *Sideways* was 97 percent fresh versus 3 percent rotten.[16]

Looking over the Rotten Tomatoes "pull quotes" for the reviews of *The Passion,* one is struck by the hostility directed toward the movie, coupled with the belief that it would surely flop. In the *New Yorker* David Denby opined, "The movie Gibson has made from his personal obsessions is a sickening death trip, a grimly unilluminating procession of treachery, beatings, blood, and agony." *Entertainment Weekly* reviewer Lisa Schwarzbaum wrote that "Gibson has made a movie for nobody, really, but Gibson." The *Los Angeles Times*'s Kenneth Turan declared it "a film so narrowly focused as to be inaccessible to all but the devout."

Gibson the Storyteller

Movie critics and the broader working press utterly failed to understand *The Passion* as a work of art with popular heft. As Armond White said, few reviewers were willing to try to understand the movie's "basic, powerful imagery." Instead, they carped about the film's violence and fired every arrow in their quiver at it. None of these criticisms managed to deflate ticket sales, but one charge, in particular, is worth examining in order to understand what White described as "the lack"—the inability of journalists and critics to "get" what the massive audience saw in the film.

One of the worries about Gibson's film was that it would be an absurdly literalist project. By hewing too closely to the text and texture of the gospels, *The Passion* would, at best, become an anti-Semitic un-nuanced mess. The scholars alleged it, the reporters reported it, and the reviewers duly read this dangerous literalism right into the film and warned us against it. A few critics alleged that by portraying Jesus's last, terrible hours in the way that he did, Gibson was effectively making an anti-gospel—one that replaced love with hate and compassion with suffering.

This criticism flew wide of the target. Gibson's film had all the trappings of authenticity—it was in Aramaic and Latin and clocked in at more than two hours long—but it was not, and did not aim to be, a literal reproduction of the portions of the gospels related to Jesus's trial and crucifixion. We don't have to wonder what kind of ticket sales a more literal interpretation would have generated because we have actual measurable evidence in the form of another film. *The Gospel of John,* a movie released in September 2003 with dialogue that was taken, word-for-word, from the fourth book of the New Testament as translated in the *Good News Bible,* did slightly more than $4 million in domestic box-office sales.

In fact, *The Passion* was a highly theological interpretation of the story it portrayed. Go into any American Catholic church and take a look around. Nearly all of the churches, from grand cathedrals to those happy-clappy A-frame buildings that were put up in the 1970s, share a few basic features. Obviously, there's an altar and a center aisle and a crucifix, but the visitor will also find fourteen placards posted around the church. These are the Stations of the Cross, a development of the late Middle Ages that became part of the popular piety of the Church and were slowly incorporated and then formalized into church architecture.

The stations are markers on the Via Dolorosa, the "way of suffering." They begin with Pilate sentencing Jesus to death and end with his body being laid in the tomb. In between are a dozen events from a mixture of the gospels and what is called sacred tradition: Jesus stumbles and Roman soldiers drag an African Jew named Simon in to help carry the cross; St. Veronica wipes the carpenter's bruised and battered face; he is stripped and nailed to the cross. The stations allow the pious, in a spiritual sense, to follow Jesus through his struggles, meditate on this, and deepen their faith.

These ubiquitous stations, well known to most Catholics if not to movie critics, just happen to be the rough outline of much of the movie, which gave Catholic moviegoers a leg up on stunned Protestants in the audience. Far from being a leaden literalist flick, *The Passion* was a bloody, violent meditation not only on what happened but what it meant. Gibson freely tweaked details of the story to fit with his sense of what was important and underscored this with flashbacks to Jesus's life and ministry.

In the most famous example of his storytelling license, Gibson decided to drop from the captions the line from Matthew in which the Jewish mob accepts responsibility for Jesus's death and wishes a curse upon their own children. That was an interesting, if grudging, concession. But more important, to my mind, was the way Gibson chose to shoot the unexpurgated scene. In his version, the high priest Caiaphas was the only member of the crowd to accept responsibility. This helped shift responsibility from the rabble to a few powerful leaders who were skilled at working the crowds.

This is not the place for an exhaustive examination of the imagery of *The Passion*, but there were a number of details that the news coverage and critical writing about *The Passion* either missed or downplayed: the active, in-your-face role of the devil; the utter brutality of the Romans (this brutality, strangely, was occasionally used to bolster charges of anti-Semitism); and what most Catholics would recognize as the very strong Eucharistic undercurrents of the film.

Mass Appeal

Indeed, *The Passion* is a very, very Catholic film—to such an extent that it should have had a difficult time attracting such a catholic audience. I wrote on the eve of the movie's release that while the talking heads were bobbing to the controversies that swirled about the movie, observant Christians were "busy buying out screenings in record numbers." I noted, "Local, mostly Protestant congregations have purchased so many tickets that this independently distributed film will open on at least 2,800 screens. . . . Many fundamentalist children and teens are about to see their first R-rated movie, and they're bringing friends."[17]

At the time, I was dismissive of the effects of the pre-release coverage on the broader audience of moviegoers clamoring to get into *The Passion*. The press, I thought, had made itself irrelevant to this story by focusing relentlessly on small details while failing to show us the bigger picture, like a microscope stuck on too high a magnification. I wrote that "[if] most journalists didn't focus on the anti-Semitism angle, they wouldn't know what else to say."

But now, in sifting through the reviews and the press accounts and other ephemera, it occurs that I was not just wrong but badly wrong about the effect of the press on *The Passion*. With a few notable exceptions—Peter Boyer's profile in the *New Yorker* being one—news coverage of the movie was bad, the opinion writing was clichéd, and the movie criticism was worse. But it was perhaps precisely because the press botched *The Passion of the Christ* so badly that the audience decided to give the movie a chance.

Evangelicals might have had serious theological difficulties with this film: the focus on the suffering of Jesus was too intense and unrelenting; the identification of bread and wine with body and blood was so very transubstantial; and the movie drew heavily on the traditions of the Church, rather than relying only on the bare text of the gospels, to determine the content and structure of the story. These things might not have been deal breakers, but they would have dampened enthusiasm, even if Gibson did let Protestant ministers in to advance screenings.

By repeatedly reporting concerns over the movie's literalism, the press did yeomen's work to put these concerns to rest. And, in fact, the charges of anti-Semitism may have done more to bring Christians of various confessions together than the last thirty years of ecumenical dialogue have done. *The Passion* became a rallying point for these believers not because they especially liked Mel Gibson's oeuvre ("If you liked *Mad Max,* you'll love *The Passion!*") but because they continued to read allegations that any rendition of the story of Jesus Christ that is true to the sense of scripture would be anti-Semitic. The moviegoers took this to mean that the faith itself was being charged with anti-Semitism, and they didn't like it one bit, and responded with a show of solidarity.

In one sense, the story of the success of *The Passion of the Christ* is really about the press's failure to honestly grapple with broader questions of religion. In another sense, the story is about the estrangement of American journalists from their audience. The movie did not lead to the rise in anti-Semitic sentiment that the critics had predicted. The fact that the predictions were broadcast as widely and loudly as they were (see the "anti-Semitism" chart above) bespeaks a troubling willingness by journalists to believe the worst of religious would-be moviegoers. And so I leave future journalists with the following story—something to keep in mind when the next *Passion*-like event occurs.

Rev. Maurice Gordon was the pastor of the hundred-member Lovingway United Pentecostal Church in Denver, Colorado. To coincide with the release of *The Passion,* he arranged the following five-word polemic on the church message board: "Jews killed the Lord Jesus." The incident was widely reported and touted by *Passion* critics as evidence that the movie was hardening American hearts toward Jews. Less widely reported was the thundering response. The small church drew something on the order of two hundred protesters—twice the size of the congregation. The marquee was changed to read: "I am deeply sorry for offending the Jewish people, whom I love. Brother Gordon." Within a month, Gordon announced his retirement at a special church meeting. One of the members of the congregation said of the pastor's resignation, "I think it sends a message—that not only is he sorry but there are consequences when you make a mistake of that magnitude."[18]

PART III

Getting It Right

8

Getting Religion
in the Newsroom

Terry Mattingly

Roy Peter Clark, a senior scholar at the Poynter Institute, didn't like
the headlines on the morning after the election. His journalistic
instincts, along with his progressive Catholic convictions, had led
him to believe that Sen. John Kerry would win the White House.
Then the "values voters" showed up. It was one thing to see his candidate lose. While that bothered him, it didn't scare him. What left him
staring at his face in the mirror was a disturbing sense that there was
a big story hiding in the 2004 election that the mainstream media
had missed. That made him ask tough questions. He questioned the
contents of his own head and his assumptions about his work. He
wrote, "I am now taking seriously the theory that we mainstream
journalists are different from mainstream America." But the problem
was not "difference" per se but "alienation." He wrote, "We may live
in the same country, but we treat each other like aliens. Maybe it's
worse than that because we usually see and suspect the alien in our
midst. The "churched" people who embrace Bush, in spite of a bumbling war and a stumbling economy, are more than alien to me. They
are invisible." Clark admitted his expertise on slutty MTV videos and
the fine details of *Queer Eye for the Straight Guy*. But don't ask him
how to click with tuna-casserole people at church suppers. Going to
Mass Sunday after Sunday, he said, has not taught him the doctrinal
differences between an "evangelical" and a "charismatic." The people
in those pews were a confusing blur and, to be honest, he didn't
think much of them and their values, stating, "I can't see what is in

the hearts and minds of so many working class and rural Americans attracted to George W. Bush as a defender of moral values. In my skeptic's mind, the expression 'moral values' is nothing more than code language for showy piety and patriotism, with more than a dash of racism and homophobia." Nevertheless, Clark realized that he needed help. "I'm a journalist," he confessed. "I once was blind—and still can't see. My blind spots blot out half of America. And that makes me less of a citizen, and less of a journalist."[1]

The response, in the age of e-mail and weblogs, was immediate. Some liberals said they felt his pain. But it was the conservatives who got his attention. Some religious readers dismissed him as just one more biased lefty journalist. But others wrote thoughtful letters and genuinely seemed to want to know more about his point of view. Some suggested information sources, scholars, think-tank contacts, and helpful Web sites. Some sent books. In a few cases, the exchange of letters evolved into a real dialogue. In an interview Clark stressed to me that his basic political and religious views remained the same but that there were large segments of the American population that he knew nothing about and, for a journalist, that was bad. His bottom line was that journalists frequently get big religion stories wrong or miss them altogether. Once that was accepted, they could start talking about ways to improve their work.

> I'm talking about fairness and balance. But I'm also talking about
> things like empathy—the ability to identify with another person's
> experiences and point of view. I'm talking about paying attention to
> what is going on around you. Journalists also need to be self-critical
> and have a sense of self-doubt, which is the opposite of arrogance.
> We need tolerance, which is not the same thing as acceptance. We
> need to be able to cover all kinds of people whose viewpoints we don't
> accept. But we have to be able to write about them in a way that they
> can recognize their own values.[2]

If we first recognize that religion is a crucial force at local, national, and global levels, that it is not going to go away, and that covering it is hard work, then I suggest four basic things need to be done.[3]

- Journalists need to be more careful about religious language and labels.
- We need real diversity in our newsrooms.
- Editors need to offer better training and resources both to religion reporters and others whose work veers into religious territory.
- We must strive to get inside the daily lives and stories of the people we cover.

When journalists cover protests, near the top of their to-do list is finding a quotation to capture the protesters' style. With religious groups this can be harder than it sounds, as illustrated by one disaster story. When a flock of Pentecostal Christians gathered at the Capitol for yet another rally about sex, abortion, and family values, a *Washington Post* reporter wrote the following to capture the mood: "At times, the mood turned hostile toward the lawmakers in the stately white building behind the stage." Then, the *Post* quoted an onstage exclamation from one of the religious broadcasters: "Let's pray that God will slay everyone in the Capitol."[4] Since the quote appeared without any explanation, the reader, and presumably the reporter who wrote the story and the editors who handled it, is not made aware of the experience that millions of Pentecostal Christians call being "slain in the Holy Spirit," in which they believe they are transformed by a surge of God's power. Kovach and Rosenstiel comment: "The reporters didn't know, didn't have any Pentecostals in the newsroom to ask, and were perhaps too anxious for a 'holy sh-t' story to double-check with someone afterward whether the broadcaster was really advocating the murder of the entire Congress."[5]

It's hard to cover religious events and trends if we don't know what the words mean, especially if one is parsing Vatican documents, the sermons of Iraqi clerics, prayer-breakfast meditations by Baptists who sit in the Oval Office, Buddhist references in Hollywood scripts, and canon laws that affect millions of dollars in pensions and properties during global schisms. But many journalists keep getting the words wrong. Sociologist Christian Smith said he is tired of calls from journalists who don't know that Episcopalians are not "Episcopals" or who confuse evangelicals with "evangelists" or even, God forbid, "evangelicalists." "I find it hard to believe that political journalists call Washington think tanks and ask to talk with experts on background about the political strategies of the 'Democrizer' or 'Republication' parties, or about the most recent 'Supremicist Court' ruling. So why do so few journalists covering religion know religion?"[6]

Some do. Richard N. Ostling, best known for his work with *Time* and the Associated Press, consistently got it right but has also read more than his share of messed-up religion stories, and still winces. "Sometimes we are talking about things that can get complicated. But it isn't good when people read their newspaper and say, 'Wait a minute. That's just wrong.'" One prime example is a mistake he describes seeing countless times in news reports about the sharp decline in the number of priests being ordained in the Catholic Church, especially in North America and Europe. This mistake usually appears in reports about two of the hottest subjects in Catholic news today—mandatory celibacy for priests and the scandals of clergy sexual abuse: journalists often report that

Rome does not ordain married men. He notes: "It would be accurate to say that the overwhelming majority of men ordained as Catholic priests are not married. It would even be accurate to say that 'almost all' priests are not married. But what about Eastern Rite Catholicism, where you have married priests? Then there are the married men who have been ordained in the Anglican Rite, who used to be Episcopal priests. You have a few Lutherans, too. Now some people would say that little mistakes like this do not matter all that much. Well, they matter to the people who read the story and know that what they are reading is wrong. What does this say about our journalistic standards?"[7]

One problem is that journalists who cover religion news—like those who cover other complicated beats, such as science, sports, law, and the arts—must write stories that work on two levels: they must be accessible to general readers yet accurate enough to pass muster with clergy, scholars, and devout believers. This is especially a challenge on a beat that is not only complex but emotional. Consider one of the most loaded terms in religion news—"fundamentalist." In a *New York Times* story, reporter Jodi Wilgoren described the beliefs of Discovery Institute fellows highly critical of Darwinian evolution. In the final-edition version of the story, Wilgoren wrote: "Their credentials—advanced degrees from Stanford, Columbia, Yale, the University of Texas, the University of California—are impressive, but their ideas are often ridiculed in the academic world. . . . [Most] fellows, like their financiers, are fundamentalist Christians, though they insist their work is serious science, not closet creationism."[8] But the group included Episcopalians, Catholics, Jews, Eastern Orthodox Christians, Baptists, and several strains of Presbyterian. What does the word "fundamentalist" mean in this context? On top of that, a bible of journalism—the *Associated Press Stylebook*—warns against using the divisive term in precisely this manner. It states: "fundamentalist: The word gained usage in an early 20th century fundamentalist-modernist controversy within Protestantism. In recent years, however, fundamentalist has to a large extent taken on pejorative connotations except when applied to groups that stress strict, literal interpretations of Scripture and separation from other Christians. In general, do not use fundamentalist unless a group applies the word to itself."[9]

In this case, the *New York Times* had to retreat. Its digital archives contain an altered version of the story, and the following correction: "A front-page article on Sunday about the Discovery Institute, which promotes the concept known as intelligent design to explain the origins of life, referred incorrectly to the religious affiliation of the institute's fellows. Most are conservative Christians, including Roman Catholics and evangelical Protestants—not fundamentalist Christians." To avoid having to make that correction, all that was needed was to consider the *Associated Press Stylebook* or allow members of the group to describe their own ideas and beliefs, rather than using labels assigned to them by their enemies.

Another example is given by Aly Colon, a leader in the Poynter Institute diversity programs. It helps to know that Colon is active in the Presbyterian Church (U.S.A.). In 2003 he wrote a column entitled "Preying Presbyterians," which was about news coverage of the execution of Paul Hill, who was sentenced to death by the State of Florida for the 1994 murders in Pensacola of an abortion clinic doctor and his guard. Almost all the stories mentioned that Hill was a "former Presbyterian minister." Colon writes: "All the stories I read via the *New York Times, Washington Post, St. Petersburg Times,* the Associated Press, and the *Los Angeles Times* sought to give me background on Hill. . . . Some offered more than others. But none of them explained, at least to my satisfaction, why they felt it important to note why they used the term Presbyterian as a description."[10] What did they think that "Presbyterian" means? Did his denominational ties have anything to do with the murders?[11]

In this case, an even more basic fact was missing. Was Hill a member of the Presbyterian Church (U.S.A.), or was he part of the more conservative Presbyterian Church in America, or the even more conservative Orthodox Presbyterian Church? Isn't it significant that, because of his extreme views, Hill had in fact been expelled from both of those conservative churches? The bottom line is that, while it may be accurate to say that Hill was a "Presbyterian," such a shallow and incomplete reference would mystify, if not infuriate, the vast majority of Presbyterians—Left and Right—who happened to read it.

The question can be extended. Does an Orthodox rabbi have the same beliefs as a rabbi in a liberal, Reconstructionist congregation? Do "moderate" Baptists (think Bill Moyers) have the same beliefs as "conservative" Baptists (think Rick Warren)? Will an Anglican bishop in Nigeria have the same beliefs as one in New Jersey? Will a Sufi mystic in Bosnia have the same understanding of the word "jihad" as a violent Islamist in the mountains of Pakistan? Colon suggests: "When we use religious terms, especially designations of denominations, sects, or groups, we need to offer more clarity about what they are and what they believe. . . . We need to define denominations. Context and specificity help news consumers better understand the religious people in the news and how religion affects what they do." When in doubt, journalists should let religious believers define themselves. Humility is a virtue, especially when writing about the religious beliefs of other people.

Of course, it also helps if newsrooms contain more reporters and editors who already knew what many of the words mean, and this makes hiring people who are sensitive to religion news important. William R. Burleigh, who spent more than fifty years at the E. W. Scripps Company, including as president, chief executive officer, and chairman of the board at Scripps Howard Inc., for decades tried to convince editors to improve their religion-news coverage. While he is a traditional Roman Catholic, he didn't do this because he wanted to see more journalists in church. He simply didn't want to see his reporters and editors keep missing news stories that, nationwide, affected millions of people and billions of dollars, and he thought that journalists could do important stories about the "big questions" that linger behind the everyday events of birth, life, marriage, joy, suffering, pain, and death. He maintains that far too many editors get sweaty palms when it comes time to dedicate time, ink, and money to these complex and volatile issues. Few would want to ask religion-related questions during job interviews with prospective reporters and editors. "The prevailing ethos among most of our editors is that the public square is the province of the secular and not a place for religious life and for religious messages to be seen or heard. . . . As a result, lots of editors automatically think religion is out of place in a public newspaper. That's what we are up against."[12]

Let me reemphasize that this is a journalism problem, not a religion problem. If newsroom managers are going to make improvements, one way is through the hiring process. Efforts to improve religion coverage will fail if the people who gather day after day in the newsroom are, as commentator Bill Moyers likes to put it, "tone-deaf" to the music of religion in public life. The laws and structures that govern religious life can be just as complicated and technical as the U.S. government, and there are hundreds of different religious movements and factions in the typical news market, not one or two.

And there is more to religion than laws, facts, creeds, and ecclesiastical structures. Every now and then, a reporter will be covering a picky, boring, tense religious meeting and someone will stand up and start to preach or even pray. The words can be folksy or Byzantine, inspiring or downright strange. Then people may start crying and hugging, or screaming and walking out. Reporters may wonder what they missed. They were covering what appeared to be a political meeting and then someone started to sing sacred songs. They could hear the words but not some of the music that others apparently heard.

Editors do not need to try to hire more reporters who are religious believers, though they shouldn't go out of their way to avoid hiring believers, either. There are religious believers who are good religion-beat specialists, and also total skeptics who are good religion-beat writers. There are believers more committed to plugging their own religious beliefs than to mastering journalistic skills, and skeptics whose skepticism yields more condescension than insight. The goal is to hire journalists who take religion seriously, reporters who know, or are willing to learn to hear the music.

Burleigh found "that it was interesting to talk to reporters and editors about their education. How many people in our newsrooms have actually studied history and art and philosophy and even some theology? How many of them have had any exposure at all to the ultimate questions that people have asked through the ages? I have to admit—quite frankly—I always showed a partiality toward people with that kind of educational background. I didn't do that because I am a big religious guy. I did it because I wanted to know if we were dealing with well-rounded people who could relate to the big questions in life." This may threaten many news professionals who fear that personal interest in or commitment to religious faith is a threat to journalistic objectivity. But it's also possible to turn the equation around. Journalists have to be able to cover stories of faith and also of doubt. They must be able and willing to report accurately the views of people they believe are wrong or even intolerant. It's hard for a newsroom to do a good job of covering religion when it contains few, if any, people who can identify with the lives of believers. We need journalists who can treat religion with empathy and also skepticism, quote people accurately, show respect for the lives of their sources, and stop mangling the technical, yet often poetic, language of religious life.

It will help if editors try to hire reporters who want to do this. Burleigh noted that this strategy makes sense in this era of declining readership and revenues, while the news industry makes a painful transition to digital media. If they care about the future, journalists cannot afford to ignore or misreport stories that are important to the lives of so many readers and viewers. "With editors and publishers, you have to push things back a step or two for them," he said. "When they realize that there is a large and valid audience for solid religion coverage then the economic imperative will kick in and then they will care more about the religion beat. It's that simple or, at least, it should be."

In recent decades, newspaper executives have focused on diversity categories such as race, gender, age, and class. This is important, but many journalists seem unaware of just how much religious diversity exists in most communities. "In most cities, the religious community is like a solar system," says Colon. "You may have one group that is so large that it is almost like the sun. You have to dedicate much of your coverage to that group or you are not doing your job. You have to do a good job there. Then you have other groups that are like planets—large and small—and some of them even have moons that revolve around them. The goal is to cover all of these groups to some degree. Of course, this means that your editors and reporters have to know their way around the solar system." Indeed, it may help if the newsroom contains journalists who are natives of some of these planets or who have visited them from time to time. It would be hard to cover New York City without a few reporters who regularly attend a synagogue or to appeal to readers in Dallas without a reporter or two who frequents the pews of a Southern Baptist church. Do Los Angeles bureaus contain any Hispanic Pentecostals, either Catholic or Protestant?

Of course, each media market offers its own challenges, its own combination of religious groups, and it's hard to navigate all of these complex religious systems without knowing the language, the culture, the doctrines, the history, and the phobias of the people who live there. How are reporters and editors supposed to get up to speed and learn all of that? There are resources such as the Poynter Institute, the Religion Newswriters Association, the Pew Research Center, the Ethics and Public Policy Center, the Oxford Centre for Religion and Public Life, and ReligionLink.org, in addition to colleges and university programs to help journalists serious about getting additional training, if editors will let them. There are also on-the-job educational opportunities.

Kelly McBride, who teaches ethics at Poynter, recounts writing a series of news features about life for gay and lesbian Christians in a wide range of pews—from mainline Presbyterians to Baptists, Unitarians to Catholics. She had articulate sources on the liberal side, people willing to state their views and share details of their lives, but was weak on the Christian conservative side. So she called a trusted evangelical Protestant source and asked: "What am I missing? How would people in your church talk about these issues?" The evangelical pastor called a husband and wife who had both struggled with homosexuality in their own lives. Now, in addition to being the parents of six children, they were counselors in a ministry working with others wrestling with same-sex attractions. The couple agreed to talk to McBride and that led to an interview with another evangelical who agreed to discuss his struggles. This gave a new perspective to the series, one very controversial in liberal churches.[13]

She says the success of the series was that she questioned her own research by using what her colleagues call the "stakeholder" principle. McBride teaches students that in most news stories there are people uniquely invested in the subject being reported. These "stakeholders" are not merely interested in a story, they are deeply touched by it, and "the hotter the story, the more you want to make that 'stakeholder' group as big as possible." "Knowing who the stakeholders are is one of the skills of making good ethical decisions. You can get better at ethical decision-making—period—and you will do better journalism around religious and cultural issues, because you will start to anticipate the negative consequences of your stories. . . . If your stakeholders keep saying that your stories don't ring true, you need to listen to them."

Ostling is convinced that editors who truly want high-quality coverage will strive to build a team of professionals to handle religion news, including at least one trained, experienced specialist. This may be impossible at smaller newspapers and in almost all broadcast newsrooms. But that doesn't mean that editors and producers have to settle for a haphazard approach. The key is to designate at least one person who will remain connected to the beat as a reporter or editor, serving as an "institutional memory." "You have to have someone who is taking the calls, filing the information and following local trends. . . . If you don't do that, then you are going to have stories explode on you. You're going to miss stories and make mistakes that you don't need to make. It's like politics or business or education or any other important beat. You have to have some kind of continuity."[14]

The same is true in television and radio. The number of reporters working in the typical broadcast newsroom is usually small, but this doesn't mean that managers cannot find reporters interested in religion news, get them the extra training they need, and then allow them to serve as resources to the larger news operation. Ostling says, "So many television stations are stuck in the dark ages when it comes to religion. You have to have someone who keeps a file of telephone numbers. You have to have someone who knows how to spell words like 'pope' and 'archdiocese.' . . . There are religion stories, after all, that you must cover. You may not be able to afford a specialist, but you have to have *someone* who will not mess up the basics."

Part of the problem is that many senior editors reach their posts by excelling as political reporters. Thus, elite newspapers emphasize political news. Most editors also see waves of focus-group statistics about the importance of high-quality coverage of sports, entertainment, and "lifestyle" news and so try to improve coverage on these beats, and every editor knows she can't afford to botch local news stories. However, Steven Waldman, previously national editor of *U.S. News & World Report* and national correspondent for *Newsweek,* now editor-in-chief of Beliefnet.com, maintains that religion is harder for editors to grasp. They see church disputes and try to turn them into political stories. They see stories about the growth of new congregations and movements and turn them into stories about polls, statistics, and trends. Some religion stories are off their radar screens. "Some of the best religion stories have to do with the most mundane, everyday, ordinary events in life—birth, death, marriage, depression, hope, thanksgiving, salvation. That's not the stuff of breaking news," he notes. "But editors have to grasp that . . . to get at the stuff of people's lives, then we are going to have to find a way to cover the big stories that are not hard news. This is where religion has its power and that cuts against everything that editors are taught to believe. . . . How do you keep score when you are talking about stories of faith? How do you determine who won and who lost? What's the final score, when you are talking about issues that people have been wrestling with for centuries and centuries? . . . If you are covering the election of a new pope, then where do you go to cover the Iowa caucuses? That's how editors think."[15]

Editors and publishers can insist that their company's research departments ask questions about religious affiliations, activities, and beliefs and have the results circulated in their newsrooms. "Editors shouldn't even be in a newsroom if they aren't doing this," says McBride. "When you are seeking to serve your community, one of the things that you have to know is who *is in* your community. What does it mean if you cannot look at your community and have some idea what the largest faith group is? . . . If you cannot answer these kinds of basic questions then you have a knowledge gap in your newsroom and you need to fix it." Editors hire consultants all the time to help their newsrooms improve skills and solve problems. There is no reason that this approach cannot be applied to religion news.

McBride thinks that there are, however, journalists who have serious hang-ups. "I think that some newsrooms have a clear *inhibition* about covering religion, which is different from just ignorance," she said. "Sometimes it comes from a couple of people who are personally inhibited about religion. They find it distasteful, mysterious, intimidating, weird, silly. . . . If that person is your city editor, then you either have to get that individual some training or figure out another way to balance that out." One way to shed these inhibitions is to escape the newsroom and rub shoulders with true believers. This may be frightening, but it often works.

One example of this is Mark Pinsky, who grew up as a Jew in the Miami and New Jersey suburbs. In the mid-1980s, he began covering religion in Orange County for the *Los Angeles Times*. This was the era of the great televangelism scandals, and Pinsky was covering Robert Schuller of the Crystal Cathedral, Paul and Jan Crouch of the Trinity Broadcasting Network, and other top evangelicals. For him it was like covering an exotic tribe, and he says he assumed that he could get to know the faithful by studying the superstars. This top-down approach seemed natural, since he lived in what he called a "quaint, cosmopolitan beach community" in Los Angeles County—far from the evangelical fortresses.

Then, in 1985, he traveled across the country to cover religion for the *Orlando Sentinel*. Suddenly, evangelicals were next door, in the same PTA meetings, chatting with him in grocery checkout lines ("Where do *you* go to church?") and organizing most of the birthday parties in his zip code. The Pinsky family doctor kept a New Testament in each dressing room and loved to talk about church missionary projects. Even the local Catholics spoke in tongues and waved their hands in the air when they prayed. He wrote, "While evangelicals are part of a varied theological landscape in California, they *are* the landscape in

Florida. . . . I found myself in a very different Orange County. The most ubiquitous bumper sticker was not for a commercial rock station; it was for one
devoted to contemporary Christian music. In addition to being a tourist Mecca,
Orlando was becoming a New Jerusalem for international evangelical organizations, much like Colorado Springs. Reflexively, I returned to my top-down
ways, making up for lost time by doing articles about influential para-church
organizations like Campus Crusade for Christ and Wycliffe Bible Translators
that had by then migrated from southern California to central Florida."[16]

However, he began to move beyond the top-down model and began visiting local churches, listening to what people said and comparing this to how
they lived. As it turned out, his neighbors were rather complex. They were
"more likely to be overzealous than hypocritical" and, although they shared
a conservative approach to faith, he found interesting variations in how this
affected their views of politics, culture, and other newsworthy topics. And, to
his shock, Pinsky discovered that, as a parent, he identified with many of their
fears about a "pervasive, popular culture" that baptizes children in a "toxic mix
of loveless sexuality and senseless violence." He concluded that evangelicals
were a "discrete universe" that deserved in-depth coverage, especially if he
wanted his newspaper to attract and retain Orlando readers.

> Evangelicals were no longer caricatures or abstractions. I learned
> to interpret their metaphors and read their body language. From
> personal, day-to-day experience I observed what John Green at
> the University of Akron has discerned from extensive research:
> evangelicals were not monolithic nor were they, as the Washington
> Post infamously characterized them, 'poor, uneducated and easy
> to command.' . . . This is not to say that I agree with them. . . . Yet
> neither does it keep me from understanding the sincerity of their
> beliefs, or from reporting them fairly. I may be flattering myself, but
> over time I think I have developed a relationship of mutual trust and
> mutual respect with the evangelical community and its leaders.[17]

He also, while maintaining his journalistic independence, decided to try to
write stories that evangelicals themselves would see as accurate and insightful.

Many believers are convinced that most reporters are biased against all
religious-truth claims, especially those based on personal experience. One reason is that many reporters strongly believe that their stories must be based on
facts and that personal claims of religious experience don't really qualify. Faced
with people who say that God answers their prayers, reporters often close their
notepads. The late Peter Jennings of ABC News Tonight put it the following

way. Everyone has seen camera crews descend on the wreckage after a disaster. Inevitably, a reporter confronts a survivor and asks: "How did you get through this terrible experience?" As often as not, the survivor replies: "I don't know. I just prayed. Without God's help, I don't think I could have made it." What follows, noted Jennings, is an awkward silence. "Then reporters ask another question that, even if they don't come right out and say it, goes something like this: 'Now that's very nice. But what *really* got you through this?'" For most viewers, he said, that tense pause symbolizes the "faith gap" between journalists and, statistically speaking, most of the ordinary Americans that they cover day after day.[18]

Many religion stories involve different kinds of "facts" and different kinds of truth claims. It may be impossible to verify that God answers prayers, but it's certainly possible to verify the fact that millions of people believe in answered prayers and that this affects their actions in private and in public life. Journalists who ignore religious-truth claims will be flying blind and missing many important religion stories on the religion beat. As McBride puts it, "We miss a lot of stories because . . . not everybody thinks that everything has to have a scientific cause and effect, a proven relationship. So part of what we have to do . . . is to stop looking for some kind of an a plus b plus c equals d sequence and start asking questions that elicit stories about faith and religious experiences."

Although this storytelling approach is valid, it obviously has its dangers, perhaps producing fuzzy stories about the private beliefs of individuals or small, eccentric flocks. Steward Hoover suggests the danger with this approach is that "you turn religion totally into something completely private and personal. You ignore its power in the public square and you fail to deal with reality." This is why some journalists say they want to write about "spirituality" instead of "religion." Hoover notes that journalists might use a " 'just let people talk about what faith means to them' approach to minimize the public power of religion. You end up with lots of individual religious voices, but very few facts." It's important to escape the old straitjacket in which all religion news was crafted to resemble political reports about denominational infighting, and important to write about spiritual trends in popular culture, but it's also important to report on religious leaders and their organizations marching into the public square. "The stereotype is that religion news is all about the heart and that journalism is supposed to be all about the head. The reality is that religion news, and lots of other kinds of stories worth telling, is about both."[19]

To return to the question of hiring. When trying to land my first religion-writing job, I called the late George Cornell of the Associated Press for advice on what it takes to be a good religion-beat reporter. The first thing he said was that you had to prove that you were a good reporter—not a religion reporter, but a reporter. It also helped to have studied religion, formally or on your own: the beat was complex, and it was hard to avoid mistakes. But it was worth the effort, although it might be hard to convince some editors of that. He also suggested studying the annual list of the Associated Press's top ten news stories and noting how, year after year, most seemed to have some kind of religion hook.

There are, however, newsroom managers who believe that religion news is best covered by reporters who are not specialists, by newcomers who offer what some consider a fresh, blank-slate approach and fewer preconceptions. Debates on this issue often return to a highly symbolic event in 1994, when *Washington Post* editors posted a notice for a religion reporter, seeking applicants from within the newsroom. The "ideal candidate," it said, is "not necessarily religious nor an expert in religion."[20] Professional religion writers often argue about the pluses and minuses of religious believers working on this beat, and the arguments won't end any time soon. Since believers and non-believers can both do excellent work, including fair and accurate coverage of faiths radically different from their own, the *Post* editors are correct that the "ideal candidate" is "not necessarily religious." What is controversial is the statement that the "ideal candidate" is not necessarily "an expert in religion." They were, in effect, arguing that a lack of expertise and experience can be a plus—a virtue—when covering religion news.

It's hard to imagine *Post* editors seeking a Supreme Court reporter and posting a notice saying that the "ideal candidate" is one who is "not necessarily an expert on legal issues," or similar notices seeking reporters to cover professional sports, opera, science, film, and politics. Russell Chandler, a pioneer religion reporter who won numerous national awards for his work with the *Los Angeles Times*, argues, "The religion beat is too complicated today for this kind of approach to be taken seriously. You need experience and if you don't have experience you have to pay your dues and get some. Then you have to keep learning. . . . I have never really understood what this argument is about. It's like saying that we want to sign up some people for our basketball team and we don't really care whether or not they can play basketball or even if they want to play at all. Everything will be OK, because we'll teach them to play the way we want them to play."[21] The way for newsroom executives to improve religion coverage is to take precisely the same steps they would take to improve coverage on any other complicated, crucial theme: hiring qualified specialty reporters and giving them the resources necessary to do their jobs. If there are no such applicants, find a dedicated reporter interested in learning.

Chandler maintains that, in an era in which religious facts, symbols, and themes are woven through story after story in both international and domestic news, editors should be raising the bar for qualifications, not lowering it.

Religion is almost always part of trends from fashion to family life, from popular culture to business, from science to diplomacy, and the very nature of religious belief and practice may be changing as well. "I don't mean to sound like Armageddon, but we are seeing how people differ not only in what they believe, but how they get the information that informs those beliefs. This is going to affect every single world religion and the turf that it occupies. You cannot talk about globalization without facing the religious component of all of these changes."

America's best-known commentator on religion goes further. Martin Marty of the University of Chicago says there was a time when editors could afford to debate questions such as "What is religion news?" and "Do we need to hire a specialist to cover it?" But now journalists should be asking a more demanding question: "In the wake of September 11, is there any news today that *is not* religion news?" He thinks the question is especially intimidating for mainstream journalists who tended to believe that every time they looked out their newsroom windows "there was going to be less religion around than there was before." These journalists were wrong and they were also wrong if they believed that whatever "leftover religion" survived in the postmodern age was "going to be tolerant, concessive, mushy and so on. . . . We are past that, right now. We are now dealing with issues that all journalists are going to have to try to understand. . . . The horizons of religion and the news have touched and we all have to realize that."[22]

9

Getting It Right

Roberta Green Ahmanson

When I walked into the newsroom on October 31, 1984, my editor called me over and said something like: "Whatever you planned for today, forget it. Indira Gandhi was shot by her Sikh guards. Find out why. Find the Sikhs in Orange County and see what they think about it. Then find the Hindus and see what they think. By six." It never occurred to me to wonder why I, a religion reporter, got the biggest story of the day, though, clearly, whatever else it was, it was a religion story. It wasn't until about twenty years later that a friend who had been managing editor at a Gannett paper said to me: "Rob, don't you realize you were probably the *only* religion reporter in the whole country who got that story?"

I still don't know why I got it. Maybe they figured I was the only one in the newsroom who had any idea what a Sikh was. Or knew how to find them, let alone Hindus, in Orange County, California.

Since at least I knew that Singh was a common Sikh last name, I opened the phone book and started dialing Singhs. Because the first five or six people I called referred me to a spokesman for the community, a Dr. Wadhwa, I called him. I got one quote that hit the wires and crossed the country. "I would have been surprised if no assassination attempt was done within the next few months," he said. "Indira Gandhi was a bad politician. She was like a Hitler."[1] There it was, the lead quote, the top of the story. Then I had to find out the rest.

The story was that Indira Gandhi had died for her faith: not her Hindu faith, for she had little, if any. Certainly not her Sikh faith, for she had none. Instead, she died for her faith in the necessity and healing power of secularism. That is a story most of the press missed. Instead, the dominant story line was a political one. A paragraph from *Newsweek* on November 12, 1984, was repeated in various forms in every press report I read, from the *New York Times* and the *Washington Post* to the *Los Angeles Times*, the *Boston Globe*, *Time*, and *U.S. News:*

> The assassination of Indira Gandhi was an act of pure and pointless vengeance—the life of India's prime minister in payment for the lives that were lost last June when she sent her Army to root out the armed Sikh separatists who had holed up in the Golden Temple of Amritsar, their holiest shrine. "We have taken our revenge," boasted the inevitable anonymous caller. "Long live the Sikh religion!"[2]

The quote did point out that her killers had killed in the name of Sikh religion, but in the story line this was subordinated to the idea that it was a political fight: the story was covered as politics, as political revenge for attacks. But it didn't explain why many so many Sikhs actually thought they needed to be at war with Indira Gandhi nor why she was in a war with Sikhism, a faith that proved stronger than her guards' loyalty to secular tradition. Nor was the story connected to the growing worldwide struggle between deepening religious faith and the not-infrequent rigidity of secular intellectual elites in the face of this explosion.

I think that, for at least that day, we got the story right, and have wondered in the years since why others did not recognize what was going on in India. In Chapter 8, "Getting Religion in the Newsroom," Terry Mattingly described some of the problems in the newsroom that get in the way of reporting on religious matters and made some suggestions for improving coverage. Here I would like to look at some of the newsroom habits of the mind, and maybe of the heart, that get in the way, and make some suggestions for how we should think about religion.

The Road to Assassination

The Indira Gandhi assassination story began in 1500, when Guru Nanak melded Hinduism and Islam to create the new Sikh religion affirming one god, reincarnation, and an end to the caste system. Persecuted by Muslim Mogul emperors, Sikhs responded by becoming strong warriors and created a fighting brotherhood called the Khalsa. For a time in the nineteenth century they controlled the Punjab state. The British defeated them in 1848, and from that time

Sikh warriors were loyal soldiers of the British Crown. In the early twentieth century, however, Sikhs supported independence, hoping for greater autonomy for their region. In 1966, shortly after Indira Gandhi first became prime minister, her government separated the Punjab into two states, the "Punjab," which was majority Sikh, and "Haryana," which was majority Hindu. They shared a capital, Chandrigarh.

In the 1970s the Punjab and its Sikh farmers nurtured the "green revolution" that enabled India to feed its own population without imports, and the state became wealthy.[3] However, Sikhs were troubled by several things. They resented the federal government investing in industry in poorer areas and not in the Punjab, they didn't like having their river water diverted to other provinces, they weren't happy about sharing their capital city, and they wanted recognition for their Punjabi language. But, underneath all these concerns was their unhappiness that India's 1947 constitution had defined their religion merely as a sect within Hinduism. Sikhs feared being absorbed into Hindu culture and losing the meaning of their history, and, as one step in self-protection, they wanted their religion to be independently recognized in the constitution. As they saw it, they were fighting for their identity.

In the late 1970s, a Sikh party, Akali Dal, took a nonviolent approach to greater autonomy. But after it was defeated in 1980 by Indira Gandhi's Congress Party, a more militant movement arose, led by Jarnail Singh Bhindranwale, who some reporters have compared to a Sikh version of radical Islamists.[4] Often called "the guiding light," Bhindranwale used Sikh temples, including the most important one, the venerable Golden Temple, as sanctuaries and military training grounds to further his goal to free Sikhs from the corrupting influences of both Hindus and the West through self-rule, either as an independent state or as an Indian province with great autonomy.[5] In 1983 a series of strikes followed by off-and-on talks between Akali Dal and the national government, and Sikh attacks on Hindus—including pulling them off trains to beat or murder them—led to the Punjab being put under direct rule from Delhi in October. Violence increased and militant Sikhs said they would continue until concessions were made; they also threatened to burn the offending Article 25 of the constitution. After more than 570 people had been killed, in June 2004, Indira Gandhi placed the army in charge of security in the Punjab.[6]

After days of fighting, on June 6 Gandhi ordered the Army, which included soldiers of all religions and was led by a Sikh general, to attack the Golden Temple. When the dust settled, Bhindranwale was dead, as were at least 500, perhaps 1,000, others.[7] In the following days, the State was shut down, borders sealed, and all press excluded except by special invitation. Thousand of Sikhs were rounded up. Across northern India, between 2,000 and 5,000 Sikh soldiers mutinied, one group even killing their commanding officer.[8] Of course, Gandhi received death threats, but that was nothing new; she had been hit by bottles and debris in every one of her political campaigns.[9] When warned by her advisors to take the precaution of transferring her Sikh guards, she refused. She replied with a scrawled note saying that if she dismissed her guards on religious grounds, "How can we claim to be secular?"[10]

On the morning of October 31, on her way to an interview with British actor Peter Ustinov, Gandhi greeted her familiar guards—Beant Singh and Satwant Singh. Beant then fired his pistol and Satwant immediately pumped thirty rounds from an automatic into her. She was rushed to a nearby hospital and pronounced dead later in the day.[11] One the same day, Hindus attacked Sikhs in at least eight cities.[12] Nationwide the death toll was more than one thousand, while sixteen thousand or more fled to refugee centers.[13]

What Reporters Missed

A November 1 *Washington Post* editorial said that "ethnic strains" produced Gandhi's murder, though the Sikhs' concerns had more to do with religion than ethnicity.[14] Most papers described Gandhi's commitment to the secular nature of India's democracy, and many editorials praised it. The *Boston Globe* concluded that "all Indians of good will" would be likely to support Rajiv Gandhi's goal of "defending secularism in Indian society."[15]

But "secularism" can have a wide range of meanings. Behind Gandhi's scrawled note was the fact that, like her father Nehru, India's first president, she had no time for religion. Nehru was convinced that a secular state was the only solution to the deep rifts between religious communities. Similarly, Indira often cited her own family as a model of modern India; Hindu by birth, she had married a Parsi, and each of her sons had married outside Hinduism, one to an Italian Catholic. Her refusal to remove Sikh guards came out of a lifelong commitment to secularism as the foundation of the new India and of her political life.[16] But a wise secularism should govern with recognition of the power of religion, and India has many other currents that need to be recognized. A little more than a decade later, from 1998 to 2004, the Hindu nationalist Bharatiya Janata Party (BJP) came to power at the federal level—and the BJP is still dominant in several governments at the state level. Under the BJP the persecution of India's religious minorities deepened.

In the years before Gandhi's death, religious questions and conflicts had increased throughout the world: 283 American soldiers were killed in Lebanon; the Ayatollah Khomeini consolidated his power in Iran; in Egypt Anwar Sadat was assassinated. These events gave reason to wonder about and recognize the connections between religion and public life, even terrorism. As I researched the Gandhi story, Lewis Snider, chair of International Relations at Claremont Graduate School, told me, "There was a perception on the part of a large number of Sikhs that Indira Gandhi's policy was threatening their identity. . . . Because their culture is so closely bound up with their religion, you get such fervor."[17] Then he added something that situated Gandhi's murder, back in 1984, at the heart one of the major factors fueling conflict across the globe to this day: one root of "religious terrorism" is a growing rift between leaders trying to create a secular state, and the deepening religious commitments of the majority of their people.[18] Secular ruling elites often do not know how to cope with or even comprehend the increasingly religious human beings in their own countries or around the world. A similar comment can be made about many journalists; they often do not know how to cope with or comprehend the increasingly religious human beings in their own countries or around the world.

Looking for Answers

One reason that many in the media, not to mention political leaders such as Gandhi, act as if and, in her case, stake their lives on the idea that religion does not, or at least should not, matter in public life is suggested in the sociology of religion. In 1967 the American sociologist Peter Berger wrote that, as modernity advanced, religion would die away. He defined secularism as "the process by which sectors of society and culture are removed from the domination of religious institutions and symbols."[19] He added that this generally meant that the more education, the less need for religion, and so the future would be secular. However, Berger now admits, quite bluntly, that he was wrong.

> The idea was very simple: the more modernity, the less religion. . . .
> I think it was wrong. And I, along with most people in the field,
> changed my mind about 25 or so years ago, not for some philosophi-
> cal or theological reason, but simply because the empirical evidence
> made it impossible to adhere to this theory.

He also emphasizes that every major religion is globalizing, and that this is particularly so with Islam and Pentecostalism. "We don't live in an age of secularity, we live in an age of explosive, pervasive religiosity."[20] "Strongly felt religion has always been around. . . . [T]he phenomena under consideration here on one level simply serve to demonstrate continuity in the place of religion in human experience." In other words, from sociology's point of view, religion has always been part of the landscape, so it should be no surprise that it continues to be. What is mysterious is why some people, particularly in the academy, had not recognized this.[21]

One reason is that, alongside massive global religion, there are also other groups, particularly "a relatively thin, but very influential, stratum of people internationally, broadly speaking an intelligentsia, who is secular. . . . In many countries, including the United States, this intelligentsia or cultural elite . . . is very much in conflict with the religious populace."[22] There are, in turn, several reasons that this elite, which includes many journalists, is secular, and also often threatened by religion. To begin with, religion's content is no longer considered a genuine source of knowledge. In some places this line of thinking goes even further, and even the concept of knowledge itself is considered a problem: particularly in parts of the academy, it may be regarded as hegemonic and imperialistic, a means of control, a limit to freedom, something bad. This gives two strikes against religion, and there is also a third: Since religion is usually also inextricably intertwined with morality, another means of control, the very suggestion that religion might be a proper source of knowledge, and of power, can be terrifying.

There have been many stages to this process. The European "wars of religion" broke up the more or less unified Western church into competing denominations and gave a sharper edge to the already existing medieval quest to justify political authority in ways apart from revelation. The growth of industrialization and capitalism produced a new and complex world very different from the agrarian context in which much of Christian ethics had been shaped, and so made them seem irrelevant. Education began to take on a life of its own apart from ecclesiastical control.[23] Though there were arguments and debates, this change in the understanding of religion did not come about through a concrete series of arguments that one side won and the other lost. It happened more because of a cultural shift, a change in the zeitgeist. Although until the nineteenth century, it was thought that there was a body of knowledge about how to lead a moral life, today that idea often is treated as ludicrous. Today ethics is commonly perceived as a set of issues to be examined, certainly not a set of principles that could be agreed on as authoritative. And religion itself is thought no longer to have anything to say about reality.

In the United States, since major religious groups supported the idea of individual freedom, including religious freedom, and were open to modern developments, ideas critical of religion had much less effect. The First Amendment expressed a national consensus and, sociologically speaking, the Protestant churches functioned as the de facto state religion. But, by the end of the nineteenth century, there were gaping holes in the edifice. After the Civil War, religion rapidly lost cultural traction. First, the educated classes just didn't see what religion had to do with the needs of an expanding industrial society. Second, religion wasn't thought to foster open inquiry for meeting those needs. Third, conflicts within and between churches over doctrine and practice made it clear that lots of things churches taught had to be wrong. Finally, Christian leaders who rejected credible scientific findings, such as geological evidence about the age of the Earth, provided the last straw. Religion was thought to be superstitious and reactionary.[24] By the 1880s religious views were widely considered irrelevant to scientific knowledge, and by the 1890s a secular view governed higher education. Christian Smith concludes: "These two transformations, effectively excluding religion from the core institutions of socially legitimate knowledge production and distribution, were the most crucial in the process of secularizing American public life."[25] By the 1920s these ideas had captured American popular culture, one example being H. L. Mencken's coverage of Clarence Darrow and William Jennings Bryan in the Scopes Monkey Trial in 1925. There the school board actually won the right to fire a teacher for teaching evolution, but the Darwinists won the public relations war.

With the help of the wealth created by exploding capitalism and an expanding state, the knowledge class grew by leaps and bounds. "Between 1870 and 1930, the number of Americans gainfully employed in knowledge class occupations [editors, journalists, college professors, lawyers, welfare workers, artists] . . . grew more than nine times, an increase of more than twice the rate of growth of the total American labor force."[26] Many of them, more than ten thousand between 1815 and 1914, were educated in Germany, where the more radical changes described above had occurred. By the 1920s "the old Victorian struggles with religious doubt had finally been replaced with a distinct cultural sense, among social elites and beyond, of religion's mere irrelevance."[27] Today, those who express religious convictions are often labeled as uneducated, uncultivated people. Smith concludes: "In the end . . . becoming and remaining a good member of the intellectual community requires leaving religion behind and below—or at the very least, keeping it privately within."[28]

Journalists Take the Cue

For many journalists, who have in recent decades moved up the social scale and become part of the knowledge class, that has come to mean that religion is not a credible explanation for human behavior. Reporters often look for motives for actions in money, sex, ambition, and power, but not in religion, not in what people believe about God. Religion is thought to be properly private, having nothing to do with wider realities, and when it does intrude on those realities it is usually perceived as dangerous.

I felt this personally when, in 1983, as a fellow in the Program in Religious Studies for Journalists at the University of North Carolina, one night, over food and drinks, I was asked to explain my upbringing in the Baptist Church and how I had become disillusioned by the legalism of the Bible college I had attended for two years. I'd quit going to church for a while and read Camus, Sartre, Hermann Hesse, F. Scott Fitzgerald, Hemingway, and so on. This fit the dominant paradigm. But then I added that, after reading C. S. Lewis, Dorothy Sayers, T. S. Eliot, John Donne, the Bible, and biblical criticism, I thought that Christianity still offered the best explanation for reality. There was a long silence, then, Marge Hyer, then religion reporter for the *Washington Post,* said, "But you're intelligent!"

Studies back up that personal experience. There are arguments in these studies about the exact degree of secularity among journalists, but the general agreement is that they are far more secular in outlook than are their readers. This can produce problems. Richard Ostling, then religion reporter for *Time* magazine, told that same seminar group that, in the 1970s, he had repeatedly warned his editors that they should watch the Ayatollah Khomeini (then in Paris) and that something big was going to happen, but he said that they just laughed at him since they thought Shiite militancy was "just a religious movement." This had a partially happy ending, for Ostling, if not for the Iranians. In 1979 the Shah fled Iran, and the Ayatollah and his followers seized power and took Americans hostage. Ostling's stock immediately went up, and he was made a contributing editor.

The rise of militant Islam, evidenced by men willing to fly passenger airplanes into buildings, killing themselves and thousands of others, has made even secular reporters and editors think twice about ignoring religion. Michael Rubin's and Paul Marshall's essays in this book explain just how much journalists have missed. However, although we live in postmodern times, and we usually accept that each person has his or her own story, his or her own narrative, what do we do with others' narratives that we don't understand easily or like very much? What about Osama bin Laden's narrative; does it make any sense? Or a narrative that argues that same sex-unions are not equivalent to heterosexual marriage, or that there is an Intelligent Designer behind the universe? Each is a narrative and an issue rooted in a description of reality linked to religion. Will we report on them as simply irrational, or will we report the content of the arguments?

One area where this problem surfaces is in reporting on evangelicals, often described, and reduced to political terms with which journalists are more comfortable, as the "religious Right." Alan Hertzke's chapter describes one example of this: a human rights movement ignored or misunderstood because it includes supporters from the "religious Right." Hertzke's essay also provides an example of something else that Peter Berger is concerned about—the dearth of conversation between evangelical intellectuals and America's secular elite. "There are about 80 million Americans who consider themselves Evangelicals, and if they are shut out of respectable intellectual discourse, that is not a healthy situation," Berger said. He added that the term "culture war" refers to something real in the United States—"a heavily religious population with a highly secular elite."[29]

In May 2007 *Washington Post* religion writer Alan Cooperman was following up a two-year-old story about a Missouri State University student charged with discrimination by a faculty committee. Her sociology professor had assigned each student to write a letter supporting adoption by same-sex couples and to sign it. The student refused because of her Christian convictions and was brought before the faculty, but the outcry in her defense was so great that the charge was dropped and her graduate school fees were paid. This helped lead to the state's house of representatives passing a law requiring public universities to monitor "viewpoint discrimination." In his update, Cooperman reported something very troubling: 53 percent of a sample of 1,200 college and university faculty from public and private institutions across the country said they had "unfavorable feelings" toward evangelical Christians. This finding emerged from a study sponsored by the San Francisco–based Institute for Jewish and Community Research that was principally looking for signs of anti-Semitism.[30]

Those findings launched a hot debate. The institute's director and chief pollster, Gary A. Tobin, said: "There is no question this is revealing bias and prejudice." The president of the American Association of University Professors, Cary Nelson, disagreed. This wasn't prejudice, he said, but rather "a political and cultural resistance, not a form of religious bias." Nelson gave two reasons for this resistance: "the particular kind of Republican Party activism that some evangelicals have engaged in over the years, as well as what faculty perceive as the opposition to scientific objectivity among some evangelicals." Here Nelson ties evangelicals to the "religious Right" and so justifies such feelings. But would he also suggest that, since Jews and Hispanics usually vote Democratic (usually in larger proportions than evangelicals vote Republican), then someone who disagrees with Democratic policies would not be guilty of prejudice if they expressed an "unfavorable feeling" toward Jews and Hispanics? Tobin was, correctly, having none of it. "If a majority of faculty said they did not feel warmly about Muslims or Jews or Latinos or African Americans, there would be an outcry," he said. "No one would attempt to justify or explain those feelings."[31]

Similar issues have surfaced in coverage of the intelligent-design movement and led to calls for censoring reports on its proponents. In the *Columbia Journalism Review*, Chris Mooney and Matthew C. Nisbet argued that intelligent design did not deserve to be covered at all. Their concern was not whether any reporters had implied that intelligent-design arguments were true; rather, he argued that some journalists had actually reported what the arguments were. Mooney and Nisbet insisted that such arguments were really religious arguments and were, therefore, not only nonscientific, but could not be counted as arguments at all. They concluded that intelligent design is "a sophisticated religious challenge to an overwhelming scientific consensus." Therefore, "journalistic coverage that helps fan the flames of a nonexistent scientific controversy (and misrepresents what's actually known) simply isn't appropriate."[32] In their view, journalists are not to report what is happening but only what they have decided is "appropriate" for their readers and listeners to know.

Getting It Right

With this muddle, conflict, and frequent misunderstanding, is it possible to understand and report on the religious dimensions of the world and what role religion plays? Clearly, billions of people embrace some kind of faith in God or gods. In America, Gallup polls have found for the last seventy-five years that 40 percent of Americans attend a house of worship once a week. Though some dispute those figures, contending the actual number is lower, the surprising thing is the consistency of the finding over time. But, if reporters do not see religion as a legitimate way of looking at the world, then, as Richard Ostling pointed out in the late 1970s and again in 1983, it can have a high cost.

In these conflicted times and with these issues in mind, here are seven ways journalists might improve coverage of today's world, a world alive with religion.

If we see the world or, at least, human motives, as shaped only by forces of economics, politics, gender, race, and class, then it becomes hard to ask religious questions. The coverage of Indira Gandhi's death in 1984 by and large failed to consider the religious dimensions of her death and so situate the event in a larger, and more revealing, context. The same is true of the coverage of many of the stories on the 2004 election described by Vinson and Guth in their essay. *Hence, we need to broaden our own paradigm of reality so as to include religion as a motivator of human behavior.*

Reporting on religion also requires defining religion, or at least having a basic understanding of what it is. If journalists think it is only some kind of basic irrationality, a purely subjective, esoteric, ethereal flight of fancy, or else simply a mask for power and control, we won't see it as a real factor in the events of the world. Instead we will treat religious adherents as specimens whose real motivations will be revealed by psychology, or else simply as political manipulators. Of course, religion can at times be irrational. But before judging it so, it is important to know that different religions may have their own sophisticated understanding of what rationality really is. Religion can also certainly be used to mask a drive for power, as can most everything else in human life; in fact most religions have extensive and developed teachings and warnings about this danger. Hence, if there are good grounds for thinking that either of these is the case, then, of course, it should be part of the story. But we must avoid a prejudiced approach that assumes a priori that this is what religion in general, or a particular religion, necessarily is. If we instead understand religion as basically how people make sense of reality and how they should act in it, then we have the chance to take its proponents seriously and begin to factor it into the list of questions we ask as we develop a story. *Put in simple terms, religion is what makes it possible for people to get up in the morning and make sense of their reality. We must bear this in mind if we want to understand them.*

This also means that we should, as much as we can, try to describe people in terms that they themselves recognize and that make sense to them. If we, whether we are Christians or atheists, believe that our views are the best description of reality, then we should realize that others probably think the same about their own beliefs. People deserve to have their views of reality reported faithfully. Through careful and respectful listening, it is possible to understand people, from the followers of Bhagwan Shree Rajneesh, to Chan monks, Catholic bishops, Muslim mullahs, fundamentalist pastors, Hasidic rabbis, Sikh activists, and a long list of others. *The key is to be aware that we are entering into another world, likely one precious to the speaker, and to try to represent that world faithfully.*

One of the major stories in the modern world is religious conflict, or conflict between religious and secular views, whether in the former Yugoslavia or in the confrontation with radical Islamist terrorism. But it is usually a mistake to assume that this religious conflict is simply the way the world is, or simply the way that religions are. Religions have coexisted as much as they have fought. Most conflicts are not eternal; they begin somewhere, in some events. Especially in the wake of 9/11, we should surely learn that many in the Muslim world have a much deeper awareness of history than do most people in the West. This isn't to say that they necessarily know it better, but just that they have a historical awareness, and that it matters. No doubt, holding onto some one-sided version of history is one source of conflict in the world, but usually conflicts can be resolved only if we understand their roots. Religion is often one of those roots. It is a vital part of the story of human life on this planet. *We need to look for the story behind the story, the history and the religion that created the present moment.*

Getting to the story behind the story also requires *questioning our own assumptions.* These assumptions can be hard to recognize; they are part of the air we breathe, so common we don't even know we hold them. For example, in the thirteenth and fourteenth centuries, no one doubted that the Earth was in the center of the universe (though not necessarily of the solar system), and so they located themselves at the center of the universe looking out.[33] Today we tend to see ourselves on the edge of the world looking in. C. S. Lewis suggested that a good way to identify our blind spots is to read old books. Not that the old book's authors were necessarily any smarter than we are, or free of assumptions. They too had their blind spots, but the key point is that theirs were different from ours. By reading them we might be able to recognize and break through our own assumptions and get a fuller picture of reality.[34]

We also need to be careful of pack journalism or, the even deeper, tribal journalism. In the West today, tribes can usually be identified by a "shared 'knowledge' of what is taken to be good, right, and obligatory."[35] Christian Smith has argued that many secular intellectuals constitute a tribe and that journalists are a subgroup within it. Stephanie Guttman summarizes the situation this way: "Journalism has been a nervous, conformist industry for some time and is more so [now] than ever because of increased competition. Most of life is really just high school writ large—and the news industry is more high school than most. Insecure editors and publishers look to a paper like the [New York] Times to tell them what is important in the news of the day and even what to think about that news."[36] However, as C. S Lewis noted, "Until you conquer the fear of being an outsider . . . an outsider you will remain."

Finally, though it is a cliché, it still remains true that in religion, as in so much else, the devil really is in the details. It isn't possible to understand religion without making fine but important distinctions. I once did a story trying to explain the major differences between Eastern Orthodox Christians and Roman Catholics. One difference is that the Catholic pope is supreme over all other Church leaders, whereas the ecumenical patriarch is simply first among a group of religiously equal patriarchs. Someone on the night desk didn't think the distinction mattered and changed the story to say that the pope and the patriarch were basically the same. The next day phone banks lit up like Christmas trees with the Catholic and Orthodox faithful demanding a correction. This is not a trivial point—it has been one of the major disagreements and barriers between Eastern and Western Christians.

Journalists, like other human beings—believers, atheists, agnostics—have to learn humility as we learn our differences. Too often, secular people have thought that pluralism means religious people must learn to question their views in order to coexist with unbelievers; too seldom have they realized that the same lesson must be applied to their secular views. We may argue for a God or gods or no god, but we ourselves are not God. In religious terms this realization is often called humility, and it is a virtue of particular value to journalists. In our work we should take a large view, strive to understand what religion is, and try to take seriously an individual's faith or lack of it. As a journalist I thought I was paid to be the "other," standing on the outside looking in; it was my job to question my own assumptions, to get the details right, and to take history seriously. It was with these goals in mind that I determined to find out the real meaning of Indira Gandhi's death.

Afterword

John J. DiIulio Jr.

Every one of America's Founding Fathers understood about religion what too many educated elites, both secular *and* religious, in our day do not: religion, whether organized or not, whether old time or New Age, is a powerful and persistent force in moving people and nations, and is uniquely important when it comes to producing individual beneficence and individual brutality, social cooperation and social strife, civil harmony and civil war.

. Although most were, in fact, Bible-believing Christians in the Anglo-Protestant tradition, the Constitution's creators hardly all sang from the same hymnal on theology or other weighty subjects. But none, from the orthodox sectarian reverend John Witherspoon to the irrepressibly agnostic Benjamin Franklin, took the slightest issue with James Madison's formulation, in the famous tenth essay in what we know as the Federalist Papers, that a "zeal for different opinions concerning religion" merits first mention among the reasons for self-loving "factions" and the perpetual human propensity to "vex and oppress" even people with whom we have much in common and much at stake. Nor did any dispute Madison's belief that religion ranked first among the checks on human depravity that made self-government possible, nor did they doubt the wisdom he showed, in the fifty-first essay, in betting the republic's future on a constitutional regime that was intelligently designed to beget and sustain religious pluralism across a vast and varied national territory stretching from sea to shining sea:

In a free government the security for civil rights must be the same as that for religious rights. It consists in the one case in the multiplicity of interests, and in the other in the multiplicity of sects. The degree of security in both cases will depend on the extent of the country and the number of people comprehended under the same government.

As this book's diverse chapters have combined to argue, for roughly a half century now, our country's leading journalists and top media outlets, print and electronic, have frequently missed or misconstrued just about every significant story about religion in everyday American life, about religion and science, about religion and politics at home, and about religion in world affairs.

This may have happened because many journalists have been led by political ideology or pseudoscientific pretense to castigate religion rather than understand it; or because they have innocently but foolishly imbibed the ahistorical, unempirical, anti-anthropological, and outdated sociology predicting that "modernity" would render religion irrelevant in the near future; or because, even as leading secular and nonsectarian scholars in just about every field, including the natural sciences, social sciences, and humanities, have begun to take religion seriously, they have lacked the intellectual self-confidence to do the same. Whatever the reasons, nobody can reasonably doubt either that religion *has* been routinely relegated by even many otherwise admirable and fair-minded journalists to a limbo of lesser civic significance than its sheer importance commands, or that religion *has* been more doubted or damned than dispassionately researched and reported on by lesser journalists whose actual knowledge, as distinct from their prejudices, concerning religion is next to nil.

Rather than rework what the reader already knows from this volume's authors, and with due regard for the differences in emphasis and outlook that attend but do not attenuate their overarching consensus on the subject, permit me to briefly flesh out three "headline" stories about religion that journalists need to work on but generally have missed or misconstrued. I will also seek to pluck the beam from my own first "faith czar's" eye and underline the need for not only the "secular" but also the now-extensive "religious press" to do a better, more responsible job too.

Headline: Evangelicals Everywhere, Orthodox Believers Here to Stay

As numerous scholars, led by Penn State's Philip Jenkins, have documented, orthodox Christianity is the world's fastest-growing religion. Its growth in the southern hemisphere is all the more impressive because it encompasses diverse denominations, from Catholics to Pentecostals.[1] Europe is the secularized exception, not the twenty-first-century rule. Even Europe is undergoing in-migration and other changes that might well bring it back into the religious community of nations.

Even though ostensibly sharp geopolitical thinkers such as former U.S. secretary of state Henry Kissinger failed to adequately account for religion's importance in international affairs (his thousands of pages of memoirs and related books contain few references to religion), the prolific and prudent senior fellow at the Council on Foreign Relations (CFR) whose fellowship chair carries Kissinger's name, Walter Russell Mead, gets religion. So does his colleague at the CFR, and the author of this volume's foreword, Michael Gerson. And so do ever more foreign policy experts who are inclined to practice what I have written and preached about under the rubric *spiritualpolitique*, a "soft power" approach to America's role abroad. This approach calls for a big push for unilateral humanitarian intervention projects (for example, multi-billion-dollar anti-malaria initiatives and other huge public health projects) mediated by religious nongovernmental organizations.

Here in America, most citizens believe in God and are affiliated with a particular religion. Evangelical Christians, in every valid survey and demographic measure, number well above fifty million. Depending on definitional boundaries, born-again believers have as many as eighty million (and counting) co-religionists. In-migration and higher-than-national-norm birthrates ensure that this population will be larger, in both red states and in blue states, in the decades ahead.

Within the socioeconomically vast and varied evangelical citizenry, there have been, and continue to be, intergenerational differences in opinions on many issues, and there are new, younger leadership cadres who care lots about fighting poverty and environmental protection, known as "creation care." D. Michael Lindsay's excellent recent study, *Faith in the Halls of Power*,[2] captures many important lessons about the nation's old and new evangelical elites. Still, evangelicals in America, both elites and average citizens, remain conservative on most cultural and social issues and are especially likely to retain pro-life majorities.

In the face of this multitude, many journalists and media outlets seem to bounce between, on the one hand, denying that orthodox believers exist in such huge numbers and spread-out geographies both at home and abroad and, on the other, fearing that they are not only everywhere but also about to take over the country or the world and ravage nonbelievers.

Notably, the *New York Times* seems unable to decide which of these wishes or fears should shape its editorial thoughts about religion in general and evangelicals in particular. For decades it has often downplayed or denied evangelical America's scope, with page-one reporters like Linda Greenhouse giving speeches at secular universities denouncing "fundamentalists" and getting wrist-slapped for the offense. The paper then featured a page-one series "In God's Name" that made erroneous claims about how radically faith-friendly and accommodating toward religion governments at all levels have ostensibly become. In late 2007, it ran a magazine cover story questioning whether it was "End Time for Evangelicals?"[3] What led to this question, echoed the same day on the *Times* editorial page, was that Republicans lost the 2006 midterm congressional elections, born-again Christians had no clear-cut favorite among presidential candidates, and many in the media realized that not all Bible-believing Christians had followed the Moral Majority, marched with the Christian Coalition, or held uniformly ultraconservative or reactionary views.

Headline: Many Top Scientists Love God, Find Faith to Be Pro-Social

Another common assumption is that what separates the secular or nominally religious or mainstream from the untutored and unintelligent is not lifestyle choices, antireligious hang-ups, or secularism, but whether people know and accept science. Journalists may write about evolutionary biology but usually have read little of Darwin or of serious works on science and religion. When faced with a term like "theistic evolution," they often reject it as simply old-time religious "creationism" by another name. But the concept reappears in the 2006 book by Francis Collins, *The Language of God*.[4] Collins is not a "Reverend Collins" but the man who led the international human genome project. Nor is this intelligent design by another name. Collins rejects intelligent design: he is, however, a Bible-believing Christian.

If we turn to medical science, the late, great Dr. David Larson had 270 professional publications, most suggesting that there are links between religion and a variety of positive physical and mental health outcomes, including prevention, recovery, and coping with chronic and serious illness. He, too, was an evangelical. One media figure said to me in 2002 that "real medical researchers" don't buy such spirituality and health findings. Well, the findings are not definitive (nothing much in actual scientific research is), but consider that in 1992 only three medical schools in America had Larson-style spirituality and health programs, but today more than 140 do, schools with nonsectarian names such as Harvard and Penn among them.

In social science, eminent scholars from Harvard's Robert D. Putnam to UCLA's James Q. Wilson have summarized the massive evidence suggesting that religion, whether measured by association memberships, philanthropy, or volunteering, is by far America's most significant, pro-social civic seedbed. That includes faith-based organizations that produce what Putnam calls "bridging social capital" by serving nonbelievers or other nonmembers who differ from affiliates by race, socioeconomic status, and other characteristics. Post-1990 "faith factor" research has made converts among cynics and skeptics on topics ranging from crime and delinquency to effective social services delivery. Faith-based organizations and programs, religious individuals and institutions, are among the hottest topics in several social science disciplines.

Headline: The Religious Press Sins, Too

During my time in the White House in 2001, I kept trying to provide journalists with facts not only about community-serving religious congregations, but also on the relevant constitutional "neutrality" law (I've coauthored a leading U.S. government college textbook for years). I also tried to outline the then recent history of the four faith-friendly charitable choice laws signed by President Bill Clinton and how, or, rather, how little, those laws had been implemented via our complex, intergovernmental administrative systems. This, in fact, was my job number one!

With few exceptions, the secular press did not heed my political science lectures and bipartisan sentiments. Indeed, the *Times* would not use the term "faith-based," since that might point toward the truth that most community-serving religious nonprofit organizations, even without any public money or hope of it, served people in need without regard to anybody's religion. Most of those people were, as studies by my Penn colleague Dr. Ram Cnaan have documented, neighborhood children and youth who were not members of the congregations that served them.[5]

There were literally hundreds of stories and broadcasts about the faith-based initiative, but my favorite appeared in *Christianity Today* magazine. John Wilson, the evangelical organ's editor-at-large, entitled it "DiIulio Keeps Explaining, but Is Anybody Listening?"[6] Describing me as "fat, rumpled, plainspoken, funny, and seemingly possessing total recall of hundreds of policy studies," he wrote:

> (Many) of the media queries proceeded as if DiIulio had said nothing, as if the most obvious church-state issues hadn't already been addressed. . . . [He was asked] "what would happen if a church said we will help you, but you have to accept Jesus as your savior." Well, said DiIulio pleasantly, as if this were a perfectly reasonable question, churches can't do that in the context of federally funded programs. And so it went.

But as bad as the secular press often was, the religious press—with the foregoing notable exception and others—was rarely much better and, in fact, was often even worse. For example, it persistently misstated facts about everything from religion in the United States to the evidence on whether spiritual-transformation programs are uniquely efficacious or supremely cost-effective in curing drug addiction and other problems. For almost every ignorant and biased orthodox secularist story about this or that related policy issue, there was an equally ignorant and biased orthodox sectarian story that had the opposite, but no less false, take on the same issue. If the *Times* led the secular media in distorting the initiative as "religion-based," several evangelical-press organs in print, radio, and television used terms like "Christophobic" and played into stereotypes suggesting that faith-based organizations were all indivisibly conversion-centered or faith-saturated.

As former Pennsylvania senator Rick Santorum, a Catholic Republican admired by Christian conservatives, has since remarked, and as Michael Gerson writes in his recent book, *Heroic Conservatism*,[7] the faith-based initiative needlessly became fodder in elite culture-war politics when it could have instead begotten a bipartisan effort to help truly disadvantaged children, youth, and families while reinforcing the religious-freedom rights enjoyed by citizens who lead or staff grassroots religious groups and other community-serving religious nonprofits, large and small, national and local.

For that sinful outcome, the so-called religious press bears as much blame as the so-called secular press. It serves to remind us that good journalism on religion, like civic good works and partnerships involving religion, can be produced by Methodists, Mormons, Muslims, Catholics, Quakers, Jews, people of other faiths, and people claiming no faith at all, including even those who sincerely see religion as a decidedly undesirable or negative force. The same holds for journalism regarding religion, whether secular or sectarian, that misreports unto metastasizing, rather than moderating, the political, social, and other cleavages that are inevitable in a healthy, representative democracy such as ours.

We are one nation, under God, for all. The "all" includes citizens who espouse no religion or strongly eschew religion. While seeking to pluck the beam from secular journalism's eye, religious believers must first pluck the beam from their own. As Madison knew, no faith is beyond faction. Wouldn't it be wonderful if diverse journalists came together to parse a phenomenon like Rick Warren's *Purpose-Driven Life*, or a controversial federal court case like the one involving the Prison Fellowship Ministry program in Iowa, or the results of the 2008 national elections? If secular liberal wordsmiths sat for several days in intellectual and civic fellowship, disagree though they might, with Christian conservative ones? Is that impossible? Memo to all journalists: Most Americans believe in miracles.

Notes

INTRODUCTION

1. Jeff Sharlot "Killing Religion Journalism," *The Revealer*, October 7, 2004.

2. Edward Luttwak, "The Missing Dimension," in Douglas Johnston and Cynthia Sampson, eds., *Religion: The Missing Dimension of Statecraft* (New York: Oxford University Press, 1994), pp. 9–10.

3. Quoted by *Los Angeles Times* media columnist Tim Rutten, March 6, 2004.

4. E. J. Dionne, "A Papacy of Spirit," *Washington Post*, April 5, 2005.

5. "A Chinese Dissident's Faith," *Washington Post*, May 28, 2006.

6. "Don't Say We Didn't Warn You, Lessons They Won't Learn from November 2," *CounterPunch*, November 6/7, 2004. For a good argument that "Anti-fundamentalism" is the only significant form of religious prejudice in America, see L. Bolce and G. DeMaio, "Religious Outlook, Culture War Politics, and Antipathy Toward Christian Fundamentalists," *Public Opinion Quarterly*, vol. 63 (1999), pp. 29–61.

7. "Confessions of an Alienated Journalist: How one journalist sees—or doesn't see—the world," *PoynterOnline*, November 4, 2004.

8. Nicholas Kristof, "A Slap in the Face," *New York Times*, April 12, 2005.

9. Quoted in *Editor and Publisher*, June 26, 2005.

CHAPTER I

A shorter version of this piece appeared as an article in *Foreign Policy* in summer 2006 (see note 3). For help on the article and this chapter, the authors gratefully acknowledge Rachel Mumford, who provided superb research assistance and editorial suggestions, and the participants in the Harvard University Religion in Global Politics Project, from which this paper emerged: Samuel Huntington, Daniel Philpott, Bryan Hehir, Jessica Stern, David Little, James Kurth, Christopher Queen, Sohail Hashmi, and Assaf Moghadam. We also gratefully acknowledge the generous financial support of the Smith Richardson Foundation and the Weatherhead Center for International Affairs.

1. Scott Wilson, "Hamas Sweeps Palestinian Elections, Complicating Peace Efforts in Mideast," *Washington Post,* January 27, 2006; Associated Press, "Bush Urges End to Cartoon Violence," February 8, 2006, available at http://www.iht.com/articles/2006/02/08/news/web.0208bush2.php (accessed June 15, 2008).

2. Sabrina Tavernise, "Alliances Shift as Turks Weigh a Political Turn," the *New York Times,* July 20, 2007. Tavernise notes that "Turkish society has significantly changed in recent decades, with religious Turks gaining wealth and status and moving into public view. Women in head scarves—precisely those whom early Turkish legislation singled out—are in shopping malls, on motor scooters and behind the wheels of cars, and rules against them seem woefully outdated." The article notes the observation of one young person opposed to the military's role in politics "that educated women in head scarves were more likely than their less religious counterparts to know that "Marx" refers to a German philosopher, not the British department store, Marks and Spencer." "This narrow shirt of secularism has become a little too tight and choking for Turkish society," said one policy researcher.

3. Timothy Samuel Shah and Monica Duffy Toft, "Why God is Winning," *Foreign Policy* (July/August 2006): 39–43.

4. Steven R. Weisman, "Rice Admits U.S. Underestimated Hamas Strength," *New York Times,* January 30, 2006.

5. K. M. Panikkar, *Asia and Western Dominance: A Survey of the Vasco Da Gama Epoch of Asian History, 1498–1945* (1952; repr., London: G. Allen & Unwin, 1959).

6. Daniel Lerner, *The Passing of Traditional Society: Modernizing the Middle East* (New York: Free Press, 1958), 45–48, 230.

7. Arnold Toynbee, "Preface," in John Cogley, *Religion in a Secular Age* (New York: Frederick Praeger, 1968), p. xvi. The emphasis is ours.

8. Gilles Kepel, *La Revanche de Dieu: Chrétiens, juifs et musulmans à la reconquête du monde* (Paris: Éditions du Seuil, 1991). Published in English as *The Revenge of God: The Resurgence of Islam, Christianity and Judaism in the Modern World* (Cambridge, UK: Polity, 1994).

9. The religious motivations of many of the 9/11 hijackers are amply documented and perceptively analyzed in Terry McDermott, *Perfect Soldiers: The 9/11 Hijackers: Who They Were, Why They Did It* (New York: HarperCollins, 2005).

10. This view is particularly characteristic of studies that interpret religion's global political resurgence under the rubric of "fundamentalism." See, for example, Martin E. Marty and R. Scott Appleby, eds., *The Fundamentalism Project,* vol. 3, *Fundamentalisms and the State: Remaking Polities, Economies, and Militance* (Chicago: University of Chicago Press, 1993), and Steve Bruce, *Fundamentalism* (Cambridge, UK: Polity, 2000). It is also characteristic of numerous studies of U.S. evangelicalism, such

as those by Randall Balmer: *Blessed Assurance: A History of Evangelicalism in America* (Boston: Beacon, 1999) and *Thy Kingdom Come: How the Religious Right Distorts the Faith and Threatens America, An Evangelical's Lament* (New York: Basic, 2006). For a powerful contrasting perspective, see Christian Smith, *American Evangelicalism: Embattled and Thriving* (Chicago: University of Chicago Press, 1998).

11. R. Scott Appleby, "Religions, Human Rights and Social Change," in Gerrie ter Haar and James J. Busuttil, *The Freedom to Do God's Will: Religious Fundamentalism and Social Change* (London: Routledge, 2003), 200–201.

12. Jim Hoagland, "Facing Faith as Politics," *Washington Post*, January 15, 2006.

13. Assaf Moghadam, "A Global Resurgence of Religion?" (WCFIA working paper 03–03, Weatherhead Center for International Affairs, Harvard University, Cambridge, Massachusetts, September 2003).

14. David B. Barrett, George T. Kurian, and Todd M. Johnson, *World Christian Encyclopedia,* 2nd ed. (New York: Oxford University Press, 2001), p. 4. For our purposes, we have combined the *World Christian Encyclopedia*'s figures for Protestants, Anglicans, and Independent Christians into one "Protestant" category.

15. On recent Protestant growth worldwide and its political implications, see Timothy Samuel Shah, "The Bible and the Ballot Box: Evangelicals and Democracy in the 'Global South,'" *SAIS Review* 24, no. 2 (2004): 117–32.

16. Philip Jenkins, *The Next Christendom: The Coming of Global Christianity* (New York: Oxford University Press, 2002), 79–105.

17. Barrett, Kurian, and Johnson, *World Christian Encyclopedia*, 13–15. Numbers compiled from figures in Table 1–4.

18. Pew Global Attitudes Project, "Among Wealthy Nations, U.S. Stands Alone in Its Embrace of Religion," December 19, 2002, at http://pewglobal.org/reports/display.php?ReportID=167 (accessed June 15, 2008). Argentina was the exception among Latin American countries surveyed, with only 39% responding that religion is "very important" to them.

19. For a summary analysis of the World Values data that draws this conclusion, see Assaf Moghadam, "A Global Resurgence of Religion?"

20. Pew Global Attitudes Project, "Among Wealthy Nations."

21. Assuming the median variant of growth. Population Division of the Department of Economic and Social Affairs of the United Nations Secretariat, *World Population Prospects: The 2004 Revision—Highlights* (New York: United Nations, 2005), 1, 6. At http://www.un.org/esa/population/publications/WPP2004/2004Highlights_final revised.pdf (accessed June 15, 2008).

22. Pippa Norris and Ronald Inglehart, *Sacred and Secular: Religion and Politics Worldwide* (Cambridge: Cambridge University Press, 2004). Also on the correlation between religiosity and fertility rates, see Phillip Longman, "The Return of Patriarchy," *Foreign Policy* (March/April, 2006): 56–65; and Monica Toft, "Differential Demographic Growth in Multinational States: The Case of Israel's Two-Front War," *Journal of International Affairs* 56, no. 1 (2002): 71–94. At the same time, based on the positive link between religiosity and fertility, some scholars argue that even in Europe the religious proportion of the population will grow—perhaps dramatically—in the coming

century. See, for example, Eric Kaufmann, "Breeding for God," *Prospect Magazine* 128 (November 2006), available at http://www.prospect-magazine.co.uk/pdfarticle. php?id=7913 (accessed July 19, 2007).

23. "Is There a Global Resurgence of Religion?" Symposium with Ronald Inglehart and Andrew Kohut, cosponsored by the Pew Forum on Religion and Public Life and the Council on Foreign Relations, National Press Club, Washington, DC, May 8, 2006; transcript available at http://pewforum.org/events/?EventID=116 (accessed July 20, 2007).

24. "Is There a Global Resurgence of Religion?" Symposium with Inglehart and Kohut.

25. For example, see Reginald W. Bibby, *Restless Gods: The Renaissance of Religion in Canada* (Toronto: Stoddart, 2002).

26. Pew Global Attitudes Project, "Among Wealthy Nations"; Pew Global Attitudes Project, "Views of a Changing World," June 3, 2003, T–64, at http://pewglobal. org/reports/display.php?ReportID=185 (accessed June 15, 2008).

27. Andrew Kohut, John C. Green, Scott Keeter, and Robert C. Toth, *The Diminishing Divide: Religion's Changing Role in American Politics* (Washington, DC: Brookings Institution Press, 2000): 28–29.

28. Under the headline, "God Really Is Winning," *Christianity Today* reported on its Web site in 2006 on a major Baylor University survey of religion in the U.S. that found strong evidence of continuing religious vitality among the American people. Among its most interesting findings was that "a fair number of those who claimed 'no religion' in [the] sample were actually active, engaged affiliates of evangelical congregations who were 'screened out' by previous surveys that concentrated on denominational affiliation." Available at http://www.christianitytoday.com/ct/2006/ septemberweb-only/137–21.0.html (accessed July 20, 2007).

29. Freedom House, "Freedom in the World 2007," at http://www.freedom house.org/uploads/press_release/fiw07_charts.pdf (accessed June 15, 2008).

30. United Nations Educational, Scientific and Cultural Organization, Press Release No. 2005–134, "Literacy: A Right Still Denied to Nearly One-fifth of the World's Adult Population," November 9, 2005, at http://portal.unesco.org/en/ev. php-URL_ID=30708&URL_DO=DO_TOPIC&URL_SECTION=201.html (accessed June 15, 2008).

31. United Nations, "The Millennium Development Goals Report 2006" (New York: United Nations), p. 4, at http://mdgs.un.org/unsd/mdg/Resources/Static/ Products/Progress2006/MDGReport2006.pdf (accessed June 15, 2008).

32. Lerner, *Passing of Traditional Society*; Karl W. Deutsch, *Nationalism and Social Communication*, 2nd ed. (Cambridge: MIT Press, 1966); Deutsch predicted the demise of national identity with modernization.

33. Alexis de Tocqueville, *Democracy in America*, trans. and ed. Harvey C. Mansfield and Delba Winthrop (Chicago: University of Chicago Press, 2000), vol. 1, p. 282.

34. Manjari Katju, *Vishva Hindu Parishad and Indian Politics* (Hyderabad, India: Orient Longman, 2003).

35. Monica Duffy Toft, "Religion, Civil War, and International Order," BCSIA Discussion Paper 2006–03 (Cambridge, MA: Belfer Center for Science and International Affairs, John F. Kennedy School of Government, Harvard University, July 2006), available at http://belfercenter.ksg.harvard.edu/publication/2962/religion_civil_war_and_international_order.html (accessed June 15, 2008).

36. Assaf Moghadam, "Suicide Terrorism, Occupation, and the Globalization of Martyrdom: A Critique of *Dying to Win*," *Studies in Conflict & Terrorism* 29 (2006): 707–29; Jessica Stern, *Terror in the Name of God: Why Religious Militants Kill* (New York: Ecco/HarperCollins, 2003); Mark Juergensmeyer, *Terror in the Mind of God: The Global Rise of Religious Violence*, 3rd ed. (Berkeley and Los Angeles: University of California Press, 2003).

37. Mark Juergensmeyer, *The New Cold War?: Religious Nationalism Confronts the Secular State* (Berkeley and Los Angeles: University of California Press, 1993).

38. "Remarks by George W. Bush to the National Endowment for Democracy," October 6, 2005, Ronald Reagan Building and International Trade Center, Washington, D.C., at http://www.ned.org/events/oct0605-Bush.html (accessed June 15, 2008).

39. Paul R. Brass, *Ethnicity and Nationalism: Theory and Comparison* (New Delhi: Sage, 1991), especially chapter 3; and Monica Duffy Toft, "Getting Religion? The Puzzling Case of Islam and Civil War," *International Security* 31, no. 4 (2007): 97–131. In addition, political scientist Robert Pape argues in *Dying to Win: The Strategic Logic of Suicide Terrorism* (New York: Random House, 2005) that militant elites sometimes use religious rhetoric to mobilize followers to engage in suicide terrorism, although the strategic goals these elites thereby seek to secure—above all the expulsion of occupying forces from territory deemed important by the elites in question—are entirely secular.

40. This is a core premise of the revised secularization theory in Norris and Inglehart, *Sacred and Secular*.

41. For a powerful argument that the global "deprivatization" of religion cannot be adequately explained either as an instrumentalist mobilization of the masses or as a "fundamentalist" reaction against modernity, see José Casanova, *Public Religions in the Modern World* (Chicago: University of Chicago Press, 1994): 211–34.

42. Pew Global Attitudes Project, "Views of a Changing World," T–120. As noted in the Pew report, the U.S. Department of State provided the 1999 survey trends.

43. "Arab Attitudes towards Political and Social Issues, Foreign Policy and the Media: Public Opinion Poll conducted jointly by the Anwar Sadat Chair at the University of Maryland and Zogby International," at http://www.bsos.umd.edu/SADAT/pub/Arab%20Attitudes%20Towards%20Political%20and%20Social%20Issues,%20Foreign%20Policy%20and%20the%20Media.htm (accessed June 15, 2008).

44. On the Shia resurgence in Iraq and elsewhere, see Seyyed Vali Reza Nasr, *The Shia Revival: How Conflicts within Islam Will Shape the Future* (New York: Norton, 2006).

45. Marie-Louise Moller, "EU Ministers Prepare Disputed Turkey Decision," *Reuters News*, December 13, 2004.

46. Pew Global Attitudes Project, "Among Wealthy Nations."

47. Anthony Faiola, "Japan's Draft Charter Redefines Military," *Washington Post*, November 23, 2005. On the larger issues and trends, see Harry Harootunian, "Memory, Mourning, and National Morality: Yasukuni Shrine and the Reunion of State and Religion in Postwar Japan," in Peter van der Veer and Hartmut Lehmann, eds., *Nation and Religion: Perspectives on Europe and Asia* (Princeton, NJ: Princeton University Press, 1999): 144–60.

48. According to the distinguished sociologist of religion Peter Berger, the "classical task" of religion is "constructing a common world within which all of social life receives ultimate meaning binding on everybody": Peter Berger, *The Sacred Canopy* (New York: Anchor), p. 133.

49. For a clear statement of this view, see Robert Audi, "The Separation of Church and State and the Obligations of Citizenship," *Philosophy & Public Affairs* 18 (1989): 259, 278–79.

50. "It belongs to the *religious convictions* of a good many religious people in our society that *they ought to base* their decisions concerning fundamental issues of justice *on* their religious convictions. They do not view it as an option whether or not to do so. It is their conviction that they ought to strive for wholeness, integrity, integration, in their lives. [emphasis in the original]": Nicholas Wolterstorff, "The Role of Religion in Decision and Discussion of Political Issues," in Robert Audi and Nicholas Wolterstorff, *Religion in the Public Square: The Place of Religious Convictions in Political Debate* (Lanham, MD: Rowman & Littlefield, 1997), p. 105.

51. Pew Global Attitudes Project, "Views of a Changing World," T–12.

52. Public Agenda, "For Goodness' Sake: Why So Many Want Religion to Play a Greater Role in American Life," Survey Report (2000), available at http://www.public agenda.org/specials/religion/religion.htm (accessed July 21, 2007).

53. The claim that religion is a danger to liberal democracy that must be contained has become a cardinal premise of American liberal political and constitutional theory in recent years. For examples, see Audi, "Separation of Church and State"; John Rawls, *Political Liberalism* (New York: Columbia University Press, 1993); Stephen Macedo, *Diversity and Distrust: Civic Education in a Multicultural Democracy* (Cambridge, MA: Harvard University Press, 1999); and Stephen G. Breyer, *Active Liberty: Interpreting Our Democratic Constitution* (New York: Knopf, 2005).

54. Judith N. Shklar, "The Liberalism of Fear," in Nancy L. Rosenblum, ed., *Liberalism and the Moral Life* (Cambridge, MA: Harvard University Press, 1989): 21–38.

55. Daniel Philpott, *Revolutions in Sovereignty: How Ideas Shaped Modern International Relations* (Princeton, NJ: Princeton University Press, 2001).

56. Michael W. McConnell, "Five Reasons to Reject the Claim That Religious Arguments Should Be Excluded from Democratic Deliberation," *Utah Law Review* 1999 (3): 639–57; Robert D. Woodberry and Timothy S. Shah, "The Pioneering Protestants," *Journal of Democracy* 15, no. 2 (2004): 47–61.

57. Stathis N. Kalyvas, *The Rise of Christian Democracy in Europe* (Ithaca, NY: Cornell University Press, 1996).

58. Jonathan Fox, "Do Democracies Have Separation of Religion and State?" *Canadian Journal of Political Science* 40, no. 1 (March 2007), p. 19.

59. Edmund Sears Morgan, *Inventing the People: The Rise of Popular Sovereignty in England and America* (New York: Norton, 1988), and Gordon S. Wood, *The Radicalism of the American Revolution* (New York: Knopf, 1992).

60. Nathan O. Hatch, *The Democratization of American Christianity* (New Haven, CT: Yale University Press, 1989).

61. Adrian Hastings, *The Construction of Nationhood: Ethnicity, Religion, and Nationalism* (Cambridge: Cambridge University Press, 1997).

62. Samuel P. Huntington, *Who Are We?: The Challenges to America's National Identity* (New York: Simon & Schuster, 2004), 356–57.

63. On Mexico, see Vikram Chand, *Mexico's Political Awakening* (Notre Dame, IN: University of Notre Dame Press, 2001); on Nigeria, see Paul Freston, *Evangelicals and Politics in Asia, Africa and Latin America* (Cambridge: Cambridge University Press, 2001), 181–90; on Turkey, see Jenny White, *Islamist Mobilization in Turkey: A Study in Vernacular Politics* (Seattle: University of Washington Press, 2002); on Indonesia, see Robert Hefner, *Civil Islam: Muslims and Democratization in Indonesia* (Princeton, NJ: Princeton University Press, 2000); and on India, see Thomas Blom Hansen, *The Saffron Wave: Democracy and Hindu Nationalism in Modern India* (Princeton, NJ: Princeton University Press, 1999).

64. "The assimilation of evangelical voters into the GOP's ranks in the late 1970s was a result of their power in newly expanded Republican primaries, as well as the rise of organized movements like the New Right": Mark Stricherz, "Primary Colors: How a Little-Known Task Force Helped Create Red State/Blue State America," *Boston Globe*, November 23, 2003; available at http://www.boston.com/news/globe/ideas/articles/2003/11/23/primary_colors (accessed July 21, 2007). See also Mark Stricherz, *Why the Democrats Are Blue: Secular Liberalism and the Decline of the People's Party* (New York: Encounter, 2007).

65. Peter L. Berger, Brigitte Berger, and Hansfried Kellner, *The Homeless Mind: Modernization and Consciousness* (New York: Random House, 1973), p. 81.

66. Smith, *American Evangelicalism*, p. 218.

67. Smith, *American Evangelicalism*, p. 218.

68. Samuel P. Huntington, "Religion and the Third Wave," *National Interest*, Summer 1991, 29–42; John Anderson, ed., *Religion, Democracy and Democratization* (London: Routledge, 2006).

69. Daniel Philpott, "The Catholic Wave," *Journal of Democracy* 15, no. 2 (2004): 32–46.

70. Daniel Philpott and Timothy Samuel Shah, "Faith, Freedom, and Federation: The Role of Religious Ideas and Institutions in European Political Convergence," in *Religion in an Expanding Europe*, ed. Timothy A. Byrnes and Peter J. Katzenstein (Cambridge: Cambridge University Press, 2006), 34–64, and Daniel Philpott, "Explaining the Political Ambivalence of Religion," *American Political Science Review* 101, no. 3 (August 2007): 505–25.

71. We are grateful to James Kurth for suggesting this way of formulating the distinctive capacities of the Catholic Church to promote transitions from authoritarianism to democracy.

72. Philpott, "Explaining the Political Ambivalence of Religion"; Alfred C. Stepan, "Religion, Democracy, and the 'Twin Tolerations,'" *Journal of Democracy* 11, no. 4 (2000): 37–57; and Robert W. Hefner, *Civil Islam: Muslims and Democratization in Indonesia.*

73. Toft, "Getting Religion," p. 128.

74. Monica Duffy Toft, *The Geography of Ethnic Violence: Identity, Interests, and the Indivisibility of Territory* (Princeton, NJ: Princeton University Press, 2003).

75. Jim Hoagland, "Facing Faith as Politics," *Washington Post,* January 15, 2006.

76. James A. Bill, *The Eagle and the Lion: The Tragedy of American-Iranian Relations* (New Haven, CT: Yale University Press, 1988).

77. "We relied heavily on impressions we had of Iraq before the war of 1990–91. Iraq at that time . . . had a highly secular society and was pluralistic. . . . What we did not adequately gauge was how Iraqi society had changed in the 1990s. . . . So we ended up not only with a society that was more religious than we thought, that had become more lower and lower-middle class than we thought, but also a society whose leadership was more clerical than we thought, assumed or hoped for": Vali Nasr, Interview with the Pew Forum on Religion and Public Life on the topic "Islam and Democracy: Iraq, Afghanistan and Pakistan," November 4, 2005, Washington, DC; available at http://pewforum.org/events/?EventID=91 (accessed July 21, 2007).

78. David Brooks, "Kicking the Secularist Habit: A Six-Step Program," *Atlantic Monthly* vol. 291, No. 2, March 2003, available at http://www.theatlantic.com/issues/2003/03/index.htm (accessed June 14, 2008).

CHAPTER 2

1. Apart from articles cited elsewhere in the notes, this chapter also draws on my articles "The Next Hotbed of Islamic Radicalism" (*Washington Post,* October 8, 2002); "Political Leaders Can No Longer Ignore Religion" (*Dallas Morning News,* April 5, 2003); "World Silence over Slain Muslims" (*Boston Globe,* October 13, 2003); "Radical Islam's Move on Africa" (*Washington Post,* October 16, 2003); "The Southeast Asian Front" (*Weekly Standard,* April 5, 2004); "Four Million: The Number to Keep in Mind This November" (*National Review Online,* August 27, 2004); "The Islamists' Other Weapon" (*Commentary,* April 2005).

2. "Declaration of Jihad against the Americans Occupying the Land of the Two Sacred Mosques," August 23, 1996, in Brad K. Berner, ed., *Jihad: Bin Laden in His Own Words* (Charleston, SC: Book Surge, 2006), pp. 40, 36–37; "Declaration of Jihad," in Bruce Lawrence, ed., *Messages to the World: The Statements of Osama Bin Laden* (New York: Verso 2005), pp. 25, 28.

3. "Declaration of Jihad," in Berner, *Jihad,* p. 59.

4. In a December 2001 interview, Zawahiri acknowledged that he and his confreres had been "the least active in championing the Palestinian cause."

5. CNN, March 1997, quoted in Peter L. Bergen, *Holy War, Inc.: Inside the Secret World of Osama bin Laden* (New York: Free Press, 2001) p. 53.

6. "Jihad against Jews and Crusaders," *Washington Post,* September 21, 2001; "The World Islamic Front," in Lawrence, *Messages,* pp. 58–60; "Declaration of the

World Islamic Front for Jihad against the Jews and Crusaders," in Berner, *Jihad*, pp. 78, 80.

7. Interview with bin Laden in December 1998, broadcast on Al Jazeera on September 20, 2001; "A Muslim Bomb," in Lawrence, *Messages*, p. 73.

8. Zarqawi, who professed allegiance to bin Laden in October 2004, refers in a September 11, 2004, audiotape to Musa Ibn Nusayr, the conqueror of Spain.

9. " 'This War Is Fundamentally Religious' November 3, 2001, Address of Osama Bin Laden," *Washington Post*, November 7, 2001. It was originally broadcast on Al Jazeera satellite television channel on November 3. The date and location of the recording was not given; "Crusader Wars," in Lawrence, *Messages*, pp. 134–37; "Speech against the Crusaders and the U.N.," in Berner, *Jihad*, pp. 145–48.

10. "To the Americans," in Lawrence, *Messages*, pp. 166–68; "Letter to the American People," in Berner, *Jihad*, pp. 194–97. The October 6, 2002, date is given by Lawrence, while Berner lists the address under September/October 2002. In November the message appeared in the British press; see the *Guardian* (UK), November 24, 2002. A year later, his October 18, 2003, "Message to the American People" told Americans "you are vulgar and without sound ethics or good manners" and referred to Vietnam, the Zionist lobby, Palestinians, oil, and the situation of Native Americans (Al Jazeera, October 18, 2003). This uncharacteristic campaign to connect U.S. preoccupations to his jihad reemerged in the run-up to the 2004 U.S. elections. In October he stressed that he had been deeply affected by the Israeli invasion of Lebanon—an issue he had strangely neglected in his previous hundreds of pages of grievances. For the benefit of the U.S. electorate, he also added boilerplate about the Patriot Act, electoral fraud, campaign finance, the deficit, Halliburton, and President Bush's reading of *My Pet Goat* on 9/11 (Al Jazeera, October 29, 2004); MSNBC, October 29, 2004; The Middle East Media Research Institute, *Special Dispatch Series* 811, November 5, 2004. Zawahiri has also castigated "usurious banks, giant companies, misleading media outlets, homosexual marriage, American support for the Copts [the indigenous Christian of Egypt]" and called for shari'a law (Joseph Braude, "On Message," *New Republic Online*, February 11, 2005). Bin Laden, in his January 19, 2006, Al Jazeera audio address referenced Vietnam and opinion polls; "Osama bin Laden," Laura Mansfield, ed., *Al Qaeda 2006 Yearbook* (Old Tappan, NJ: TLG Publications, 2007), pp. 43–52. Zawahiri's September 29, 2006, broadcast is particularly revealing because one half is subtitled in English and has references to Iraq and weapons of mass destruction. The second half has no subtitles and he goes on at length about the faults of Christianity, calling on Christians to convert to Islam., His May 5, 2007, interview, also subtitled in English, includes environmental themes and plays to the underprivileged (see "Third Interview with Dr. Ayman al-Zawahiri," As-Sahab, May 5, 2007, http://www.archive.org/details/Third-Interview [accessed June 15, 2008]). The same combination of themes occurred in the flurry of tapes issued by bin Laden, and also ones by Zawahiri, in September 2007. These tapes, usually posted to Islamic Web sites, combined criticisms (likely to resonate with many Americans) of "neoconservatives like Cheney, Rumsfeld, and Richard Pearle [Perle]" and of Democrats in Congress with praise for books by Michael Scheuer and Noam Chomsky. They also

include much longer, specifically Islamist denunciations of United Nations involvement in Darfur and rejection of those who "separate state from religion." Finally, they
include criticism of purported Christian polytheism, a declaration that, unlike the
Qur'an, the Torah and the Bible had been corrupted by Jews and Christians, and a call
for Americans to "embrace Islam."

11. Fifteen minutes of this address was broadcast by Al Jazeera on January 4,
2004, and the Web site of the Islamic Studies and Research Center published a
translation of the entire text on March 7, 2004; "Resist the New Rome," in Lawrence,
Messages, pp. 214, 216–17; "Message to the Islamic Nation," in Berner, *Jihad,* pp. 266,
268–69.

12. JihadUnspun Web site, December 16, 2004, http://www.jihadunspun.com/
BinLadensNetwork/statements (accessed June 15, 2008); excerpts in MEMRI *Special
Dispatch* 838, December 30, 2004; "Depose the Tyrants," in Lawrence, *Messages,*
pp. 250–51; "To the Muslims of Saudi Arabia in Particular and to the Muslims of
Other Countries in General," in Berner, *Jihad,* pp. 317–18.

13. MEMRI *Special Dispatch* 837, December 30, 2004; "To the Muslims in Iraq,"
in Berner, *Jihad,* pp. 331–33. Iraq's terrorist Ansar al-Sunnah Army, a longtime ally of
al Qaeda, also warned Iraqis not to vote because "democracy is a Greek word meaning
the rule of the people. . . . This concept is apostasy."

14. Apparently, the rumor that Abbas is really a Baha'i is widespread in the
Middle East, though Baha'i organizations have repeatedly affirmed that there is no
truth to it.

15. Bruce Loudon, "Terror Group's Threat Raises Dalai Lama Alert," *Australian,*
April 3, 2007.

16. See MEMRI *Special Dispatch* 1153, May 3, 2006: "Bin Laden's 'State Of Jihad'
Speech," by Walid Phares, Counterterrorism Blog, April 24, 2006, http://counterter
rorismblog.org/2006/04/bin_ladens_state_of_jihad_spee.php; "Osama bin Laden:
O, People of Islam," in Mansfield, *Al Qaeda,* pp. 111–48.

17. BBC, June 9, 2006; "Dr. Ayman al Zawahiri: Supporting the Palestinians,"
in Mansfield, *Al Qaeda,* pp. 180–81; "Supporting the Palestinians," in Laura Mansfield,
ed., *His Own Words: A Translation of the Writings of Dr. Ayman al Zawahiri"* (Old Tappan,
NJ: TLG Publications, 2006), p. 347.

18. Al Jazeera, June 23, 2006; "Dr. Ayman al Zawahiri: Elegizing the Ummah's
Martyr and Commander of the Martyrdom-Seekers," in Mansfield, *Al Qaeda,*
pp. 190–93.

19. See SITE Institute, September 27, 2006; "Bush, the Pope, and Darfur," in
Mansfield, *Al Qaeda,* pp. 465–80.

20. Except where indicated, bracketed inserts are the translator's, MEMRI *Special
Dispatch* 731, June 15, 2004.

21. Edward Wong, "Iraqi Video Shows Beheading of Man Said to Be American,"
New York Times, September 21, 2004.

22. Paul Marshall, "This War We're In," *National Review Online,* November 26,
2002; Al Jazeera, October 14, 2002; Nadia Abou El-Magd, "Bin Laden Statement
Praises Attacks," Associated Press, October 14, 2002.

23. Pamela Constable, "Proposed Afghan Constitution Fits U.S. Model," *Washington Post*, November 4, 2003; Carlotta Gall, "Afghans' King Receives Draft of Constitution," *New York Times*, November 4, 2003; Burt Herman, "Afghanistan Unveils Long-Delayed Draft Constitution, Key Step on Road to Recovery," Associated Press, November 3, 2003; Paul Marshall, "Taliban Lite: Afghanistan Fast Forwards," *National Review Online*, November 7, 2003.

24. Lisa Miller and Mathew Philips, "Caliwho? Why Is President Bush Talking about an Islamic Caliphate? And What Does the Word Mean?" *Newsweek*, October 13, 2006 http://www.newsweek.com/id/45294 (accessed June 15, 2008).

25. Paul Marshall, "Terrorism's Not New to Indonesia," *New York Post*, October 15, 2002, and "This War We're In."

26. "Against the Crusaders," *Washington Post*, November 7, 2001; "Crusader Wars," in Lawrence, *Messages*, p. 137; "Speech against the Crusaders and the U.N.," in Berner, *Jihad*, p. 148.

27. Al Jazeera, November 12, 2002; "To the Allies of America," in Lawrence, *Messages*, p. 175; "Message to U.S. Allies," in Berner, *Jihad*, p. 204; "To the Allies of the United States," in Raymond Ibrahim, ed., *The Al Qaeda Reader* (New York: Doubleday, 2007), p. 232. On April 23, 2006, bin Laden stressed the role of India and referred to a "Crusader-Zionist-Hindu war against the Muslims," and even ties Hindus to the alleged conspiracy to separate East Timor from Indonesia. See bin Laden's "State of Jihad" speech in MEMRI *Special Dispatch* 1153, May 3, 2006; "Osama bin Laden: O, People of Islam," in Mansfield, *Al Qaeda*, pp. 111–48.

28. Rajiv Chandrasekaran, "Purported Bin Laden Tape Lauds Bali, Moscow Attacks," *Washington Post*, November 13, 2002.

29. Jonathan Steele, "De Mello Killer Revealed," *Guardian* (UK), July 10, 2004 (bracketed text is the Guardian's).

30. "Crusader Wars," in Lawrence, *Messages*, p. 136; "Speech against the Crusaders and the U.N.," in Berner, *Jihad*, p. 147; Mansfield, *Al-Qaeda*, pp. 123–24.

31. See Paul Marshall, "Motive for Massacre," *Wall Street Journal*, September 27, 2002.

32. David Rohde, "Gunmen Kill 7 Workers for Christian Charity in Pakistan," *New York Times*, September 26, 2002; Khawaja Hussain, "Pakistani Police Probe Christian Charity Massacre," Agence France-Presse, September 26, 2002; CNN, September 26, 2002.

33. "Pakistan Attack Seen Aimed at West, Not Christians," Reuters, August 6, 2002; BBC, August 5, 2002; Lisa J. Adams, "Gunmen Storm Christian School in Pakistan, Killing Six," Associated Press, August 5, 2002; Zahid Hussain, "Six Shot Dead in Raid on Pakistan Christian School," *London Times*, August 9, 2002; "Attackers Kill Three at Pakistan Christian Church," *Los Angeles Times*, August 9, 2002.

34. David Blair, "Three Christians Killed in Hospital Chapel Raid," *Daily Telegraph*, August 10, 2002; Farhan Bokhari, "Four Die in Pakistan Missionary Hospital Attack," *Financial Times*, August 10, 2002.

35. "Four Dead after Grenade Attack on Pakistan Christian Hospital," Agence France-Presse, August 9, 2002.

36. Paul Marshall, "Misunderstanding al Qaeda," *Weekly Standard*, December 1, 2003; "War against the Infidels: The Message Behind the Beheadings," *Weekly Standard*, July 5, 2004.

37. "Al Qa'ida Commander in Iraq," MEMRI *Special Dispatch 609*, November 14, 2003.

38. CNN, November 11, 2003; ABC, November 11, 2003; Peter Slevin, "Saudi Bombing Blamed on Al Qaeda; Officials Point to Parallels with May 12 Attacks," *Washington Post*, November 10, 2003; Donna Bryson, "Arabs Recoil from Attack in Saudi Arabia Blamed on Muslim Extremists," Associated Press, November 11, 2003; Martin Walker, "Saudi Bombing a Message to Army," United Press International, November 11, 2003; BBC, November 11, 2003.

39. CNN, November 11, 2003; Bryson, "Arab Recoil," Associated Press, November 11, 2003; John R. Bradley, "Saudis Outraged at Muslims Casualties," *Washington Times*, November 10, 2003; Patrick E. Tyler, "Stability Itself Is the Enemy," *New York Times*, November 10, 2003; CBS, November 12, 2003.

40. CNN, November 12, 2003.

CHAPTER 3

1. John F. Burns, "Iraqi Conference on Election Plan Sinks into Chaos," *New York Times*, August 16, 2004.

2. Extract from *Kashf al-Asrar* (*Revelation of Secrets*), in Imam Khomeini, *Islam and Revolution*, trans. Hamid Algar (London: Kegan Paul, 1981), 170.

3. Ruhollah Khomeini, *Hukumat-i Islami* (Najaf: Nahzat-i Islami, 1391 [1971]); for an English translation, see Imam Khomeini, *Islam and Revolution*, trans. Hamid Algar (London: Kegan Paul, 1981), 27–166.

4. Khomeini, "The Incompatibility of Monarchy with Islam," October 31, 1971, in Algar, 204.

5. Khomeini, "Message to the Muslim Students in North America," July 10, 1972, in Algar, 210–11.

6. Khomeini, "In Commemoration of the First Martyrs of the Revolution," February 19, 1978, in Algar, 213.

7. *Le Journal*, November 28, 1978.

8. *Le Monde*, January 9, 1979.

9. One exception, albeit too late, was in the Associated Press, March 31, 1980.

10. Jonathan C. Randal, "Huge March in Tehran Is Peaceful," *Washington Post*, December 11, 1978.

11. Ira Klein, "The 70-Year Roots of Iran's Turmoil," *Washington Post*, December 24, 1978.

12. Steven Erlanger, "Iran's Shaky Theocracy," *New Republic*, November 10, 1979, pp. 12–13.

13. *Ettela'at*, February 2, 1979.

14. Joe Strupp, "Pentagon Releases Reporters' Iraq Slots," *Editor & Publisher*, February 13, 2003.

15. "Ayatollah Sadeq Khalkhali," *Daily Telegraph*, November 28, 2003.

16. See, for example, "Spiritual Leader," *Washington Post*, April 8, 1979, http://www.loc.gov/rr/print/swann/herblock/one.html.

17. Patrick E. Tyler, "U.S. Forces at Edge of a Blacked-Out Baghdad," *New York Times*, April 4, 2003.

18. See, for example, James Dao and Eric Schmitt, "U.S. Taking Steps to Lay Foundation for Action in Iraq," *New York Times*, November 18, 2002.

19. Nazila Fathi, "Iraqi Cleric in Iran Welcomes Plans to Oust Hussein," *New York Times*, August 4, 2002.

20. For a good overview, see Moojan Momem, *An Introduction to Shi'i Islam* (New Haven, CT: Yale University Press, 1985), 203–206. Moomen describes the historical evolution of the terms, the latter two of which are relatively recent innovations.

21. For example, the pro-Islamic Republic Ahl ul-Bayt Islamic Organization Official Web site (www.fabonline.com) lists eight "grand scholars alive in the Shi'a world," although most mainstream Shiites would dispute the inclusion of Khamene'i. *Washington Post* staff writer William Booth listed only four: Sistani; Muhammad Sa'id Tabataba'i al-Hakim; Ishaq Fayadh; and Bashir Najafi, although he arbitrarily limited his list to those resident in Najaf.

22. Craig Smith, "A Long Simmering Power Struggle Preceded Killings at an Iraqi Holy Shrine," *New York Times*, April 13, 2004.

23. George Packer, *Assassins' Gate* (New York: Farrar, Straus, and Giroux, 2005); Thomas E. Ricks, *Fiasco: The American Military Adventure in Iraq* (New York: Penguin, 2006).

24. Husayn 'Ali Montazeri, *Matn-i kamil-i khatirat-i Ayatallah Husayn 'Ali Muntazir* (Spånga, Sweden: Baran, 2001).

25. Youssef M. Ibrahim, "Grand Ayatollah Ali Araki," *New York Times*, December 1, 2004.

26. "Iran Intervenes, Names its Top Cleric Head of World's Shiite Muslims," *Chicago Tribune*, December 7, 1994.

27. While many journalists misunderstood the nature of Shiism, editorial pages did publish contributors who offered greater nuance. See, for example, Frank Smyth, "Iraq's Forgotten Majority," *New York Times*, October 3, 2002.

28. Most analysts suspect that Saddam's regime ordered the 1980 assassination of Ayatollah Muhammad Baqir al-Sadr, then the Shiite world's most prominent *marja' at-taqlid*. See "Statement of Mr. Max Van Der Stoel," Special Rapporteur of the U.N. Commission on Human Rights on the Situation of Human Rights in Iraq (New York: United Nations, 1999).

29. "Reuters Bureau Chief; IHT Correspondent in Tehran expelled," Agence-France Presse, February 4, 2001.

30. Susan Sachs, "The World: Theocracy and Democracy," *New York Times*, January 18, 2004.

31. Edward Wong. "Iran Is in Strong Position to Steer Iraq's Political Future," *New York Times*, July 3, 2004.

32. The only Western news agency to pick up the controversy over dates was Agence-France Presse, "Iran's Religious Leaders Divided over Eid Start," November 25, 2003. Their report, however, did not appreciate the full ramifications of the controversy given the public dispute between Sistani and Khamene'i.

33. Cameron Khosrowshahi, "Iraqi Shiism Could Topple the Mullahs," *International Herald Tribune,* March 24, 2005.

34. Anthony Shadid, "Shiite Clergy Push Vote in Iraq," *Washington Post,* December 7, 2004.

35. Article 100, Constitution of the Islamic Republic of Iran. For an English translation, see Hamid Algar, trans., *Constitution of the Islamic Republic of Iran* (Berkeley: Mizan, 1980).

36. Article 91, Constitution of the Islamic Republic of Iran.

37. "A New Chapter," *Daily News* (New York), May 27, 1997.

38. Kathy Evans, "Iranian Youth Celebrate Khatami's Clear Mandate for Social Change," *Guardian* (London), May 26, 1997.

39. Meg Laughlinby, "Shiites Show Strength through Pilgrimage," Knight Ridder Foreign Service, April 22, 2003; "Clerics Ascend to Power," *St. Petersburg Times,* April 22, 2003; John Daniszewski, "Shiites Get Their Shot at Power," *Los Angeles Times,* April 21, 2003.

40. Robert Collier, "Religious Frenzy and Anger on Once-Banned Pilgrimage," *San Francisco Chronicle,* April 23, 2003.

41. Meir Litvak, *Shi'i Scholars of Nineteenth-Century Iraq* (London: Cambridge University Press, 1998), 99.

42. Hamza Hendawi, "Powerful Iraqi Shiite Cleric al-Sistani's Iranian Citizenship Slowly Becoming an Issue," Associated Press, January 26, 2004.

43. Anthony Shadid, "Shiite Clerics Emerge as Key Power Brokers," *Washington Post,* December 1, 2003.

44. Larry Kaplow, "Iraq Blast Linked to al-Qaida; Bomb Is Like One That Hit U.N. Complex," *Atlanta-Journal Constitution,* August 31, 2003; Neil MacFarquhar, "After the War: Funerals," *New York Times,* August 31, 2003.

45. Douglas Frantz and James Risen, "A Nation Challenged: Terrorism," *New York Times,* March 24, 2002.

46. "Iran's Al-Qaeda Link: What the 9-11 Commission Found," *Middle East Quarterly* (Autumn 2004), 71–74.

47. Maureen Fan, "Ayatollah Complicates U.S. Plans," Knight Ridder News Service (as cited in *Miami Herald*), December 7, 2003.

48. Aamer Madhani, "Clerics Flex Political Muscles," *Chicago Tribune,* March 25, 2004. National Public Radio's "All Things Considered" also featured Karbala'i in a March 8, 2004, report.

49. Dan Murphy, "View Emerging of Shiite-Ruled Iraq," *Christian Science Monitor,* February 7, 2005.

50. Tyler Marshall and Ashraf Khalil, "Aide to Top Shiite Cleric in Iraq Slain," *Los Angeles Times,* January 14, 2005, p. A1.

51. Interview with Ladan Archin, Iran Country Director in the Office of the Secretary of Defense, Washington, DC, March 27, 2005.

52. Edward Wong, "Iran Is in Strong Position to Steer Iraq's Political Future," *New York Times*, July 3, 2004.

53. Dogen Hannah and Hannah Allam, "U.S., Iraq Skeptical as Cleric Accepts Deal," *San Jose Mercury News*, August 19, 2004.

54. Paul Wiseman and David Enders, "Al-Sadr's Intentions, Ambitions Unclear," *USA Today*, July 16, 2004.

55. Nimrod Raphaeli, "Understanding Muqtada al-Sadr," *Middle East Quarterly* 11, no. 4 (Autumn 2004), 33–42.

56. Patrick Cockburn and David Enders, "Shia's Make Their Choice for Iraq's New Prime Minister," *The Independent*, February 23, 2005; Alissa J. Rubin, "Iraq Shiites Offer Election Slate," *Los Angeles Times*, December 10, 2004.

57. For an explanation of American attempts to marginalize Chalabi, see Brian Bennett and Michael Weisskopf, "Inside the Takedown," *Time*, June 7, 2004.

58. Yitzhak Nakash, *The Shi'is of Iraq* (Princeton, NJ: Princeton University Press, 1994), 23.

59. Hanna Batatu, *The Old Social Classes and the Revolutionary Movements of Iraq*, 3rd ed. (London: Saqi, 2004), 315.

60. Tom Lasseter and Nancy A. Youssef, "Shiite Alliance Will Lead Iraq," *Kansas City Star*, February 14, 2005.

61. Leslie H. Gelb, "The Three-State Solution," *New York Times*, November 25, 2003.

62. Drake Bennett, "The Day After," *Boston Globe*, January 16, 2005.

63. Alissa J. Rubin, "The Iraqi Elections: Shiites Likely Victors, but Path is Unknown," *Los Angeles Times*, January 31, 2005.

64. Eric Davis, "Iraqi Sunni Clergy Enter the Frey," *Religion in the News* 7, no. 3 (Winter 2005), http://www.trincoll.edu/depts/csrpl/RINVol7No3/IraqiSunnisJoinFray.htm.

65. "Second Iraqi Bombing Kills Dozens," Associated Press, February 12, 2006.

66. Dexter Filkins and Warren Hoge, "As January Nears, Iraq Waits for Promised Election Assistance," *New York Times*, October 21, 2004.

67. Charles Clover and Dhiya Rasan, "The Chance to Take Part in the Planned Election Could Be Tempting to Some Anti-Coalition Leaders," *Financial Times*, October 21, 2004.

68. "Another Year of War; The Iraqi Election offers Ample Reason for Hope, Still the Insurgency Shows No Signs of Abating," *Cleveland Plain Dealer* March 20, 2005.

69. Liz Sly, "With Assembly Shaped, Iraq Constitution Next," *Chicago Tribune*, February 18, 2005.

70. Patrick J. McDonnell, "Key Sunni Arab Group Predicates Its Participation on Troops' Leaving," *Los Angeles Times*, February 16, 2005.

71. *Kurdistani News*, July 20, 2002.

72. Nicolas Pelham, "Siege of Falluja Ignites Wrath of Iraq's Mystical Sufi Masters," *Financial Times*, April 21, 2004.

73. For a detailed chronicle of ethnic cleansing in and around Kirkuk, see Nouri Talabany, *Arabization of the Kirkuk Region* (Uppsala, Sweden: Kurdistan Studies Press, 2001).

74. Asla Aydintasbas, "City Limits," *New Republic,* August 19, 2002.

75. Agence-France Presse, October 7, 2003.

76. Thanassis Cambanis, "Fractured Iraq Sees a Sunni Call to Arms," *Boston Globe,* March 27, 2005.

77. Nibras Kazemi, "Kurds Marching Off," *New York Sun,* March 31, 2005.

78. Christine Chinlund, "Dateline: Baghdad," *Boston Globe,* June 21, 2004.

79. Jonathan Foreman, "Bad Reporting in Baghdad," *Weekly Standard,* May 12, 2003.

CHAPTER 4

I wish to acknowledge the wonderful assistance of University of Oklahoma student Heather Stephenson in researching this chapter.

1. Allen D. Hertzke, *Freeing God's Children: The Unlikely Alliance for Global Human Rights* (Lanham, MD: Rowman & Littlefield, 2004).

2. This theme is developed in *Freeing God's Children,* especially chap. 6.

3. Such outlets as *Catholic News Service, Religious News Service, Christianity Today,* and *World* often provided fuller, more accurate coverage of these stories than does the secular press. Readers of such religious publications would often have been more informed about movement battles than, say, subscribers of the *New York Times.*

4. The following are examples of such columns: Charles Jacobs and Mohamed Athie, "Bought and Sold," *New York Times,* July 13, 1994; Michael Horowitz, "New Intolerance between Crescent and Cross," *Wall Street Journal,* July 5, 1995; Nina Shea, "A War on Religion," *Wall Street Journal,* July 31, 1998; Paul Marshall, "Motive for Massacre," *Wall Street Journal,* September 27, 2002. Those who produced multiple columns were Abe Rosenthal (see endnote 14), Nicholas Kristof (see endnote 62), and Eric Reeves, who penned no fewer than eighty editorials on Sudan, as I summarize on page 261 of *Freeing God's Children.* A sample of Reeves's editorials include: "Sudan's Genocidal Oil: It's Time to Divest," *Los Angeles Times,* August 30, 1999; "Capital Crime in Sudan," *Washington Post,* August 20, 2001; and "The Terror in Sudan," *Washington Post,* July 6, 2002.

5. Stories reporting on repression of Buddhists, Muslims, and underground Christians include: Erik Eckholm, "Wary Flock: A Special Report," *New York Times,* June 17, 1997; Steven Mufson, "Churches Brace for Darker Day," *Washington Post,* June 26, 1997; Robert S. Greenberger, "As Summit Nears, U.S. View of China Remains Harsh," *Wall Street Journal,* October 24, 1997; Dexter Filkins, "The Long Trek Out of Tibet," *Los Angeles Times,* April 14, 1998. Several op-ed pieces also covered the religious scene in China. See Andrew Nathan, "Clinton Can't Ignore Beijing's Thuggery," Commentary, *Wall Street Journal,* October 17, 1997, and "Religion in China," Editorial, *Wall Street Journal,* September 19, 1996; Gerald F. Seib, "A Bishop's Tale and Its Meaning for U.S., China," *Wall Street Journal,* October 22, 1997. Stories capturing alliances include: Erik Eckholm, "A Look at Religion in China by 3 U.S. Clerics," *New York Times,* February 8, 1998; Tyler Marshall, "Clinton to Nudge China on Rights

Reform, Officials Say," *Los Angeles Times*, June 17, 1997 (in this piece Marshall refers to "labor unions and the Christian Right"); Sara Fritz, "Religious Right Enters Fray over Trade Status for China," *Los Angeles Times*, May 2, 1997.

6. Laurie Goodstein, "Religious Leaders Urge Clinton to Press China on Persecution," *New York Times*, June 8, 1998.

7. On two of the legislative champions, see Megan Rosenfield on Chris Smith, "The Congressman's Faith Accompli; Don't Accuse Christopher Smith of Being Narrow on Issues: His Principles are Catholic," *Washington Post*, June 10, 1997; and Mary McGory on Frank Wolf, "The Man Who Won't Give Up," *Washington Post*, August 31, 1997. Fred Hiatt, in an op-ed piece, "So Religions Can Be Free," *Washington Post*, May 10, 1998, went beyond other disparate reporting for the *Post* in noting broad support for the legislation. Other reporting stressed the Christian Right angle. See Ceci Connolly, "Religious Persecution Tops Christian Coalition List," *Washington Post*, August 26, 1997; Megan Rosenfield, "Donald Hodel: A Belief in Belief," *Washington Post*, May 4, 1998; Juliet Eilperin, "House Overwhelmingly Passes Anti-Religious Persecution Bill," *Washington Post*, May 15, 1998; Thomas Edsall, "GOP Angers Big Business on Key Issues," *Washington Post*, June 11, 1998. Efforts by the Christian Coalition were not the predominant evangelical backing for the legislation, and an emphasis on this group also led to erroneously categorizing legislation as deriving from the "religious Right."

8. Janet Wilson, "Buddhists Decry Fate of Monks," *Los Angeles Times*, April 27, 1998.

9. The *Los Angeles Times* had particularly good coverage of religious persecution in Vietnam. See Janet Wilson, "Buddhists Decry Fate"; Tini Tran, "A Call for Human Rights in Vietnam," *Los Angeles Times*, December 14, 1997; Liz Seymour, "Envoy to Vietnam Urged to Focus on Rights Issues; Lorenza Munoz, "Protestors Accuse Vietnam of Rights Violations," *Los Angeles Times*, November 24, 1997. On coverage of activists and alliances for the broader religious freedom campaign, see Lee Romney, "Battle Urged against Religious Persecution," October 20, 1997; Norman Kempster, "Religious Persecution Bill Attracts Converts, Repels Pragmatists," September 22, 1998; Teresa Watanabe, "People of Diverse Faiths Battle Scourge of Religious Persecution," *Los Angeles Times*, October 17, 1998; John Daniszewski, "In Sudan, Hope Has a Hard Time," October 14, 1998; Norman Kempster, "U.S. to Name Official to Focus on Religious Liberty Issues," January 24, 1998; Norman Kempster, "Congressman Slips into Tibet, Slams China," August 21, 1997; Larry B. Stammer, "Bishop's Tale Stresses Plight of Christians in Other Nations," August 2, 1997; Norman Kempster, "State Dept. Urges INS to Ease Granting of Asylum to Christians Persecuted Abroad, July 23, 1997; Larry B. Stammer, "U.S. Urged to Fight Religious Persecution, January 27, 1996. The *Times* also published an opinion piece by Nina Shea, "Oppression of Christians Is Ignored," March 17, 1997.

10. Peter Steinfels is author of *A People Adrift: The Crisis of the Roman Catholic Church in America* (New York: Simon and Schuster, 2003).

11. Peter Steinfels, "Evangelicals Ask Government to Fight Persecution of Christians," *New York Times*, January 23, 1996; Peter Steinfels, "Evangelicals Lobby for

Oppressed Christians," *New York Times,* September 15, 1996; Peter Steinfels, "Beliefs," *New York Times,* November 16, 1996.

12.   Steven A. Holmes, "GOP Leaders Back Bill on Religious Persecution," *New York Times,* September 19, 1997. Holmes noted that the thirty organizations backing the bill represented, "with a few exceptions," "fundamentalist and evangelical denominations." Jeffrey Goldberg, "Washington Discovers Christian Persecution," *New York Times,* December 21, 1997; Eric Schmitt, "House Votes to Bar Religious Abuses Abroad, *New York Times,* May 15, 1998; Eric Schmitt, "Bill to Punish Nations Limiting Religious Beliefs Passes Senate," *New York Times,* October 10, 1998. Goldberg's piece was exceptional in noting that evangelical Christians were joined by "Reaganite conservatives, labor activists, veterans of Soviet Jewry movement," though he mentioned no other religious allies beyond such activists as Shea and Horowitz. In his May piece, Schmitt noted support from B'nai B'rith, while in his October piece he noted the Episcopal Church and the American Jewish Committee. But this was the sum total of references to other religious groups during 1998 campaign for legislation. The pivotal work of the Catholic Church, the Union of American Hebrew Congregations, and the Campaign for Tibet was not acknowledged.

13.   David E. Rosenbaum, "Senate Puts Aside Bill to Punish Nations the Persecute Religion: Measure Doomed by Split among Republicans, *New York Times,* July 24, 1998, p. A1; and "Republican Infighting," Editorial, *New York Times,* July 26, 1998. Rosenbaum seemed to strain to reach beyond the facts at hand, the failure of the Senate Foreign Relations Committee to act on the legislation, to draw the conclusion that there was no time for a bill with any teeth to pass the Senate and be reconciled with the House. Activists I interviewed felt the headline and interpretation were gratuitously pessimistic and tainted by bias against the campaign at the *Times.* Like his colleagues at the *Times,* Rosenbaum only stressed the backing of the legislation by conservative Christians but ignored the broader coalition.

14.   A. M. Rosenthal's columns in the *New York Times* include the following: "Persecuting the Christians: The Book of Daniel," February 11, 1997; "Questions Unasked about Persecution of Christians," February 14, 1997, A37; "The Chinese Christians," April 4, 1997, A29; "The Double Crime: Persecution and Acceptance," April 25, 1997, A31; "The Well Poisoners: Copts, and Other Christians," April 29, 1997, A25; "Chance for Americans to Help Persecuted Christians," May 13, 1997, A25; "Questions from West 47th Street: Why So Much about Christians?" June 10, 1997, A35; "The City and the Kingdom: The Royal Embassy Lies," June 17, 1997, A23; "The Position of Worship: A Letter for Congress and the China Lobby," July 25, 1997, A29; "The Right Message: The Importance of the Religious Persecution Bill," September 16, 1997; "Gutless in New York: But Courage in Washington," October 10, 1997; "Shatter the Silence: Two Videos, Two Moralities," October 21, 1997, p. A21; "Is This a Story?: Eight Million Prayers," December 2, 1997; "A Year of Awakening: America and Human Rights," December 30, 1997; "Feeling Clean Again: Fighting Religious Persecution," February 6, 1998; "The Simple Question: Voting on the American Purpose," May 12, 1998, "Clinton Policies Explained: The Values of Persecution," April 24, 1998; "Clinton's Fudge Factor: Operating for Religious Persecutors," May 1, 1998; "Freedom From

Religious Persecution: The Struggle Continues," August 7, 1998, p. A25; "They Will Find Out," October 2, 1998, p. A27; "Secrets of the War: Refugees Sold into Slavery;" April 23, 1999; "Slaves Stay Out: The U.N.'s New Human Rights Policy," June 25, 1999, p. A27. After he left the *Times*, Rosenthal continued write periodically. See A. M. Rosenthal, "Ignoring Religious Persecution Overseas," *Washington Times Weekly Edition*, November 13–19, 2000; "Of Slavery, Oil Money and Human Rights," *Washington Times*, July 20, 2001.

15. The quote is from a letter, signed by a distinguished group of religious leaders and human rights activists, nominating Rosenthal for the Pulitzer. Letter from Elie Wiesel and others to the Pulitzer Prize Board, January 14, 1999.

16. Steven Erlanger, "U.S. Assails China over Suppression of Religious Life," *New York Times*, July 21, 1997; Steven Le Myers, "Word for Word/Religious Freedom," *New York Times*, July 27, 1997; Jeffrey Goldberg, "Washington Discovers Christian Persecution," *New York Times Magazine*, December 21, 1997. Goldberg catalogued opposition from business interests and the Clinton administration, and skepticism from secular human rights groups.

17. A. M. Rosenthal, "Is This a Story?" *New York Times*, December 2, 1997.

18. Laurie Goodstein, "Evangelicals Mount Campaign against Oppression of Christians," *Los Angeles Times*, September 26, 1996. Writing for the *Los Angeles Times*, Goodstein catalogued examples of Christians jailed or killed.

19. Laurie Goodstein, "A Move to Fight the 'Persecution' Facing Christians," *New York Times*, November 9, 1998.

20. As Pakistan has cracked down on its own Islamists militants, conditions have improved for Christian minorities.

21. Mark O'Keefe, "Violence and Injustice Keep Pakistan's Christians Living in Fear in a 'Lawless' Society," *Oregonian*, October 25, 1998.

22. Mark O'Keefe, "Burma's Christians Caught in War," *Oregonian*, October 26, 1998.

23. Mark O'Keefe, "Egypt's Christian Converts Risk Abuse," *Oregonian*, October 27, 1998.

24. Mark O'Keefe, "In China, A Church Divided," *Oregonian*, October 28, 1998.

25. Mark O'Keefe, "Religion Inflames Sudan War," *Oregonian*, October 27, 1998.

26. Eric Schmitt, "Bill to Punish Nations Limiting Religious Beliefs Passes Senate," *New York Times*, October 10, 1999; "Religious Persecution Bill Clears the House and Senate," *Wall Street Journal*, October 12, 1998.

27. Karl Vick, "Powell Calls for Reconciliation in Sudan," *Washington Post*, May 27, 2001. Vick's acknowledgment of this is telling for two reasons: first, it occurred several years after extensive publicity in religious outlets, and second, Vick's reporting, as the section shows, was among the least sympathetic toward faith-based initiatives on Sudan.

28. Paul Marshall documents these patterns in *Their Blood Cries Out* (Dallas: Word, 1997), a book published before mobilization for the Sudan Peace Act.

29. The 2002 Report of the U.S. Commission on International Religious Freedom charged Sudan as "the world's most violent abuser of the right to freedom of

religion and belief," and in *Freeing God's Children*, I elaborate on the culpability of the Khartoum regime with a host of other national and international reports.

30. Charles Jacobs and Mohamed Athie, "Bought and Sold," *New York Times,* July 13, 1994; Abe Rosenthal, "Secrets of the War: Refugees Sold into Slavery," *New York Times,* April 23, 1999; Abe Rosenthal, "Slaves Stay Out: The U.N.'s New Human Rights Policy," *New York Times,* June 25, 1999; Dean E. Murphy, "Neighbors Lose No Love Over Sudan Regime," *Los Angeles Times,* August 22, 1998; John Daniszewski, "In Sudan, Hope Has a Hard Time," *Los Angeles Times,* October 14, 1998.

31. Interview with Nina Shea, 2003; Nina Shea, "A War on Religion," *Wall Street Journal,* July 26, 1998.

32. Allen D. Hertzke, "On This They Do Agree," *Wall Street Journal,* October 10, 2003.

33. Jane Perlez, "U.S. Weighs Using Food As Support for Sudan Rebels, *New York Times,* November 28, 1999.

34. Richard John Neuhaus, *First Things* 115 (August/September, 2001):100.

35. Eibner uses an elaborate system of photographs and fingerprinting to ensure against abuse, and those who have traveled with him note that it would be impossible for the thousands of people interviewed to fake stories, emotional reunions, or scars that were unlikely to have been made been by rebels engaged in a ruse. Eibner has repeatedly challenged any press organization to find a single example of fraud in the thousands of individual files he has.

36. Karl Vick, "Ripping Off Slave Redeemers," *Washington Post,* February 26, 2002, p. A1.

37. Indeed, official news releases by the Sudanese government played on the same themes as Vick's article. See "Fraud and Bigotry: Attempts to Resurrect Claims of Slavery," Press Release, Embassy of Sudan, Washington, DC, June 26, 2003,

38. Charles Jacobs, "Redeeming Values: Media Says Slave Redemption Is Fiction," *National Review Online,* June 4, 2002; *60 Minutes II* with Dan Rather, CBS, May 15, 2002; Nate Hentoff, "Major Papers Get Sudan Slavery Story Wrong," *Editor & Publisher Online,* June 4, 2002; Tony Norman, "Turning a Profit on the Price of Freedom," *Pittsburgh Post-Gazette,* March 1, 2002. Macram Gassis, the Catholic bishop for southern Sudan and the Nuba Mountains, who for years has served as a major voice informing the West about the plight of his people, was especially outrage at the *Post* report, as noted by Charles Jacobs.

39. Charles Jacobs, "Redeeming Values."

40. Tony Norman, "Turning a Profit on the Price of Freedom," *Pittsburgh Post-Gazette,* March 1, 2002. Norman's retraction occurred in Tony Norman, "Student's Journey to Sudan Sheds Light on Slavery," *Pittsburgh Post-Gazette,* April 16, 2002.

41. Jane Perlez, "Candidate as Envoy for Sudan Wants a Shield from Politics," *New York Times,* May 31, 2001; "Fraud and Bigotry: Attempts to Resurrect Claims of Slavery," Press Release, Embassy of Sudan, Washington, D.C, June 26, 2003.

42. Marc Lacey, "Sudan's 2 Sides Take Big Step Toward Peace: A Security Pact," *New York Times,* September 26, 2003.

43. I make this case in Allen D. Hertzke, "On This They Do Agree," *Wall Street Journal*, October 10, 2003.

44. Ian Fisher, "Oil Flowing in Sudan, Raising the Stakes in Its Civil War," *New York Times*, October 17, 1999; Ian Fisher, "Sudan's Slavery and War Get a Second Look from Americans," *New York Times*, November 14, 1999. Fisher's reports lacked the kind of biases found in those by Goodstein and Perlez but failed to capture the true nature and depth of the movement for southern Sudanese.

45. Davan Maharaj, "U.S. Asks Sudan to Resume Talks," *Los Angeles Times*, September 4, 2002; Andrew England, "Sudanese and Rebels Exchange Accusations," *Washington Post*, October 26, 2002; Michael Phillips, "Bush Diplomats Gain in Sudan," *Wall Street Journal*, October 22, 2003; Solomon Moore, "Powell to Take Part in Sudan Peace Talks," *Los Angeles Times*, October 21, 2003. Of these the pieces, the ones by Moore in the *Los Angeles Times* and Phillips in *Wall Street Journal* were particularly valuable, as they captured the religious dimensions of both the war in Sudan and American efforts to end it.

46. "Washington in Brief," *Washington Post*, October 22, 2002.

47. The Reuters photo caption read "President Bush greeted Sudanese guests yesterday in the Roosevelt Room of the White House after signing the Sudan Peace Act, a resolution authorizing $300 million over the next three years for peace efforts in Sudan," *New York Times*, October 22, 2002, p. 18.

48. "Bush Meets Former Slave for Signing of Sudan Peace Act," News Release, American Anti-Slavery Group, Boston, Massachusetts, October 21, 2002.

49. Jeffrey Zaslow, "Francis Bok's Story: Former Slave in Sudan Turns American Celebrity," *Wall Street Journal*, May 23, 2002.

50. Marc Lacey, "Sudan and Southern Rebels Sign Deal Ending Civil War," *New York Times*, January 10, 2005; Glenn Kessler, "Sudan, Southern Rebels Sign Accord to End Decades of War," *Washington Post*, January 10, 2005.

51. Michael Specter, "Traffickers' New Cargo: Native Slavic Women," *New York Times*, January 11, 1998.

52. Between September 1, 2000, to November 30, 2000, the *Wall Street Journal* contained 10 stories citing trafficking; the *Washington Post* had 65, the *New York Times* 75, and the *Los Angeles Times* 97.

53. Melissa Lambert and Josh Meyer, "House OKs Crackdown on Trafficking in Sex," *Los Angeles Times*, October 7, 2002.

54. *NBC Evening News* and *Dateline* presented an expose of Cambodian child prostitution and featured the work of Haugen and the International Justice Mission on June 13, 2003. I cover how Haugen's exposure helped lead to the crackdown of child-prostitution rings in Cambodia and elsewhere in *Freeing God's Children*, chap. 8.

55. Phillip Shenon, "Feminist Coalition Protests U.S. Stance on Sex Trafficking Treaty," *New York Times*, January 13, 2000.

56. William J. Bennett and Charles Colson, "The Clinton's Shrug at Sex Trafficking," *Wall Street Journal*, January 10, 2000. Bennett and Colson outline the arguments against the relaxed definition and cite their agreement with feminists on the issue.

57. Shenon, "Feminist Coalition Protests U.S. Stance."

58. Shenon used Kay Coles James's signature on a letter signed by a broad range of religious leaders and turned that fragment into a broad statement about "leaders of the Heritage Foundation and other politically conservative groups."

59. I treat this alliance more fully in *Freeing God's Children*, chap. 8.

60. Peter Waldman, "Evangelicals Given U.S. Foreign Policy an Activist Tinge," *Wall Street Journal*, May 26, 2004. Waldman's account covered well the diverse initiatives pressed by religious allies and included a one-paragraph reference to the North Korean Human Rights Act before Congress. Oddly, the *Journal* did not subsequently post a story when that legislation passed.

61. The Korean-American Church Coalition held its meeting in late September 2004, on the eve of final deliberations that passed the legislation.

62. Nicholas D. Kristof, "Following God Abroad," *New York Times*, May 21, 2002; Nicholas D. Kristof, "God on Their Side," *New York Times*, September 27, 2000; Nicholas D. Kristof, "When the Right is Right," *New York Times*, December 22, 2004. Kristof's column on Brownback was not without oddities, as he described Brownback as "to the right of Attila the Hun," and then catalogued his broad work for human rights, humanitarian causes, prison reform, increased funds for AIDS, and even the construction of an African American museum (while quoting Brownback as saying that God's heart is "with the downtrodden"). Kristof also failed to note that Brownback converted to Roman Catholicism after being inspired by Mother Theresa. Perhaps Kristof felt the need to qualify his praise lest he be seen as too soft on the "Christian Right" for readers of the *Times*.

63. Peter Waldman, "Evangelicals Give U.S. Foreign Policy An Activist Tinge," *Wall Street Journal*, May 26, 2004. Waldman chose to use Michael Horowitz's work with evangelicals as the hook for his piece.

64. Elisabeth Bumiller, "Evangelicals Sway White House on Human Rights Issues Abroad: Liberals Join Effort on AIDS and Sex Trafficking," *New York Times*, October 26, 2003.

65. Bumiller, "Evangelicals Sway White House on Human Rights."

66. Murray Hiebert, "Christian Right Focuses on North Korea," *Wall Street Journal*, May 13, 2005; John Cochran, "New Heaven, New Earth," *CQ Weekly*, October 17, 2005; Matt Steams and Shashank Bengali, "Senator's Interest in Africa Turns into a Campaign Weapon," Knight Ridder Newspapers, December 15, 2005; Paul Starobin, "Isolationism Redux," *National Journal*, March 31, 2006; Marisa Katz, "A Very Long Engagement," *New Republic*, May 15, 2006.

67. Susan Page, "Christian Right's Alliances Bend Political Spectrum," *USA Today*, June 14, 2005.

CHAPTER 5

1. S. Robert Lichter, Stanley Rothman, and Linda S. Lichter, *The Media Elite: America's New Powerbrokers* (Bethesda, MD: Adler & Adler, 1986). Some recent surveys have found that most journalists say religion is important to them and more are willing to claim a religious affiliation, but an update of Robert Lichter's 1986

survey still found 70 percent of elite journalists attending religious services rarely if ever (see Stanley Rothman and Amy Black, "Elites Revisited: American Social and Political Leadership in 1990s," *International Journal of Public Opinion Research* 11 (June 1999):169–91).

2. Daniel Okrent, "Is the *New York Times* a Liberal Newspaper?" *New York Times*, July 25, 2004.

3. "The 25 Most Influential Evangelicals in America," *Time*, February 7, 2005.

4. Louis Bolce and Gerald De Maio, "The Political of Partisan Neutrality," *First Things*, no. 143 (May 2004):9.

5. Wilgoren and Keller, "Kerry and Religion," *New York Times*, October 7, 2004.

6. Julia Duin, "Bush, Kerry Turn to Religion in Final Weeks," *Washington Times*, October 22, 2004.

7. David E. Sanger, "At All Bush Rallies, Message Is 'Freedom Is on the March,'" *New York Times*, October 21, 2004.

8. Richard Stevenson, "Bush's Talks May Vary, but Always a Reminder: Sept. 11," *New York Times*, October 27, 2004.

9. Nicholas Lemann, "Fear and Favor," *New Yorker*, February 14–21, 2005, p. 170.

10. David M. Halbfinger and David E. Sanger, "Kerry's Latest Attacks on Bush Borrow a Page from Scripture," *New York Times*, October 25, 2004.

11. Jim VandeHei, "Faith Increasingly Part of Kerry's Campaign," *Washington Post*, October 18, 2004.

12. Elisabeth Bumiller and Richard W. Stevenson, "A Leader Now Tested by Tragedy—George Walker Bush," *New York Times*, September 2, 2004.

13. Sheryl Gay Stolberg, "Reaganite by Association? His Family Won't Allow It," *New York Times*, June 15, 2004.

14. Arthur Schlesinger Jr., "The White House Wasn't Always God's House," *Los Angeles Times*, October 26, 2004.

15. Maureen Dowd, "Casualties of Faith," *New York Times*, October 21, 2004.

16. Paul Kengor, "What Bush Believes," *New York Times*, October 18, 2004.

17. Laurie Goodstein, "Personal and Political, Bush's Faith Blurs Lines," *New York Times*, October 26, 2004.

18. Jim VandeHei, "Events Forcing Abortion Issue on Kerry; Reticence as Much Personal As Political, His Aides Say," *Washington Post*, June 3, 2004.

19. Stephan Dinan, "Kerry Says Social Justice Would Guide Presidency," *Washington Times*, October 25, 2004.

20. Pam Belluck, "Vatican Says Kerry Stance on Abortion Is Not Heresy," *New York Times*, October 20, 2004.

21. Liz Sidoti, "Political Notebook—Catholics and Kerry," Associated Press, October 19, 2004.

22. Charles J. Chaput, "Faith and Patriotism," *New York Times*, October 22, 2004.

23. Wilgoren and Keller, "Kerry and Religion," October 7, 2004.

24. Roger Cohen, "Ardent Faith Squares Off against Earnest Reflection," *New York Times*, October 24, 2004.

25. Robert Wright, "Faith, Hope and Clarity," *New York Times*, October 28, 2004.

26. Eleanor Clift, "Faith versus Reason," *Newsweek*, August 13, 2004.

27. Wilgoren and Keller, "Kerry and Religion," *New York Times*, October 7, 2004.

28. Maureen Dowd, "Vote and Be Damned," *New York Times*, October 17, 2004.

29. Maureen Dowd, "Casualties of Faith," *New York Times*, October 21, 2004.

30. Ron Suskind, "Without a Doubt," *New York Times*, October 17, 2004.

31. Wilgoren and Keller, "Kerry and Religion," *New York Times*, October 7, 2004.

32. David Brooks, "A Matter of Faith," *New York Times*, June 22, 2004.

33. "GOP the Religion-Friendly Party," Pew Research Center, August 24, 2004.

34. This report from the National Survey of Religion and Politics, sponsored by University of Akron and the Pew Forum on Religion and Public Life, is available at http://pewforum.org/docs/index.php?DocID=55. James Guth was part of the research team producing this survey.

35. Andrew Welsh-Huggins, "Clergy Enter Political Arena in New Way during Close Presidential Race," Associated Press, October 13, 2004.

36. Lara Jakes Jordan, "Bush Push May Cost Churches Tax Breaks," Associated Press, June 2, 2004.

37. Alan Cooperman, "Churchgoers Get Direction From Bush Campaign," *Washington Post*, July 1, 2004.

38. David D. Kirkpatrick, "Bush Appeal to Churches Seeking Help Raises Doubt," *New York Times*, July 2, 2004.

39. David D. Kirkpatrick and Michael Slackman, "Republicans Try to Expand Appeal to Religious Voters," *New York Times*, September 3, 2004.

40. David D. Kirkpatrick, "Battle Cry of Faithful Pits Believers against Unbelievers," *New York Times*, October 31, 2004.

41. Hamil R. Harris, "From Pulpits, Faithful Rallying to Polls; Christians Seek a Voice; Evangelicals' Courting of Blacks Debated," *Washington Post*, October 28, 2004.

42. Arthur Schlesinger Jr., "The White House Wasn't Always God's House," *Los Angeles Times*, October 26, 2004.

43. Jim Dwyer, "Among Black Voters, A Fervor to Make Their Ballots Count," *New York Times*, October 11, 2004.

44. David M. Halbfinger, "Campaigning Furiously, With Social Security in Tow," *New York Times*, October 18, 2004.

45. Jim Dwyer and Jodi Wilgoren, "Gore and Kerry Unite in Search for Black Votes," *New York Times*, October 25, 2004.

46. Jim Rutenberg, "Clinton, Campaigning in Florida, Calls Kerry a Stalwart Friend of Israel," *New York Times*, October 27, 2004.

47. Sharon Theimer, "Bush Campaign Criticizes Democratic Effort to Solicit Religious Vote," Associated Press, October 8, 2004.

48. Bill Broadway, "In Election Season, IRS Sits in Judgement; Clergy Withhold Endorsements While Touting Free Speech from Pulpit," *Washington Post*, October 9, 2004.

49. David D. Kirkpatrick, "Kerry Is Criticized for Church Drive," *New York Times*, October 13, 2004.

50. Kirkpatrick, "Kerry Is Criticized," *New York Times*.

51. Paul Farhi and Vanessa Williams, "Politics and Pulpits Combine to Sway Swing-State Voters," *Washington Post*, October 25, 2004.

52. The data in this and the following paragraphs are from the authors' analysis of the University of Akron post-election survey.

53. William Safire, "Arab and Jewish Votes," *New York Times*, October 25, 2004; Carlyle Murphy, "Muslims Seen Abandoning Bush; Chagrin over President's Policies Spurs Pro-Kerry Activism," *Washington Post*, October 25, 2004; Julia Duin, "Bush Makes Significant Gains in Two Polls of Catholic Voters," *Washington Times*, October 4, 2004; Laurie Goodstein, "How the Evangelicals and Catholics Joined Forces," *New York Times*, May 30, 2004.

54. "Beliefs and the Ballot Box," *Economist*, June 3, 2004; Peter Steinfels, "Under God, but Divisible: Where Different Categories of Christians Stand on Social Issues," *New York Times*, October 9, 2004.

55. Jane Lampman, "In Final Push, Kerry Tries to Close a Perceived 'God Gap,'" *Christian Science Monitor*, October 26, 2004.

56. Peter Beinert, "The End of the 'Jewish Vote,'" *Washington Post*, October 27, 2004.

57. Steinfels, "Under God," *New York Times*.

58. R. W. Apple Jr., "With Bush Advancing, Missouri May Be a Battleground All but Conquered," *New York Times*, September 30, 2004; James Dao, "Where Kerry Is Trying to Avoid Gore's Pitfalls," *New York Times*, October 13, 2004.

59. Alan Cooperman, "Evangelical Leaders Appeal to Followers to Go to Polls; Efforts Are Planned to Amplify Religious Conservatives' Voice," *Washington Post*, October 15, 2004.

60. Walter Shapiro, "Ohio Churches Hope Marriage Ban Prods Voters to Polls," *USA Today*, September 27, 2004.

61. Mark W. Roche, "Voting Our Conscience, Not Our Religion," *New York Times*, October 11, 2004.

62. Peter Steinfels, "Religion, Politics and the Good—or Harm—That May Result from the 2004 Campaign," *New York Times*, October 23, 2004.

63. Virginia Heffernan, "True Believers Seen through Secular Eyes," *New York Times*, October 23, 2004.

64. David D. Kirkpatrick, "Robertson Says Bush Predicted No Iraq Toll," *New York Times*, October 21, 2004.

65. Timothy Egan, "Democrats in Red States: Just Regular Guys," *New York Times*, August 22, 2004.

66. Michael Hout and Andrew M. Greeley, "A Hidden Swing Vote: Evangelicals," *New York Times*, September 4, 2004.

67. James Dao, "Kerry Trying to Avoid Gore's Pitfalls," *New York Times*.

68. E. J. Dionne, "Faith without Fealty; It's Time to Free Religion from Party Politics," *Washington Post*, October 19, 2004.

69. See James L. Guth, "George W. Bush and Religious Politics," in Steven E. Schier, *High Risk and Big Ambition: The Presidency of George W. Bush* (Pittsburgh: University of Pittsburgh Press, 2004).

70. Amy Faganand and Stephen Dinan, "GOP Forcing Vote on Wedge Issues," *Washington Times*, September 26, 2004; Richard Simon, "Bill to Ban Same-Sex Marriage Falls Short: . . . Opponents Call Vote 'Election-Year Ploy,'" *Los Angeles Times*, October 1, 2004.

71. William B. Rubenstein, "Play It Straight," *New York Times*, October 16, 2004.

72. Brad Knickerbocker, "Ballot Wars over Same-Sex Marriage," *Christian Science Monitor*, October 8, 2004.

73. Laurie Goodstein, "Personal and Political, Bush's Faith Blurs Lines," *New York Times*, October 26, 2004.

74. Leon R. Kass, "Playing Politics with the Sick," *Washington Post*, October 8, 2004.

75. Sheryl Gay Stolberg, "For Stem Cell Advocates, A Death with Resonance," *New York Times*, October 12, 2004.

76. Leon Kass, "Playing Politics with the Sick," *Washington Post*.

77. For further detail on the University of Akron post-election survey and a brief interpretive essay, consult http://pewforum.org/docs/index.php?DocID=64.

78. For the internal panel's criticism of the *Times*'s coverage of religion, see Katherine Q. Seelye, "Panel at the *Times* Proposes Steps to Increase Credibility," *New York Times*, May 9, 2005.

CHAPTER 6

1. Hanna Rosin, "A Papacy and Church Transformed," *Washington Post*, April 3, 2005; Kenneth L. Woodward, "Tested Beloved and Brave," *Newsweek*, April 11, 2005; Helen Prejean, "Above All Else, Life," *New York Times*, April 4, 2005; Jaroslav Pelikan, "The Great Unifier," *New York Times*, April 4, 2005; Thomas Cahill, "The Price of Infallibility," *New York Times*, April 5, 2005.

2. Richard Boudreaux, "Innovator Revised Papacy," *Los Angeles Times*, April 3, 2005.

3. Boudreaux, "Innovator."

4. Bob Keeler, "His Profound and Lasting Impact," *Newsday*, April 3, 2005.

5. Robert McFadden, "Pope John Paul: Church Shepherd and a Catalyst for World Change," *New York Times*, April 3, 2005.

6. Michael Paulson, "A Life for History: A Polish Native Who Rose to Lead—and Reshape—a 2,000-Year-Old Church," *Boston Globe*, April 3, 2005.

7. G. Jeffrey MacDonald, "A Small, Sturdy Band of 'John Paul Priests,'" *Christian Science Monitor*, April 8, 2005; also discussed in *Newsday*, April 15, 2005, and in a segment on CBS's *60 Minutes*, April 3, 2005.

8. Andrew Greeley, "Young Fogeys," *Atlantic Monthly*, January/February 2004.

9. Larry Stammer, "Legacy of John Paul II; Attendance Is a Concern for Church," *Los Angeles Times*, April 10, 2005; Keith B. Richburg, "Church's Influence Waning in Once Fervently Catholic Spain; Religion's Decline in Europe among Biggest Challenges for Next Pontiff," *Washington Post*, April 11, 2005; John Henderson, "Italy, Catholic Church diverged; The pope couldn't stem the feminist tide that hit the nation

in the '70s; abortion, working moms and divorce are now common," *Denver Post,* April 10, 2005.

10. Dean E. Murphy and Neela Bannerjee, "Catholics in U.S. Keep Faith, but Live with Contradictions," *New York Times,* April 11, 2005; Susan Reimer, "Pope Admired If Views Not Always Shared," *Baltimore Sun,* April 5, 2005.

11. Robert D. McFadden, "Pope John Paul II, Church Shepherd and a Catalyst for World Change," *New York Times,* April 3, 2005.

12. Jeffery L. Sheler, Michael Schaffer, Joshua Kurlantzick, Linda Kulman, and Alexander Stille, "Pope John Paul II," *U.S. News & World Report,* April 11, 2005.

13. David van Biema, "Defender of the Faith," *Time,* April 3, 2005.

14. "Ousted Cardinal Will Lead Funeral," *Los Angeles Times,* April 8, 2005.

15. John Blake and Gayle White, "Liberal Catholics in U.S. Wary; Pope's Traditional Views Make Changes Unlikely," *Atlanta Journal-Constitution,* April 24, 2005; Clarence Page, "Even with Black or Latin Pope, Don't Expect Major Change," *Baltimore Sun,* April 8, 2005; Greg Barrett, "Faithful in U.S. Unlikely to See Altered Message from Vatican," *Baltimore Sun,* April 20, 2005; "A Vote for Tradition," *Houston Chronicle,* April 20, 2005.

16. Don Lattin, "U.S. Catholics Expect New Pope Benedict to Hew Hard Line," *San Francisco Chronicle,* April 24, 2005; Michael Paulson and *Boston Globe* staff, "From New Pontiff, A Vow of Openness; Remarks at Odds with Stern Image," *Boston Globe,* April 21, 2005; Michael Paulson and *Boston Globe* staff, "U.S. Prelates Seek to Dispel New Pontiff's Divisive Image," *Boston Globe,* April 21, 2005; Cathy Lynn Grossman, "For U.S. Catholics, New Pope Could Be Polarizing," *USA Today,* April 21, 2005; Elisabeth Rosenthal with Elisabetta Povoledo, "For Onlookers, Enthusiasm and Praise Tinged with Questions about Pope's Conservatism," *New York Times,* April 20, 2005.

17. William J. Kole, "Cardinal Joseph Ratzinger of Germany Elected New Pope, Takes Name Benedict XVI," Associated Press, April 19, 2005; Laurie Goodstein and Ian Fisher with Elisabetta Povoledo, "Cardinals Align as Time Nears to Select Pope," *New York Times,* April 17, 2005; Alessandra Stanley, "White or Black? Maybe Beige? As Smoke Detectors, the Anchors Were All Too Fallible," *New York Times,* April 20, 2005; Maureen Dowd, "Smoke Gets in Our News," *New York Times,* April 20, 2005; Sarah Lyall with Mark Landler, "What Does British Press See in Pope? Just a German," *New York Times,* April 22, 2005; Maureen Dowd, "Uncle Dick and Papa," *New York Times,* April 23, 2005.

18. Tracy Wilkinson, "In Pope's 1st Encyclical, Focus Is Heart and Soul," *Los Angeles Times,* January 26, 2006.

19. Lorenzo Albacete, "For the Love of God," *New York Times,* February 3, 2006; Cathy Lynn Grossman, "Benedict's Message of Love; Encyclical May Set Tone for His Papacy," *USA Today,* January 26, 2006.

20. "Pope Enjoys Private Time after Slamming Islam," Agence France-Presse, September 13, 2006.

21. Apostolic Journey to Cologne on the Occasion of the XX World Youth Day— Meeting with Representatives of Some Muslim Communities: Address of His Holiness Pope Benedict XVI, the Vatican, August 20, 2005, http://www.vatican.va/holy_father/

benedict_xvi/speeches/2005/august/documents/hf_ben-xvi_spe_20050820_meeting-muslims_en.html (accessed June 16, 2008).

CHAPTER 7

1. All box office figures, unless otherwise noted, are from www.boxofficemojo.com.

2. Jeff Jensen, "The Agony & the Ecstasy," *Entertainment Weekly*, February 20, 2004.

3. The terms were "Mel w/1 Gibson and anti-Semitism." The search was of all English news sources. If a month yielded too many results, it was sliced down into smaller cuts and the pieces were added together. So February 2004 had 379 hits between the 1st and 15th; 709 from the 16th to the 24th; and 923 from the 25th to the 29th. The combined total reported above is 2,011.

4. Gibson was arrested on a DUI charge on the early morning of July 28, 2006. He was picked up just after 2 a.m. for driving erratically on the Pacific Coast Highway in Malibu, California. The posted speed limit was forty-five miles per hour; Gibson had been bobbing and weaving his Lexus down the road at nearly ninety. His breathalyzer results put him at well over California's legal limit, and he was also in violation of the state's open-container law.

Gibson didn't resist arrest, but once he was cuffed an in the back seat of the squad car, he started to rant. One of the things he said in his inebriated state was that Jews were responsible for all the world's wars. He then asked the arresting officer, James Mee, if Mee was a Jew. Gibson also allegedly referred to a female officer as "sugar tits," though that received far less press coverage than the anti-Semitic outburst.

Gibson pled guilty to one charge of driving with a blood-alcohol level above the state's .08 legal limit. As part of that plea, he agreed to a $1,300 fine, three years probation, a ninety-day license restriction, a ninety-day rehab program, and twelve months of Alcoholics Anonymous. He also agreed to record a free public service announcement cautioning viewers against the dangers of drinking and driving.

For Gibson, those dangers included the obvious public relations hit that comes with a night of drunken ranting when you are already a lightning rod for controversy. He issued two apologies: first, a general apology to the police, the public, and his family; then an apology to the Jewish community. In the second apology, he insisted that his inebriated outburst did not represent his true feelings toward Jews. He argued his words represented "a moment of insanity" but then said that his status as a "public person" meant that his words "carry weight in the public arena." As a result, he said that he was "not just asking for forgiveness."

Gibson insisted that he "would like to take it one step further, and meet with leaders of the Jewish community with whom I can have a one-on-one discussion to discern the appropriate path for healing." He closed by reiterating the responsibility and insanity motifs: "This is not about a film. Nor is it about artistic license. This is about real life and recognizing the consequences hurtful words can have. It's about existing in harmony in a world that seems to have gone mad." For what it's worth, the ADL's Abraham Foxman, who had been very critical of *The Passion*, publicly accepted Gibson's apology.

5. The statement and other Anti-Defamation League material relating to the *Passion* controversy can be found at http://www.adl.org/Interfaith/gibson_qa.asp.

6. Paula Fredriksen, "Mad Mel," *New Republic*, July 28, 2003.

7. Frank Rich, "Mel Gibson's Martyrdom Complex," *New York Times*, August 3, 2003. My analysis is focused on the film's effects on the U.S. audience, but it's worth mentioning *The Passion*'s reception in the Middle East and the Muslim world. It was widely screened in many Muslim countries and bootlegged into countries, such as Saudi Arabia, which prohibited its public airing. According to the rough indicators available to us, it doesn't seem to have led to an uptick in anti-Semitic attitudes or anti-Jewish violence. It mainly seems to have cast the central figure of Christianity in a new light for devout Muslim theatergoers.

8. Frank Rich, "Gibson's *Passion* Publicity Juggernaut," *New York Times*, September 20, 2003.

9. Peter J. Boyer, "The Jesus War," *New Yorker*, September 15, 2003.

10. Murray Dubin, "Movie Inflames Passions," *Miami Herald*, August 30, 2003.

11. Mark Jurkowitz, "Articles Are Already Stirring Passion over Gibson's Movie," *Boston Globe*, September 25, 2003.

12. Ruthe Stein, "Daily Datebook," *San Francisco Chronicle*, October 29, 2003.

13. Lorenza Munoz and Greg Krikorian, "Flap Erupts over *Passion* Viewing," *Los Angeles Times*, November 21, 2003.

14. Rachel Abramowitz, "Gibson Talks about Film, Furor, and Faith," *Los Angeles Times*, February 15, 2004.

15. The whole exchange is available at http://www.slate.com/id/2111473/entry/2111743.

16. These ratings can be found at www.rottentomatoes.com. Click on "cream of the crop" to narrow the results to the top critics.

17. Jeremy Lott, "*The Passion* and the Fury," *American Spectator*, February 25, 2004: http://www.spectator.org/dsp_article.asp?art_id=6208.

18. Eric Gorski, "Pastor behind 'Jews Killed Jesus' Sign to Retire," *Denver Post*, March 10, 2004.

CHAPTER 8

1. Roy Peter Clark, "Confessions of an Alienated Journalist: How One Journalist Sees—or Doesn't See—the World," *PoynterOnline*, November 4, 2004, http://www.poynter.org/content/content_view.asp?id=73946.

2. Interview with the author, January 2005, in St. Petersburg, Florida.

3. Many of these suggestions are based on interviews with those working on this issue. Below, when people are quoted without other reference given, the quotations are from interviews with the author.

4. "Christian Rally Draws Ex-Sinners to Capitol," *Washington Post*, May 1, 1996.

5. Bill Kovach and Tom Rosenstiel, *The Elements of Journalism: What Newspeople Should Know and the Public Should Expect* (New York: Three Rivers Press, 2001), 85–86.

6. Christian Smith, "Religiously Ignorant Journalists," *Books & Culture*, January 1, 2004, http://www.ctlibrary.com/bc/2004/janfeb/2.06.html.

7. Telephone interview with the author, February 2005.

8. Jodi Wilgoren, "Politicized Scholars Put Evolution on the Defensive," *New York Times*, August 21, 2005.

9. Staff of the Associated Press, *The Associated Press: Stylebook and Libel Manual*, 39th ed. (New York: Basic Books, 2004), 213.

10. Aly Colon, "Preying Presbyterians," *PoynterOnline*, September 18, 2003, http://poynteronline.org/column.asp?id=58&aid=48353.

11. Interview with the author, January 2004, in St. Petersburg, Florida.

12. Telephone interview with the author, March 2005.

13. Interview with the author, January 2005, in St. Petersburg, Florida.

14. Interview with the author, 2005.

15. Telephone interview with the author, March 2005.

16. Mark I. Pinsky, "Among the Evangelicals: How One Reporter Got Religion," *Columbia Journalism Review* (Jan./Feb. 2005), http://cjrarchives.org/issues/2005/1/voices-pinsky.asp.

17. Pinsky, "Among the Evangelicals."

18. Terry Mattingly, "Peter Jennings—News Seeker," *Terry Mattingly—On Religion*, August 10, 2005, http://tmatt.gospelcom.net/column/2005/08/10.

19. Telephone interview with the author, March 2005. Hoover is the author of author of *Religion in the News: Faith and Journalism in American Public Discourse* (Thousand Oaks, CA: Sage, 1998).

20. "Inside the Beltway," *Washington Times*, November 11, 1994.

21. Telephone interview with the author, February 2005.

22. As quoted in Terry Mattingly, "What Is NON-Religion News?" *Terry Mattingly—On Religion*, http://tmatt.gospelcom.net/column/2002/09/25.

CHAPTER 9

1. Roberta Green, "Orange County's Sikhs Aren't Surprised at Assassination," *Orange County Register*, November 1, 1984.

2. Russell Watson (with Frank Gibney Jr., Edward Behr, Ray Watson, and Sudip Mazudar in New Delhi and bureau reports), "After Indira," *Newsweek*, November 12, 1984.

3. Rahul Singh, *New Republic*, July 16, 1984, and July 23, 1984.

4. James M. Markham, "Temple Raid Puts Sikhs 'In a Very Foul Mood,'" *New York Times*, June 12, 1984.

5. "Slaughter at the Golden Temple," *Time*, June 18, 1984.

6. William K. Stevens, "Indians Report Daylong Battle at Sikh Temple," *New York Times*, June 6, 1984.

7. The official government number was 492. William K. Stevens, "Aftermath at Golden Temple: Holes and a Hollow Science," *New York Times*, June 15, 1984.

8. "Angry Sikhs Stage Rallies across India," *New York Times*, June 18, 1984; Associated Press, June 18, 1984.

9. Katherine Frank, *Indira* (New York: Harper Collins, 2003), 304.

10. William E. Smith, "Death in the Garden," *Time*, November 12, 1984.

11. Frank, *Indira*, p. 493.

12. William K. Stevens, "Gandhi, Slain, Is Succeeded by Son; Killing Laid to 2 Sikh Bodyguards; Army Alerted to Bar Secret Violence," *New York Times*, November 1, 1984.

13. Tom Ashbrook, "India Violence Said to Subside; Thousands of Sikhs in Refugee Camps," *Boston Globe*, November 5, 1984.

14. "Indira Gandhi," *Washington Post*, November 1, 1984.

15. "Rajiv Gandhi Takes Over," *Boston Globe*, November 16, 1984.

16. " 'Indira Is India'; To Supporters, Gandhi Was the Glue That United a Nation," *Washington Post*, November 1, 1984.

17. Green, "Orange County Sikhs."

18. Green, "Orange County Sikhs."

19. Quoted in Christian Smith, ed., *The Secular Revolution* (Berkeley and Los Angeles: University of California Press, 2003), 13.

20. Berger, "Religion in a Globalizing World," Event Transcript, Pew Forum, Faith Angle Conference on Religion, Politics, and Public Life, December 4, 2006.

21. Peter Berger, ed., *Desecularization of the World* (Grand Rapids, MI: William B. Eerdmans, 1999), 11–12.

22. Berger, Pew Forum, 2006.

23. On these developments, see Dallas Willard, chap. 1, "Moral Knowledge Disappears," unpublished manuscript, 2007; Jacques Barzun, *From Dawn to Decadence 1500 to the Present: 500 Years of Western Cultural Life* (New York: HarperCollins, 2000), 270; Mark Lilla, "The Politics of God," *New York Times Magazine*, August 19, 2007; Simon Schama, *Citizens* (New York: Vintage, 1990), 791; Randall Collins, *The Sociology of Philosophies* (Cambridge, MA: The Belknap Press, 2000), 524.

24. Willard, "Moral Knowledge."

25. Smith, *Secular Revolution*, 27.

26. Smith, *Secular Revolution*, 36.

27. Smith, *Secular Revolution*, 28.

28. Smith, *Secular Revolution*, 46–47.

29. Berger, Pew Forum, 2006.

30. Alan Cooperman, "Is There Disdain for Evangelicals in the Classroom?; Survey, Bias Allegations Spur Debate," *Washington Post*, May 5, 2007.

31. Cooperman, "Disdain for Evangelicals."

32. Chris Mooney and Matthew C. Nisbet, "Undoing Darwin," *Columbia Journalism Review*, September/October 2005, available at http://cjrarchives.org/issues/2005/5/mooney.asp (accessed June 17, 2008).

33. C. S. Lewis, *The Discarded Image* (London: Cambridge University Press 1971), 98–99.

34. C. S. Lewis, "On the Reading of Old Books," *God in the Dock* (Grand Rapids, MI: William B. Eerdmans, 1970), 202.

35. Willard, "Moral Knowledge."

36. Stephanie Guttman, *The Other War: Israelis, Palestinians and the Struggle for Media Supremacy* (San Francisco: Encounter, 2005), 260.

AFTERWORD

1. Philip Jenkins, *The Next Christendom: The Coming of Global Christianity* (New York: Oxford University Press, 2002).

2. D. Michael Lindsay, *Faith in the Halls of Power* (New York: Oxford University Press, 2007).

3. David D. Kirpatrick, "End Time for Evangelicals?" *New York Times*, October 28, 2007.

4. Francis Collins, *The Language of God: A Scientist Presents Evidence for Belief* (New York: Free Press, 2006).

5. See, for example, Ram A. Cnaan with Stephanie C. Boddie, Charlene C. McGrew, and Jennifer Kang, *The Other Philadelphia Story: How Local Congregations Support Quality of Life in Urban America* (Philadelphia: University of Pennsylvania Press, 2006).

6. John Wilson, "DiIulio Keeps Explaining, but Is Anybody Listening?" *Christianity Today*, April 1, 2001.

7. Michael J. Gerson, *Heroic Conservatism: Why Republicans Need to Embrace America's Ideals (and Why They Deserve to Fail If They Don't)* (New York: Oxford University Press, 2007).

Index